TEST PILOT

TEST PILOT

BRIAN JOHNSON

Guild Publishing London

This edition published 1986 by
Book Club Associates
by arrangement with
BBC Publications

© Brian Johnson 1986

Typeset in 10/12pt Plantin
by Phoenix Photosetting, Chatham
Printed and bound in Great Britain by
Mackays of Chatham Ltd

CONTENTS

For the staff and students
of Fixed Wing Course No. 44
and Rotary Wing Course No. 23
of the Empire Test Pilots'
School, Boscombe Down

ACKNOWLEDGEMENTS

This book was written at the same time as I was producing the BBC series of the same name. Throughout the ten months of ETPS Course No. 44/23, I and my colleagues filmed the progress of the students. Although the presence of a BBC film crew must have been a distraction to the staff and students, we were welcomed and granted all the facilities we required. Members of the staff flew the camera aircraft with a skill that was exceptional. I would like to mention my gratitude to the Superintendent of Flying at the A&AEE, Group Captain Ron Burrows AFC, for his enthusiastic support in allowing the BBC the greatest latitude with his aeroplanes; the CO of the School, Wing Commander John Bolton, and his staff for their unfailing support, not only during the filming but after the shooting was completed and as this book was being written. Vic Lockwood was by then at Staff College but made himself available for consultation; James Giles, who succeeded Vic as the Principal Tutor, Fixed Wing, read the entire manuscript and patiently corrected my errors, additionally making several valuable suggestions about content. Hedley Hazelden, the former Chief Test Pilot of the Handley Page Company, who was a founder member of ETPS in that he was a student on the very first course in 1943, was good enough to answer my questions about that course and to allow me to quote from his logbook the details of his flights while attending the school: a unique document. Finally, may I take this opportunity to express my admiration for all the students on that difficult and demanding ETPS course, who are now the living embodiment of the title of this present volume: *Test Pilot*.

BRIAN JOHNSON
LONDON, 1986

1 Boscombe Down

To design a Flying Machine is nothing;
To build it is not much;
To test it is everything.

Otto Lilienthal (1848–1896)

Boscombe Down, a large airfield on the chalk uplands of Salisbury Plain, is the base of The Aeroplane and Armament Experimental Establishment (A&AEE). It is run by the Ministry of Defence Procurement Executive. The basic remit of the establishment, which works in close collaboration with the Royal Aircraft Establishment at Farnborough and Bedford, is to assess military aircraft in their intended role as weapons of war. To this end it tests not only the actual aircraft but also a wide range of airborne weapons, equipment and electronics, including exceedingly highly classified radars and navigation systems: it goes without saying that Boscombe Down is, and always has been, a withdrawn and Prohibited Place.

The title A&AEE was granted officially as long ago as 1924, at a time when the nascent Royal Air Force was fighting for its continued existence: the Navy and the Army considered the RAF as a

opposite, There is no doubt that the flying standards of the RAF in the inter-war years were of the highest, as epitomised by these Gloster Gladiators of No. 87 Squadron, up from Debden in the summer of 1938 to practise close formation aerobatics with the aircraft tied together by elastic ropes (*Rolls-Royce*); *left*, The Empire Test Pilots' School returned to Boscombe Down in 1968 where it has since remained (*B. Johnson*)

wartime expedient and wanted their individual Air Corps returned to their command. (The RAF had been formed from the Royal Flying Corps and the Royal Naval Air Service in 1918, the exact date, 1 April, being considered by many as significant.) Owing to the skilled lobbying of Lord Trenchard, the concept of an Independent Air Force was eventually recognised and allowed to flower, on it must be said distinctly stony ground: what at the end of the Great War had been the largest and only Independent Air Force in the world with no fewer than 22,647 aircraft formed into 188 squadrons at home and overseas, had by 1923, in the post-war atmosphere of disarmament and retrenchment, shrunk to a mere ten squadrons composed almost exclusively of wartime aircraft. However, it remains true that in 1923 a committee under Lord Salisbury had proposed a 'Fifty-two Squadron Plan' of some 600 aircraft for Home Defence.

The Salisbury Report had been accepted by a reluctant government under Stanley Baldwin and a modest start to the expansion of the RAF began with new designs at last being ordered, albeit in very small numbers. The parsimony of the inter-war governments had one unforeseen benefit: if the RAF was to be small, Trenchard was determined that it would be of the highest quality possible, both in men and machines.

Desperate manufacturers, who had seen orders drop from 3500 machines a month to virtually zero at the war's end, submitted their spindly biplanes to the newly named A&AEE for Service Acceptance Trials on that Establishment's airfield at Martlesham Heath, a desolate windswept site surrounded by marshes and saltings on the east coast of Suffolk, near Woodbridge. The A&AEE

The prototype Hurricane and Spitfire were both test flown by A&AEE test pilots at Martlesham Heath. The Hurricane depicted, PZ 865, a IIc, was the last of some 14,000 built between 1936 and 1945. The Spitfire V, AB 910, was constructed in 1941, one of a total of 20,351 Spitfires. (*British Aerospace*)

had a small staff of test pilots to investigate the tendered machines and to report on their suitability or otherwise for the slowly expanding squadrons of the RAF. The test pilots were in the main drawn from the ranks of the service; at that time they would, to a man, have had operational experience during the late war, some no doubt as squadron commanders but glad to have dropped rank to fly as Flight Lieutenants in the post-war Air Force. The system of recruiting test pilots from RAF squadrons was to continue at Martlesham Heath until the outbreak of the Second World War. It had served well enough: until the advent of the new monoplanes, service aircraft of the 1930s were simple and undemanding machines with, as perceived by the Air Staff, simple and undemanding roles. In effect, the test pilots and their aircraft developed together. By the mid-1930s when new, high-performance monoplanes appeared – both the Spitfire and the Hurricane were accepted after testing at Martlesham Heath by the A&AEE – the test pilots, in many cases guided by those of the manufacturers, had acquired the skills required to evaluate them. The number of prototypes tested, even during the panic expansion years of the late 1930s when the German *Luftwaffe* was emerging as a very serious challenge to the RAF, was still low enough for new test pilots to be trained 'on the job' on a master/pupil basis.

The RAF has always been rightly proud of its standards and in the inter-war years, when the depression had made even white-collar jobs difficult to find, there was no shortage of young fit men eager to be paid, however inadequately, to fly high-performance aircraft. The RAF could, therefore, afford to pick and choose: to train only the most able and then to the highest possible standards.

K5054, the first Spitfire, being test flown in 1936. When it arrived at Martlesham Heath for Service acceptance trials, it represented a giant step forward from the fabric-covered Gloster Gladiators which were then the RAF's front line fighters. (*Aeroplane*)

After a tour or two with operational squadrons those who had their log books endorsed 'Above average' or the extremely rare 'Exceptional' might well be invited to become test pilots with the Royal Aircraft Establishment at Farnborough or the A&AEE at Martlesham Heath.

The 1930s were 'The best of times, the worst of times', for the wooden, fabric-covered biplanes powered by engines in the 600 hp class were being supplanted by stressed skin monoplanes with 1000 hp engines. Stressing of those aircraft was at that time still to a great extent empirical and several firms submitted advanced prototypes which their test pilots found to be deficient in a number of vital ways. It was not unknown in that unenlightened age for a test pilot, on landing his disintegrating charge, to settle a fine point of design detail with the head of the Stress Office behind the nearest hangar.

The expansion of the RAF accelerated as the last years of peace dwindled and the number of aircraft requiring 'Service Acceptance' increased: there was still no shortage of young men eager to fly them, whatever the risks involved. The last words of Otto Lilienthal, one of the first pilots to die testing a prototype, were prophetic: '*Opfer müssen gebracht werden*' (Sacrifices must be made). When the Munich crisis came in September 1938, despite Neville Chamberlain's 'Peace in our time' assurances, it was realised that the isolated site at Martlesham Heath, selected in 1924 to keep prying eyes away from the aircraft being tested there, was in fact just about the nearest point of the British Isles to Germany, and presented a target of which bomber crews dream.

Britain declared war on Germany a year later on 3 September 1939; by that time the plans to move the A&AEE, lock, stock and barrel, to a safer location had been finalised. In passing, it is interesting to note that for some years between the wars, official thinking in Whitehall had considered that Britain's only potential enemy was the old one: France. As a consequence many RAF airfields were located in the south of the country; one of them, Boscombe Down, was selected for the A&AEE. The idea that France would fall and place those southern airfields within *Luftwaffe* fighter and bomber range was never given any serious consideration; so the move – on 3 September – was made and the A&AEE settled into the base on which it is still to be found.

The winter of 1939–40 was one of the coldest on record; the two bomber squadrons that had been in residence, Nos 88 and 218, must have been glad to exchange the frozen airfield for their operational bases in France to fly the largely pointless sorties of the 'Phoney War'. Tragically, when that phase ended with the German Blitzkrieg which was unleashed on the hapless French Army and the British Expeditionary Force on 10 May 1940, those two

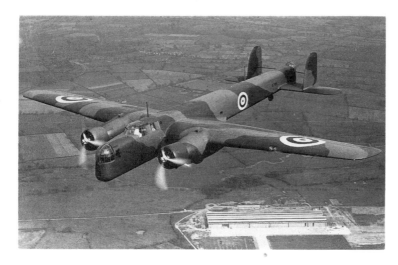

An Armstrong
Whitworth Whitley 1,
K7191, the ninth
production machine of
the original 1937 order.
The aircraft illustrated is
on a production test
flight from Baginton,
Coventry. (*Aeroplane*)

squadrons, together with No. 12, all flying their outclassed Fairey
Battle bombers, would suffer the highest loss rate to be sustained
by any unit of the RAF in Europe.

After the departure of the Battles, another unit, No. 58 Squadron, Coastal Command, was based on Boscombe Down for a short
time during the worst of that first bitter winter of the war. The
squadron was to fly convoy protection patrols over the Western
Approaches but most of the time their sixteen Whitleys, dispersed
on the open airfield, were simply frozen to the ground. After the
bombers had been prised free, the coastal squadron departed and
Boscombe Down ceased to be an operational airfield, becoming
exclusively the province of the Ministry of Aircraft Production and
their clients, the A&AEE. The tempo of test flying was soon to
increase to a level unthinkable to old Martlesham Heath hands.
Aircraft of all descriptions were being delivered from the new
Shadow factories operated by the motor car industry; many of the
aircraft being built had been ordered straight from the drawing

A Bristol Bombay.
This Bomber/Transport
represents the half-way
stage between the
lumbering biplanes of
the 1930s and the later
heavy bombers of the war
years. L5808 was the first
production aircraft,
photographed in March
1939 at Short &
Harland's, Belfast.
(*Rolls-Royce*)

board and showed it: most were constructed by a hastily trained workforce with a predominance of females who had never even seen an aircraft close to, much less helped to build one. Many of the men in the wartime factories were either unfit or too old for military service; the hours were long and the work for the most part dull and repetitive; there was a strictly enforced total blackout; from 1940 air raids disrupted production. All things considered, it is hardly surprising that among the many aircraft that came to Boscombe Down for testing, some were found to suffer from poor workmanship. All the aircraft entering service in the early years of the war were designed in the late 1930s, and the roles that they would have to fulfil would in many cases change radically; a number, like the ill-fated Fairey Battles, would be obsolete before they even saw action. Many aircraft were ordered without any clear idea as to how they could be used operationally. This was especially true of the machines bought (for hard cash) from the United States in the early days of the war. A substantial number of American aircraft arrived

Despite massive UK orders, the RAF (and more particularly the Fleet Air Arm), desperate for aircraft before Lend-Lease, had to buy American machines for cash. These Martlet II fleet fighters, together with US Navy F4F Wildcats, await assembly at the Grumman Long Island factory. (*Grumman*)

in England as a result of Britain taking over orders that had been placed by the French and Belgian governments before the occupation of those countries. In some cases – the Brewster Buffalo comes to mind – the Allied cause would possibly have been better served had the aircraft been delivered, as originally intended, to the quays of Antwerp or Brest to fall into the hands of the enemy. From whatever source, representative examples of the many aircraft ordered arrived at Boscombe Down to be tested and deemed fit or otherwise for service.

The workload on the Performance Testing Flights at Boscombe Down was very high; some idea can be gauged from the 'Aircraft on Charge' returns. In September 1939, just after the move from Martlesham Heath, the records show that the Performance Testing ('Per T') Squadron contained three flights: 'A' Flight, concerned with the testing of fighters had fourteen machines on charge; 'B' Flight, responsible for heavy bombers (in fact the heaviest were twin-engined Wellingtons), had eleven aircraft; 'C' Flight, testing naval aircraft, had eleven machines on charge. The second test squadron at Boscombe, Armament Testing ('Arm T'), consisted of two flights: 'A' Flight tested fighter armament and had fourteen aircraft (including, rather surprisingly, a Tiger Moth); 'B Arm T' Flight boasted fourteen. This gave a total of sixty-four aircraft. The returns of 'Aircraft on Charge' at Boscombe Down for May

This Brewster Buffalo I was one of a cancelled Belgian contract for twenty-eight aircraft. AS 412 was photographed at Boscombe Down in 1940, during its handling trials. These did not proceed very far, however, since the aircraft suffered engine failure on take-off at an early stage and the type was reported as unsatisfactory. (*MoD/Crown*)

1945 give a clear picture of the growth of flight testing during the war years; no fewer than 186 aircraft of all types (the figure includes 23 with ETPS though some of those, as today, were probably shared with the test squadrons).

The Performance Testing flights of 1939 had, by 1945, become full squadrons: 'A' squadron with two flights testing forty modern fighters'; 'B' squadron, again with two flights working on twenty-four bombers, all four-engined; 'C' squadron, was responsible for the testing of twenty-three assorted naval aircraft. There was also 'D' squadron with two flights of medium bombers, mainly used in the flight testing of airborne radar and radio equipment and navigation and bombing aids on behalf of the Telecommunication Research Establishment (TRE) and a Communications and Special Duties Flight. Finally, there was the Intensive Flying Development Flight (IFDF), whose aircraft included a Lincoln Bomber and six Tempest fighters. The number of skilled test pilots and, in the case of the multi-place aircraft, aircrew required to test such a large number of aircraft must have been formidable indeed. These figures only apply to Boscombe Down; service test pilots were also working at Farnborough and the Airborne Forces Experimental

Establishment at Beaulieu. Military test pilots were also seconded to the aero engine companies and the aircraft factories for proto-type and production testing, where their recent operational experience proved invaluable.

Once the Germans had defeated Poland, Belgium and France so easily, by the aggressive use of airpower brilliantly integrated with fast armour on the ground, it was obvious, even to the most obtuse of Whitehall Warriors, that the Second World War was, unlike the First, to be a conflict in which the key to success would be airpower. Without massive support from the air, no battle, whether on land or sea, could be hoped to be won. The Battle of Britain, fought during the long hot summer of 1940, was a watershed for the RAF. The warnings of a few prescient men during the last years of peace were proved true: the far-sighted provision of a radar-based ground control system, the excellent Spitfire and Hurricane fighters and, not to be forgotten, the fruits of Trenchard's insistence on the highest standards of training, undoubtedly saved the country from almost certain defeat – by a narrow margin indeed. However, fighters are defensive. When the Air Staff had succeeded in disabusing the politicians of the idea that German factories, even if engaged in war production, were private property and therefore immune from attack, Bomber Command, instead of dropping tons of useless paper in the form of leaflets, turned to the offensive against Germany. It very soon became clear that aircraft performance, tactics, even in certain respects the training of aircrew (navigators in particular), required urgent revision. The rethinking of the Air Staff resulted in an unprecedented flood of new and replacement aircraft of all types. (During the war years, the RAF had placed on charge no fewer than 55,000 aircraft, serving 487 squadrons. Of that total 22,000 aircraft were lost or damaged beyond repair.)

FR 409, a North American Mustang V, photographed at Boscombe Down during handling trials in the autumn of 1944. The hangar by the aircraft's propeller is the one used by the ETPS Flying Wing today. The building by the fin is the Officers' Mess. (*MoD/Crown*)

On 11 March 1941 President Roosevelt signed the Lend-Lease Act which enabled the United States, still ostensibly neutral, to supply Britain with an ever increasing number of aircraft. Among the early arrivals were a number of Grumman Goose flying boats, two of which can be seen surrounded by US Navy F4F Wildcats at the Grumman Bethpage works. (*Grumman*)

When it is considered that all the many aircraft types that entered service with the RAF and the Fleet Air Arm – and a good many that did not – were the subject of extensive trials by the A&AEE at Boscombe Down and the other related Establishments, it is apparent that the provision of an adequate number of trained test pilots would soon become a matter of major concern. The system of 'learning on the job', inherited from a more leisurely era at Martlesham Heath, was proving inadequate. From the end of 1941 there was no shortage of available men 'resting from operations' after the air war began to be fought in earnest; but even above average, operationally experienced pilots posted to Boscombe Down and elsewhere who had an interest in test flying could not be used straight away on a test programme. It was found that practically all required at least a year of training with the test squadrons before they could make a significant contribution to the work in hand. It is one thing to know that an aircraft is difficult to control; it is quite another to be able to write a reasoned report as to *why*. It was not a question of flying skills: to be able to put a prototype fighter into an inverted spin, and then calmly note on a kneepad the several parameters of the machine's gyrations, calls for rather special abilities which can be acquired only by specialised training. In fact, it was discovered that pilots with 'Exceptional' flying endorsements often did not make suitable candidates for test flying; their skills were such that they could take up the most ill-designed aircraft and have little difficulty in flying it, making a subsequent satisfactory report. In contrast, a trained test pilot would, on flying a deficient machine, say to himself, 'I can fly this heap, but is it reasonable to assume that an average squadron pilot with perhaps as little as 200 hours' total time, frightened, tired and perhaps wounded, would be able to cope?' Test pilots of military aircraft also have to consider the effect of combat damage; would that bomber get home on one engine? Could this fighter be safely ditched or survive total hydraulic failure when flown by a relatively inexperienced pilot?

By the end of 1942 the workload at Boscombe Down had become critical: apart from the new types from British factories and the constant modification programmes to existing aircraft, American types ordered under the provisions of Lend Lease in 1941 were arriving in large numbers. To try to alleviate the shortage of test pilots, the Commandant of the A&AEE, Air Commodore D'Arcy Grieg (who is best remembered as a member of the RAF's High Speed Flight which won the Schneider Trophy) was asked by a former Commandant of the A&AEE, Air Marshal Sir Ralph Sorley, then Controller of Research and Development, Ministry of Aircraft Production (on behalf of which the A&AEE operated), to set up a test pilots' school at Boscombe Down. The terms of reference were 'to provide suitably trained pilots for test flying duties in aeronautical research and development establishments within the service and the industry'. It was a substantial remit for which there was no precedent: such a school would be unique for, at that time, no other existed anywhere in the world.

2 ETPS

'Why,' said the Dodo,
'The best way to explain it
Is to do it.'

LEWIS CARROLL, *Alice in Wonderland*

To say that the prospect of a school for test pilots set the hard-pressed Performance Testing squadrons alight would be wide of the mark; many of the staff at the A&AEE had considerable reservations about the feasibility of training test pilots in a school. If Air Commodore D'Arcy Grieg agreed with those sentiments he did not show it; he sent for two key men: G. Maclaren Humphreys, a physicist civilian A&AEE Technical officer, whom he appointed chief (and sole) ground instructor, and Wing Commander Charles Slee, the CO of 'B' Flight (B Per T) Boscombe Down, who was offered the command of the proposed school. Both men were very keen on the idea of the new school and pleased with their appointment.

There was, however, a snag. They had previously been working together on a project which had become urgent: the clearing for service of the third prototype Avro York transport, LV663, which

opposite, G. Maclaren Humphreys lecturing in the Ground School to students of No. 7 ETPS course in 1948. This was the first course to be held at Farnborough where ETPS was to remain until 1968, when it returned to Boscombe Down (*A&AEE/Crown*); *left*, LV 633, *Ascalon*, the Avro York which was tested at Boscombe Down prior to joining the King's Flight to be used by H M King George VI and Winston Churchill. (*MoD/Crown*)

was required for the King's Flight. The aircraft had been fitted out to a high degree of luxury by austere British wartime standards. Since the three Yorks had been constructed without official sanction, using a large percentage of Lancaster bomber components, a good deal of work was involved to ensure LV663 was suitable for the King's Flight. The A&AEE acceptance trials were conducted between 30 April and 14 May 1943 and the test team, including the entire staff elect of the proposed test pilots' school, flew in the VIP York, now rather grandly named *Ascalon*, on no fewer than sixteen test flights from Boscombe Down. Fortunately, Wing Commander Slee and Maclaren Humphreys had previously spent a long time drafting a syllabus for the test pilots' course. The final test flight of the York was made, and it flew from Boscombe Down on 25 May to join No. 24 Squadron at Northolt, piloted by Wing Commander Slee who was to brief the York's prospective squadron crew on the new aircraft. Exactly what next happened is now a matter of speculation; suffice to say Wing Commander Slee remained with *Ascalon* to pilot HM King George VI on an extended tour of the North African front.

Having lost the CO of the school three weeks before it was due to open, there was little time to select a replacement; the original had been obtained from 'B' Flight, therefore Air Commodore D'Arcy Grieg sent for the CO of 'A' Flight, Squadron Leader 'Sammy' Wroath, and offered him command of the test pilots' school. He was not at all keen on the prospect, being happy at 'A Per T', and wanted to continue as the CO. After the urgency of the situation had been explained to him, he thought about it for a moment and then said to his commandant, 'Well, sir, I am not about to volunteer for the job, but if ordered to do it of course I will.' He was and did.

Sammy Wroath was a remarkable man; he had joined the RAF as an aircraft apprentice at Halton in 1925, one of the first of Trenchard's 'Brats', as they were known in the pre-war Air Force. Although Halton apprentices were trained primarily as tradesmen, a few, including Sammy Wroath, were selected to become pilots. He must have been a very good one for he later became the first sergeant pilot to undertake test flying at Martlesham Heath. At Boscombe Down he had risen to the rank of Squadron Leader and, on becoming the first CO of the still unnamed school, was promoted Wing Commander.

Sammy Wroath and Maclaren Humphreys took possession of a group of buildings situated on the south side of the airfield. Whether by accident or design, the school location was just about as far away from all the other A&AEE activities as was possible. The buildings were not ideal: they consisted of two Seco wooden huts, four Nissen huts, without which any wartime military accommodation was seemingly unthinkable, and, to look after the physical well-being of the staff and students, a brick-built wash-house adjacent to an air raid shelter. The latter was a most important consideration in early 1943, for the airfield had been bombed, though not heavily, in 1941–2, usually from single 'Tip and Run' Ju88s. (As it was to turn out, the only enemy aircraft to visit Boscombe Down from the beginning of 1943 to the end of the war were those which had been captured and sent there for evaluation.)

Sitting in the new and empty buildings, the two men set about finalising the syllabus for the first test pilots' course. All they had to go on was the already quoted terms of reference and the daunting thought that the students, on completion of the eight-month course, would be expected to be able to join a test programme without any further training. A timetable of lectures and flying exercises was prepared: arrangements were made for the students to make visits to the principal aircraft and engine manufacturers: school aircraft were wrested from Maintenance Units and COs in Home Commands of the RAF and the FAA were asked to nominate suitable candidates to apply for a place in what was simply called 'The Test Pilots' School'.

Among the eighteen candidates selected from the many nominated was a twenty-eight-year-old bomber pilot, Squadron Leader Hedley G. Hazelden, DFC and Bar. ('Hazel', as he is universally known, was to prove a good choice: he completed the course, eventually became CO of 'B Per T' and, after the war, the Chief Test

'Hazel' Hazelden in 1943 when he was a student on the first test pilots' course at Boscombe Down (*A&AEE/Crown*)

The ETPS buildings at Boscombe Down, probably at the time of the second course (1944). The aircraft visible include Harvards and various Spitfires. Though ramshackle to modern eyes, the accommodation was generous by wartime standards. (*A&AEE/Crown*)

Pilot of the Handley Page Company, testing, among other aircraft, the prototype HP Victor jet bomber.) Hazel reported to the Test Pilots' School on 19 June 1943. In a recent conversation with the author he admitted he was lucky to be there at all; he had joined the RAF Volunteer Reserve and learned to fly in the crisis year of 1939, just in time to be mobilised on 2 September, the day before Britain entered the war with Nazi Germany. He survived flying Hampdens with No. 44 Squadron, including a crash landing in fog at Boscombe Down on the night of 20 March 1941 when returning from a mine-laying operation off St Nazaire (his first, informal, visit to the A&AEE base). On the completion of a full operational tour in April 1941, he was awarded a DFC. After a 'rest', instructing on war-weary Hampdens at No. 14 Operational Training Unit (OTU), Cottesmore, his next operational posting was to No. 83 Squadron, operating the ill-fated Avro Manchesters, powered by two 24-cylinder Vulture engines; one of the few unsatisfactory powerplants produced by Rolls-Royce. This advanced engine was far from reliable and as many Manchesters were lost due to engine failure as to enemy action. Following an engine fire, Hazel brought his back from Germany on one. He received a Bar to his DFC for that. (Many Manchester pilots considered that DFCs should be awarded for simply getting back.) Hazel was particularly keen to return from a raid on the night of 8–9 March on the Krupps works at

L4032, the first production Handley Page Hampden, flown by Major Cordes, the company's Chief Test Pilot, in 1937. The Major is having some trouble in flying slowly enough for the camera aircraft and has had to open the cowl gills of the two Bristol Pegasus radials to keep the cylinder head temperatures within limits. (*Rolls-Royce*)

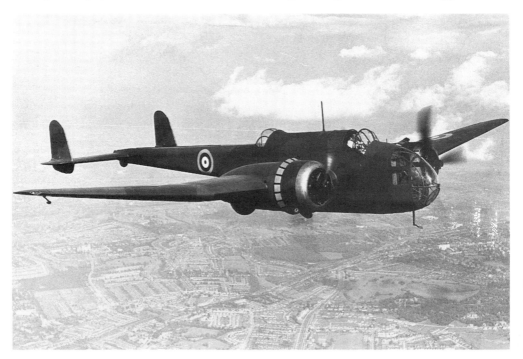

Essen as he was to marry the next day. He made it on time. Returning from his week's honeymoon, he found that the squadron had been severely hit: seven crews lost in three nights. The mounting losses and the increasing doubts about the Manchester, officially conceded after the war as 'disappointing', resulted in No. 83 Squadron being withdrawn from Bomber Command's Order of Battle, pending re-equipping with Lancasters. (These were revised Manchesters powered by four Rolls-Royce Merlins. The first operation by No. 83 Squadron with their new Lancasters was the '1000 Bomber' raid on Cologne on the night of 31 May to 1 April 1942.)

Hazel completed his second tour flying Lancasters with No. 83 Squadron, including the big Cologne raid, with another sortie deploying over 1000 bombers, this time on Bremen on 25 June 1942. He was again posted to an OTU for a 'rest', on this occasion to No. 11 at Westcott in Buckinghamshire, where he was senior instructor (on Wellingtons) at the satellite airfield at Oakley. He caused his CO, Group Captain R. W. P. Collings, so much trouble with his constant applications for a posting back to an operational unit that, when the order to nominate experienced pilots for the Test Pilots' School at Boscombe Down was received at Westcott, it was seen as a heaven-sent opportunity.

Hazel duly arrived at Boscombe Down. He soon discovered on meeting his fellow students that all seemed to have one trait in common: all were very capable pilots who had completed operational tours, yet strangely all had COs prepared to 'let them go', some with almost indecent haste. 'Mavericks' was the word Hazel used to describe his companions on the course. Hazel remembers that he was not really all that fit to begin the exacting course; he had an arm in a sling and had to walk with the aid of a stick because just before leaving Oakley he had fallen off a motorcycle, injuring his right leg, and then had fallen out of a Wellington, which fortunately was on the ground at the time, injuring an elbow.

The course of lectures began almost at once and that Achilles heel of the British educational system, the deficient teaching of mathematics, immediately manifested itself to the extent that, within the first week, no fewer than five of the students departed finding themselves unable to keep up. Hazel had worked for six years in insurance before the war and his maths was adequate; furthermore, D'Arcy Grieg had made an excellent choice in Maclaren Humphreys, who was to become a most popular lecturer. The syllabus which he and Wing Commander Slee had drawn up was to prove not only correct for Course No. 1 in 1943 but was, in essence, the one to be used for the following forty-three to the present day.

The only known photograph of No. 1 Test Pilots' course, taken on a school visit to Filton, the base of the Bristol Aeroplane Company. *Left to right, back row*, Flt Lt K. J. Sewell, Wg Cdr G. V. Fryer, E. A. Swiss (Bristol's), Sqn Ldr M. W. Hartford, Sqn Ldr D. W. Weightman; *middle row*, I. Llewellyn Owen (Bristol's), Sqn Ldr A. K. Cook, Sqn Ldr J. C. Nelson, Flt Lt R. V. Muspratt, Flt Lt J. C. S. Turner; *front row*, Lt Cdr P. H. A. Shea-Simmonds RNVR, Wg Cdr P. H. A Simmonds, Wg Cdr 'Sammy' Wroath (CO of school), A. J. 'Bill' Pegg (Bristol's), Lt Cdr G. R. Callingham RN, G. Maclaren Humphreys, Sqn Ldr H. G. 'Hazel' Hazelden. Wg Cdr P. F. Webster was 'absent flying'. (*A&AEE/MoD*)

When No. 1 course began, the popular image of the test pilot, nurtured to a great extent by Hollywood *circa* 1940, was that of a John Wayne character who socks the chief designer, leaps into the new wonder fighter and, without more ado, zooms away into the bright blue yonder, watched by a tough mechanic buddy who served as a master sergeant with our hero in the most recent war available and who has a heart of gold and a tool kit which consists of one large adjustable spanner and a wad of cotton waste, and of course by an adoring girl-friend whose blonde hair is fetchingly ruffled by the departing aircraft's slipstream. The secret 'pursuit ship' (usually played by a Seversky P-35) is then put through a series of hair-raising aerobatic manoeuvres by the pilot flying with one hand while holding a microphone to provide a running commentary over the radio. The test pilot lands the aircraft after perhaps an engine fire or trifling structural failure and tells the rueful designer how to rectify the minor faults. We then dissolve to the hero and his girl (and his mechanic buddy) as squadrons of new fighters fly away to show the peasants in Europe what real airplanes should be like. Of course that picture was as false in America as it was in Britain – or any industrial country – yet, at the same time, the image of test pilots as hell-raising daredevils persists to some extent. Test piloting is certainly not for the timid but neither is flying in general.

It is difficult to define precisely the qualities that go to make up a good test pilot; the ability to fly with confidence is clearly one essential: to possess what horsemen call 'good hands' another; to

be what John Farley, a graduate of ETPS and Chief Test Pilot of the Harrier programme, called 'good stick and rudder men', in addition to which he added that, 'A test pilot has always needed to know the theory behind the aeroplane he's testing, whether it be the aerodynamics of the aeroplane, whether it be the engine principles, the structure or the equipment fit in the aircraft.' That definition was made by John Farley for the BBC 'Test Pilot' series in 1985; it was perfectly relevant in 1943.

The thirteen (eleven RAF and two FAA) students who remained on the first course after the initial week included an American: Squadron Leader J. C. Nelson, who was serving with the 'Eagle' Squadron. He was the first of many; there have been very few courses that did not have at least one American attending. The ties between the British Test Pilots' School and the later American equivalents (particularly that of the US Navy) became and remain very close.

The students were all experienced to the extent that they had flown at least one operational tour. It should be remembered that, at that stage of the war (mid-1943), the chances of pilots surviving a tour were not high, although they did depend on the type of aircraft flown and the operational role of the squadron. A crew flying night bombers, as Hedley Hazelden had, could expect only a one in three chance of completing a thirty-sortie tour. The lowest expectation was among pilots flying Beauforts in an anti-shipping role; the highest was possibly maritime reconnaissance with Coastal Command, although individual crews' survival prospects follow-

No. 44/23 Course: *left to right, back row*, Flt Lt S. J. Moore, Cdt S. Aubert, Capt H. G. Fehl, Sqn Ldr T. L. Evans, Capt R. H. Meiklejohn, Lt R. Horton, Capt G. Yannai; *middle row*, Flt Lt C. C. Ware, Flt Lt J. S. Ludford, Flt Lt N. G. Coulson, Lt T. Koelzer, Sqn Ldr R. J. Tydeman, Flt Lt D. R. Southwood, Capt M. Zuliani, Lt A. J. Howden, Capt J. T. Koh, Flt Lt S. W. Elliott, Flt Lt P. J. Cook, Mr S. J. Kuczera; *front row*, Sqn Ldr J. D. Avery, Lt Cdr M. A. Baker, Sqn Ldr T. N. Allen, Sqn Ldr J. A. Giles, Sqn Ldr R. G. Rhodes, Sqn Ldr V. C. Lockwood, Wg Cdr J. W. A. Bolton, Lt Cdr M. R. Swales, Sqn Ldr A. W. Debuse, Sqn Ldr M. R. D. Butt, Sqn Ldr I. Young, Sqn Ldr P. A. Ashmore, Sgt R. W. Wheelhouse. (*MoD (PE)/A&AEE*)

ing a ditching far out in the North Atlantic were very low. To have survived any operational tour usually implied either exceptional luck or a high degree of flying skill, or a combination of both. That background should be borne in mind when one considers that, by modern airline captains' standards, the number of hours flown by the wartime students was not all that high. Hazel had about 1300 hours in his logbook when he arrived at Boscombe Down; he thinks the other bomber pilots on the course would have had about the same; fighter pilots on the other hand would have had a good deal less, they would probably average about 600. It was not the number of hours, it was the quality of the flying experience which counted in those days.

Although the course began with ground studies, which covered most aspects of aeronautics, basic aircraft design and control systems, as well as the related subjects of engines, propellers, instruments and the dreaded mathematics, it was essential not only to keep the students in current flying practice, but also to convert them to the school types. Bomber pilots tend to fly bombers and fighter pilots, fighters. Test pilots have to be able to fly any type. Just what types were flown on the first course at Boscombe Down is not all that clear: surviving records in the A&AEE archive reveal that the aircraft on charge to the school in the summer of 1943 included a Miles Master, a Proctor, three Hurricanes, two Oxfords, a Beaufort, a Mitchell and three Halifaxes, which seems a reasonable collection for thirteen students. Hazel's logbook for the period (see Appendix I on pages 275–8), which fortunately he has kept, shows that the first sortie he flew, on the second day of the course, was in a light aircraft, a Miles Mentor. Other aircraft in his logbook for that time included a 4-engined Stirling, a Liberator, a Lancaster, a Fortress and a Whitley. These aircraft were almost certainly 'borrowed' from 'B Per T' once the CO had been convinced that the school would not bend them. It seems incredible

L7245, the second prototype Handley Page Halifax photographed at Boscombe Down in January 1941 during the A&AEE Handling Trials. The aircraft behind the Halifax is a Wellington 1A. (*MoD/Crown*)

Two Miles Master IIIs (W8573 and T8886) were among the aircraft allocated to No. 1 Course. The aircraft illustrated, Master IIIs from an FTS, are displaying A1 roundels which date the photograph to before June 1942. (*Aeroplane*)

that the only flying instructor on the course was Sammy Wroath. Hazel cannot remember any formal conversion training in the modern sense; the single-seater aircraft were simply flown by all after a look at the pilot's notes and half an hour sitting in the cockpit to see where everything was. The standard instrument layout of British-built service aircraft must have helped. The multi-engined aircraft were flown by two students, one acting as flight engineer. Little or no radio was used, and no navigators were available; on the other hand it is doubtful if the School's aircraft, being unarmed, flew far from Boscombe Down; the chances of encountering a marauding German fighter were not entirely negligible in 1943.

Every flight had a purpose. The first one that Hazel made on the Mentor on his second day was to do 'Partial Climbs', that is, to establish the best rate of climb, after which he would have to reduce the results noted on his knee-pad and write a detailed report – the first of many. The ability to write concise reports is the cornerstone of the test pilot's art; assessment of aircraft will be made on them. The A&AEE archives contain thousands of reports, several of which are substantial documents. The fate of many aircraft has been decided on such evidence. During the war

Most British-built RAF aircraft had a standard blind flying panel, which is top centre of the photograph. The panel contains (*top left to right*) ASI calibrated up to 480 mph, Artificial Horizon (with its gyro run-down), Rate of Climb; (*bottom left to right*) Altimeter, Gyro Direction Indicator and the Turn and Slip indicator. The panel illustrated is that of a brand new Mosquito. The stick, spare bulbs for the reflector sight (not fitted in this wartime photograph), the blanked-off access to the bomb aimer's position, define this as a fighter variant. (*British Aerospace, Hatfield*)

years the pressure on the test pilots was very severe. Men's lives depended on their work but there was little time for reflection; as soon as a test programme was completed, the paperwork had to be written. The A&AEE reports were often bitterly contested by the manufacturers who tended, not unreasonably, to assume that their products were faultless, any deficiences being caused by their being employed in a role for which they had not been designed; the latter case was often true. The essential point, as far as the A&AEE were concerned, was that they had to have complete confidence in the impartial professionalism of the Performance Test Flights. Many of the men then running the aircraft and aero-engine factories were powerful and autocratic. People such as Sir Frederick Handley Page, Sir Sidney Camm, Lord Nuffield, Sir Richard Fairey and Lord Hives, not to mention sundry Air Marshals and Admirals, did not take kindly to criticism in any shape or form, certainly not that based on a report written by some obscure Flight Lieutenant at Boscombe Down. (Sir Frederick was much sought as a speaker at the annual Contractors' Dinner, held post-war in the mess at Boscombe Down. On one such occasion 'HP' remarked on 'the odd fact that the air in Wiltshire seems thinner than elsewhere, resulting in a marked loss of performance'.)

The one classic case was that of the A&AEE report No. 760. That was the bland title of an investigation into a serious fault in the design of the tail units of the Halifax I, which had caused many fatal accidents. An A&AEE test crew also lost their lives in the course of the enquiry which proved beyond doubt the nature of the trouble. At first the company was reluctant to accept this but later had to redesign the entire tail unit, resulting in the production of the Halifax MkV, a perfectly satisfactory aircraft which remained in RAF service until the end of the war.

Report writing was a major feature of the first test pilots' course and has, as we shall later see, remained so. The syllabus inaugurated the visits of the students to industry; the only known photograph of No. 1 course was taken on such a visit when the school went to Filton, the base of the Bristol Aeroplane Company. The original caption notes that one student, Wing Commander P. F. Webster, was 'absent flying', almost certainly in one of the company's aircraft. Bill Pegg and E. A. Swiss, both test pilots with the Bristol Aeroplane Company, are also in the photograph, indicating that they met the students and no doubt gave them an insight into the next phase of their course: Production Testing.

'Hazel' Hazelden spent the last month of the course at the Woodford works of A. V. Roe, where he was to test Lancasters as they came off the production line. He remembers that after a check flight with the Company's test pilot, Bill Thorne, in a Lancaster III he began work under the watchful eye of Avro's chief test pilot, Sam Brown, and was soon flying solo, testing, in all, thirty Lancasters.

Hazel and Squadron Leader A. K. Cook, a fellow student from the course who also went to Woodford to production test Lancasters, must have been good for, at the conclusion of their month's attachment, Captain Sam Brown asked both of them if they would care to stay with the company as test pilots on a permanent basis (a great compliment to the school). Hazel declined, as he had been promised that he was to join 'B Per T' when the course ended, and felt that the experience there would be more varied. Squadron Leader Cook, on the other hand, was to be posted to the Airborne Experimental Establishment at Beaulieu and, as Hazel put it, 'was less enamoured of his posting and accepted the Avro offer' as it appeared preferable to the alternative of hauling army gliders behind Dakota and Stirling tugs. In that context, it should be remembered that the test pilots' course had been held against the backdrop of the war, which in 1943 was far from won. Moreover it had by then become an air war with the American 8th Army Air Force making increasingly heavy raids over Germany in daylight. Bomber Command of the RAF was nearing the peak of the night offensive against the enemy's cities and industrial targets. Against that background, with the concomitant horrendous aircrew casualty lists, many members of the course felt, as Hazel put it, 'side-tracked away from the war . . . into a cosy little technical backwater where the risks were almost negligible'. The risks were not as negligible as the ex-students might have imagined; the work of the A&AEE and the related establishments was as vital to the war as any fighting squadron's operations.

No. 1 Test Pilots' Course formally ended on the last day of February 1944. All the remaining thirteen students had passed. Most of them had, like Hazel, flown about 130 hours in the course of their training at Boscombe Down. There were no presentations, no prizes, no dinner (food rationing was still strict), just postings and the right to add the lower-case letters 'tp' after their names in the Air Force List. Not much, one might think, for eight months of the hardest work that any of the course members could remember. Sammy Wroath and Maclaren Humphreys could be forgiven if they allowed themselves a little self-congratulation: the world's first test pilots' course had been a success; none of the aircraft used had been crashed, no one injured, despite the unlucky number thirteen. Sadly, that luck was not to hold. The day after the course ended, 1 March, one of the ex-students, the one absent from the Bristol photograph, Wing Commander P. F. Webster, DSO, DFC, took off in a Firefly 1 to begin his tour with 'A Per T' at

Boscombe Down. The test flight was to investigate spring tab elevators which had been experimentally fitted to the fleet fighter. He never returned, the Firefly Z1839 having crashed into a field at Goodworth Clatford near Andover. No cause for the fatal accident was ever discovered; the aircraft had apparently spun in. In all, five of No. 1 Course were eventually to lose their lives as test pilots.

Before the course had ended, Sammy Wroath had written a progress report on No. 1 Course and this had been forwarded to the man whose idea the school had been: Air Marshal Sir Ralph Sorley. Sir Ralph was so impressed with the work of the No. 1 Course that he submitted the report to the Minister of Aircraft Production, Sir Stafford Cripps, with the recommendation that the course should continue for at least another year. Sir Stafford returned the document with the handwritten annotation, 'A good idea, go ahead'.

Maclaren Humphreys was retained as the principal technical instructor and he was allocated assistants. Sammy Wroath, who had been, it will be recalled, a pressed man, was released and posted to Washington as chief test pilot of the British Joint Services Mission, which selected suitable American-built aircraft for the RAF and FAA. The officer who had held the appointment before

MB 727, a Firefly 1 similar to the one which crashed at Goodworth Clatford. This magnificent photograph was the work of that master of aerial photography, Charles E. Brown. (*Aeroplane*)

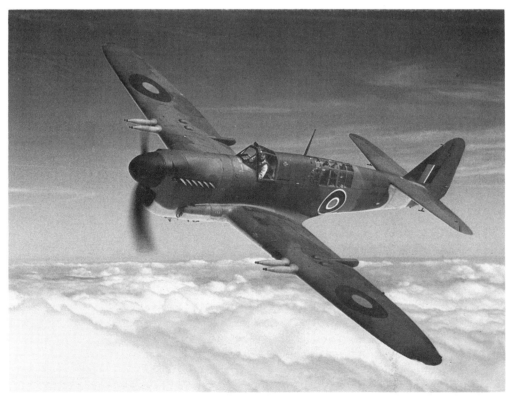

ETPS Course No. 2, 1944. Air Commodore D'Arcy Grieg, the Commandant of the A&AEE is sitting in the centre of the middle row wearing the forage cap; the officer to his right is Group Captain J. F. X. 'Sam' McKenna, the newly appointed Officer Commanding of the school; to his right is Maclaren Humphreys, the Chief Technical Instructor; the officer sitting next to him is the outstanding aerobatic pilot, Sqn Ldr J. Zurakowski, of the Polish Air Force. Another student on the course who was to attain fame as a post-war test pilot is the RNVR Lt in the front row, Mike Lithgow OBE. Other interesting students on No. 2 ETPS Course include the fourth man from the left on the top row, Sqn Ldr J. B. Starky DSO DFC RNZAF, the first student from New Zealand; the second was to be Flt Lt Steve Moore on No. 44 Course, forty-two years later! Standing just under the Mosquito's nose are the first officers from the USAAF, Major J. R. Muehlberg and Major H. Snyder. Finally, the 1944 course had two officers from the Chinese Air Force, Capt P. C. Chen and Maj C. T. Loh; they are to the right of the middle row. (*A&AEE/Crown*)

Sammy Wroath was Group Captain J. F. X. 'Sam' McKenna and he, by a pleasing symmetry, was appointed the new commandant of the Empire Test Pilots' School, Boscombe Down.

The name was to prove durable; the school still retains it despite the imperial echoes. In 1944 it was perfectly appropriate; many of the major training units of the RAF were prefixed by 'Empire', the Empire Air Training Plan, which trained over 54,000 pilots during the war years, being an example. Another cogent reason for the name lay in the fact that, of the RAF's 487 squadrons raised between 1939 and 1945, no fewer than 100 were Commonwealth units: 138,000 aircrew out of the RAF's wartime total of 340,000. Since many of the men attending the Test Pilots' School would undoubtedly be from overseas, it was a natural decision in 1944 to use the prefix Empire. (By the school's fortieth anniversary, the number of countries sending students to the ETPS was twenty-two.)

The second course got under way with twenty-seven students, four of whom were civilian test pilots sponsored by aircraft companies. The basic syllabus was retained and the new CO, 'Sam' McKenna, was to prove very popular; not only was he a most respected test pilot, he also held a First Class degree in science. The second course at Boscombe Down consolidated the growing reputation of the ETPS; the ex-students of both the courses were proving well able to fulfil the role of test pilots with the minimum of additional training; there was general acceptance of the effectiveness of the school even among the old Martlesham men. Sam McKenna and 'Humph', as Maclaren Humphreys was known, were looking forward to, and actively planning for, the third ETPS course when disaster struck.

On 19 January 1945, to keep in flying practice, Sam McKenna took off from Boscombe Down in one of 'A Per T's' aircraft, a Mustang IV, KH 648. Shortly after take-off, the single-seater fighter was seen to suffer major structural failure, shedding a wing, and crashed fatally, close to the nearby airfield of Old Sarum. The findings of the wartime RAF Courts of Inquiry remain closed for 100 years but it was thought that the access panels, used to cover the Mustang's guns which were grouped together in the wings, were improperly fastened and had become detached, precipitating the primary failure.

The popularity of Sam McKenna was such that it was decided that a suitable memorial should commemorate this outstanding airman's service to the A&AEE and ETPS. His widow donated a handsome cup, known as the McKenna Trophy, to be awarded at the conclusion of each course to the most outstanding student. The presentation is made at a farewell 'McKenna Dinner' in the Mess, a tradition founded in 1945 which continues to the present day. The first name to be engraved on the cup was that of Squadron Leader D. R. Cuming, AFC, RAAF, who graduated from the third course. That an Australian student won the first Trophy was appropriate; in succeeding years the Cup has many times been carried off overseas.

ETPS Course No. 3 was to be the last to be held at Boscombe Down for twenty-three years. All three had been successful and had fully vindicated the hopes of Air Marshal Sir Ralph Sorley, who had instigated the idea; of Sammy Wroath, Maclaren Humphreys and the late Sam McKenna, who had all worked so hard to establish that pioneer Test Pilots' School. Over seventy fully trained test pilots had been produced without any serious accidents. Among the graduates were some notable future civil test pilots whose names would become known to a wider public in the post-war years: 'Hazel' Hazelden, Peter Twiss, Mike Lithgow and the most outstanding aerobatic pilot of his generation, the Pole, Jan Zurakowski.

A detailed history of ETPS is beyond the scope of this book, but a brief outline will be of interest: Courses Nos. 4 to 6 were held at Cranfield then, when the College of Aeronautics which was also based on that airfield grew, ETPS moved once again, this time back to an Experimental Establishment: the Royal Aircraft Establishment, Farnborough. It remained there until 1968 when the growing restrictions imposed by the London Terminal Area, under whose rules flying from the RAE's airfield was controlled, together with the relatively short runways, dictated another move and ETPS went back to Boscombe Down. The school had been enlarged by that time, as the growing importance of helicopters

A Mustang IV at Boscombe Down, one of the best fighters of the Second World War. The aircraft illustrated is unusual in that it carried dual markings: an RAF serial TK 589, and its original USAAF BuNo. 413332. It is identical to the machine in which Sam McKenna so tragically lost his life. (*A&AEE/Crown*)

required the incorporation of a parallel rotary wing course, the first of which began in 1963. The rotary wing students had their own syllabus, tutors and, of course, aircraft, although many of the ground school lectures were common as was the very limited social life. The McKenna Trophy was open to the rotary wing students, many of whom have won it.

Other notable events in the history of ETPS include the granting of Armorial Bearings in 1949, with the motto 'Learn to Test, Test to Learn'. In that same year the United States Navy sent a student to No. 8 Course, Lieutenant Commander J. G. 'Joe' Smith, who was to return to America to set up a Test Pilots' Course at the Patuxent River Naval Test Center in Maryland. This school was modelled on ETPS and the closest relations established, which continue to the present day with constant interchange of students, tutors and ideas. The US Air Force also created their TPS at Edwards Air Force Base, again initially based on the experience of ETPS.

So much for the formative years. We now turn to the present and to Course No. 44, held in 1985; the subject of the BBC television series *Test Pilot*.

3 Course No. 44

*The happily married man
with a large family is
the test pilot for me.*
NEVIL SHUTE, *Slide Rule*

The 44th Fixed, and the 23rd Rotary Wing Course began at
Boscombe Down in the first week of February 1985. There were
fifteen students: four from the RAF, two from the Fleet Air Arm,
and one student each from Australia, Canada, France, Germany,
Israel, Italy, New Zealand (the first candidate from the RNZAF
since No. 2 Course in 1945), Singapore and the United States. The
six British students were selected from a short-list by a board sitting at Boscombe Down the previous summer. The basic
requirements for selection were the ability of the entrant to convince the board, by written examination and interviews, of his
future dedication to test flying; to display a wide knowledge of
aviation in general with an emphasis on future trends, particularly
in military aviation; to have sufficient educational background to
be able to absorb the high standard of the ground school lectures,
including mathematics up to at least O level. (As in 1943, this
requirement is still a major hurdle for many.) The ability to be able
to write concise, clear and accurate reports is also essential. All the
pilots selected for interview will have had a recent tour with an
operational squadron; have had their logbooks endorsed 'Above
average' or 'Exceptional'; have flown at least 750 hours P1 (Pilot in
Command); and will hold a current full flying medical category.
They should not be more than thirty-two years old at the conclusion of the course although the board has a certain discretion in this
last respect.

The type of aircraft which the interviewed student has been
flying an important bearing on his selection. While it remains
true that the successful candidates will be expected to fly at least
one exercise on all of the school's twelve types, including helicopters, generally speaking he will, on graduation, be posted to a

opposite, The Principal
Fixed Wing Flying
Tutor, ETPS, Sqn Ldr
Vic Lockwood
(*B. Johnson*)

test squadron at either Boscombe Down, Farnborough or Bedford to undertake development flying on the category of aircraft on which his main squadron experience was gained. Pilots of heavy, multi-engined aircraft will tend to go to 'B' Squadron, the unit at Boscombe Down responsible for the testing of such aircraft; and fighter pilots to 'A' Squadron. In this way all their previous experience is available, coupled with the additional skills gained from the course. This is an important point for, with the complexity (to say nothing of the cost) of modern military aircraft, many pilots arriving at ETPS will have flown only one of the current types on their operational tours, be it a Harrier, Phantom or Hercules transport. It should also be borne in mind that the great expense of training has reduced the number of hours that today's pilots fly.

The number of overseas students might at first sight seem to be surprisingly large but only about six test pilots a year are required by the Ministry of Defence Procurement Executive to replace men who have completed their mandatory three-year tour with the testing squadrons. It would be hopelessly uneconomic to train annually such a small number. Therefore candidates are invited from 'friendly governments' which is a continuation of the wartime practice of including Allied pilots. With the exception of the US Navy, which enjoys a 'no cost' reciprocity agreement, all overseas students' governments pay for their training. The MoD is very coy about putting a price tag on the ETPS course but John Farley, himself an ETPS graduate and former Chief Test Pilot on

A Sea Harrier with a Trials Squadron at Boscombe Down (*B. Johnson*)

the Harrier programme, put it this way, 'I do not know what the present price of a seat on that [ETPS] course is, but I would be surprised if it was less than a quarter of a million pounds.' He added significantly, 'Governments do not spend that sort of money lightly unless they think they are going to get some value from it.' By the school's fortieth anniversary, no fewer than twenty-two governments had thought it worth it; sending 374 students on ETPS courses.

The selection of the overseas students is left to the responsible national authorities. The system works well enough but it must be said that some countries have somewhat lower standards than ETPS can accept. When faced with a student who fails to meet the very high standards required by the course, the CO of the school has two options open to him: he can simply send the student home with regrets – although this in fact very rarely happens – or, provided the student's basic flying abilities are reasonable, he can get him posted to the RAF's Central Flying School for a short familiarisation course on British aircraft systems, cockpit layout, instruments and radio procedures.

It might, at this stage, be pointed out that the workload on the ETPS course, even for an articulate, English-speaking student, is high, even oppressive; for a man whose first language is not English it must be difficult beyond measure. The only saving grace is the fact that the lingua franca of aviation is English, a fact which the French have never found acceptable. British and American students and staff who go on exchange postings to the French Test Pilots' School, *L'École du Personnel Navigant d'Essais et de Récep-*

An F-4N and F-4J Mc Donnell Phantoms of the US Marine Corps. Every ETPS course from No. 1 to the present day has had at least one American student. (*Mc Donnell*)

tion (EPNER), at Istres have the additional difficulty of having to learn all the French aeronautical and other technical terms, which in many countries would be in English. That said, it is only fair to add that the relations between the test pilot schools of America, France and Britain remain very close, with a constant interchange of ideas, staff and students.

The Principal Fixed Wing tutor of the course, Vic Lockwood, was asked how foreign students coped:

'Well, they are fortunate in one way, in that the international language of aeronautical radio is English and most of them speak quite good English, but there is a lot of difference between speaking English and writing it and much of the course has a lot of written reports to follow each flight. That is what they find very hard. We do try to help them present their reports in good English. It is amazing [how the foreign students] speaking and writing English every day, listening to lectures, rapidly increase their command of English, very rapidly in most cases.'

There are three major testing centres in the United Kingdom. The amount of flying at just one, Boscombe Down, might seem surprising. The Superintendent of Flying there, Group Captain Burrows, revealed:

'We fly something of the order of 7000 hours per year, of which 2000 are concerned with test pilot training . . . In the three trials squadrons, twenty-four trained test pilots are actually engaged in the business of the Establishment. A further ten or so test pilots are engaged in training at ETPS. There is a philosophy of a three-year rotation and this has its strengths and its weaknesses; the weakness is, of course, the lack of continuity. We find that the first year of productive test flying tends to be somewhat of an apprenticeship

The Superintendent of Flying at Boscombe Down, Gp Capt Ron Burrows AFC in the audience at a students' presentation during Course No. 44 (*BBC*)

. . . the strength is that we are continually being refreshed by up-to-date operational experience straight off the front line. The test pilots' course is in a way an operational conversion unit to the business of trials flying; we are not a special breed by any means, we encourage operational pilots to come for test pilot training, then to go to the trial squadrons to bring their [recent] operational experience to bear on the recommendations and release of the next generation of military aviation hardware. I am looking for someone who can relate the work he does [on] the aircraft or the equipment directly to the way it will be used in the front line. It is no good having at Boscombe Down people who get stuck into academics to the extent that they lose sight of the reason for being here [which] is to ensure that we are able to make the best of the equipment which is being procured for the services . . . not only to meet the specification which may or may not be written correctly but also to ensure that the operational vehicle is a complete weapons system. The Royal Aircraft Establishment [Farnborough] is essentially an experimental establishment; it concentrates on new areas, on new technology, and on developing systems which may or may not prove useful at some future time in some new project. So the nature of the work between the RAE and the A&AEE is different. We need a more rounded person here at Boscombe Down, since he will be looking at the complete weapons systems. I am not sure that my colleagues at the other establishments would agree with that, but I certainly have a very discriminating eye when I look at the output of the test pilots' school.'

That is the background to ETPS as far as one of the end users, the A&AEE, is concerned. It might be supposed that in this day of complex and very sophisticated avionics which in many military aircraft actually fly the thing, the margins of control have become eroded to the point of vanishing altogether, or have become so small that it requires a computer to perceive them and to order the required adjustments to the aircraft's flying characteristics. Are the pilots and test pilots of the present generation of military aircraft reduced to being mere systems managers? What is the role of the test pilot in the mid-1980s?

John Farley was asked that question, to which he replied:

'Well, I think the job of the test pilot in the 1980s is exactly the same as the job of the test pilot in the 1920s or the 1940s or the 1960s; quite simply to make every aeroplane he flies as easy as possible to fly, and as safe as possible to fly, and to be as good at doing its military job as is possible. I think that applies whether he is flying a first prototype for the company that manufactured the aircraft or whether he is flying a service acceptance flight for Boscombe Down.'

John Farley
(*B. Johnson*)

As far as John Farley is concerned the computerisation of aircraft has made little difference to the role of the test pilot:

'Not to the basic job description; it makes a tremendous difference to the sort of skills the man has to bring to the job. Test pilots have always needed to know the theory behind the aeroplane that they are testing, whether it be the aerodynamics, the engines, the equipment fitted or the structure, and clearly the complexity of a modern aeroplane requires very much more study to master those topics, for example at the Empire Test Pilots' School, than it did years ago; and not only has [the test pilot] got to be a better technician, a better engineer; he has also to have considerable communication skills these days.'

That aspect of the test pilot's job is often overlooked. Not so many years ago, as John Farley recalled, the test pilot would 'get out of an aeroplane, sweaty, tired, badly frightened. The chief designer would probably be standing on the grass airfield . . . you would stick your nose in front of his, and with a few well-chosen words you would convince him that some changes were needed.'

Today, the chief designer is likely to be the chairman of a design committee in a city office miles away from the test airfield. The only contact that the test pilot will have is by appointment, at meetings based on long, written reports that would precede any action which could well take weeks, even months, to implement.

From what has been said it becomes clear that the students at ETPS have a great deal more to learn than just being able to fly aircraft well. It was interesting, therefore, to discover when talking to the students about to embark on Course No. 44 that it was the flying that seemed to have attracted the majority, the most quoted reason being the varied nature of the aircraft at Boscombe Down. One of the students put it this way, 'On a squadron one is flying the same aircraft over the same bit of country day after day . . .' and since that particular pilot's bit of country included a large area of the North Sea, one can see what he meant.

The students on the two ETPS courses which commenced in February of 1985 were as follows:

Fixed Wing Course No. 44

Commandant Serge Aubert. French Air Force. Flew Mirage IIIs and FIs. Married with two sons aged five and three.

Flight Lieutenant Nick Coulson. Royal Australian Air Force. Flew the HS 748. Married, no children.

Squadron Leader Les Evans. Royal Air Force. Hunter and Harrier. Married with a six-month-old daughter.

Captain Harry Fehl. *Luftwaffe*. Flew F-4 Phantoms and F-104s with the famed *Richthofen Geschwader*. Married. His wife, Karin, gave birth to a daughter during the course.

Lieutenant Tom Koelzer. United States Navy. Flew F-14As, TA-4Js. Married (in Salisbury) during the course.

Flight Lieutenant Jim Ludford. Royal Air Force. Hunter, Harrier. Married, no children.

Flight Lieutenant Steve Moore. Royal New Zealand Air Force. Flew UH-1H Iroquois (helicopter) and Strikemaster aircraft. Married, no children. At twenty-seven, the youngest on the fixed wing course.

Flight Lieutenant Dave Southwood. Royal Air Force. Hunter and Buccaneer. Married, no children.

Squadron Leader Robin Tydeman. Royal Air Force, senior officer on course. Flew Victor K2 tankers. Married with two sons aged three and one.

Captain Mirco Zuliani. Italian Air Force. Flew F-104s. Married with one son aged five.

Rotary Wing Course No. 23

Lieutenant Bob Horton. Royal Navy. Wessex HU-5s and Sea King
HC4s. Survived a tragic crash of Sea King while on a still-
classified sortie during the Falklands conflict. His helicopter,
carrying SAS on an undisclosed mission, is believed to have suffered a bird strike at night. Bob and his co-pilot, together with
surviving soldiers, spent a night adrift in the South Atlantic.
Bob, although badly injured, survived with undimmed enthusi-
asm for rotary wing flying. Married, no children.

Lieutenant Al Howden. Royal Navy. Flew Sea King and Gazelle
helicopters. Married with two sons aged three and one.   .

Captain J. T. Koh. Royal Singapore Air Force. Known on course
only as 'JT'. Flew UH-1B/H and Bell 212s. Married with six-
year-old son.

Captain Randy 'Mike' Meiklejohn. Canadian Armed Forces (the
Canadians do not have a separate Army and Air Force). Flew
CH-135 Twin Hueys. The only unmarried man on course.

Captain Gil Yannai. Israeli Air Force. At twenty-four, the
youngest man on the course; also, apart from Bob Horton, the
only student with battle experience. Flew Hughes 500 MDs and
Cobra AH-1S. (At the request of the Israeli Government,
Captain Yannai was not filmed for BBC programmes, as they do
not wish any of their military pilots to be identifiable, for obvious
reasons.)

This is the complete list of students who formed the 1985 ETPS
course, apart from Flight Lieutenant Andy Tailby, another helicopter pilot who was in the Falklands conflict and flew the only
Chinook that left the ill-fated *Atlantic Conveyer*, minutes before
that ship was hit by an Exocet missile. He attended the first term at
ETPS Boscombe Down, before he left to join the French test
pilots' course at Istres.

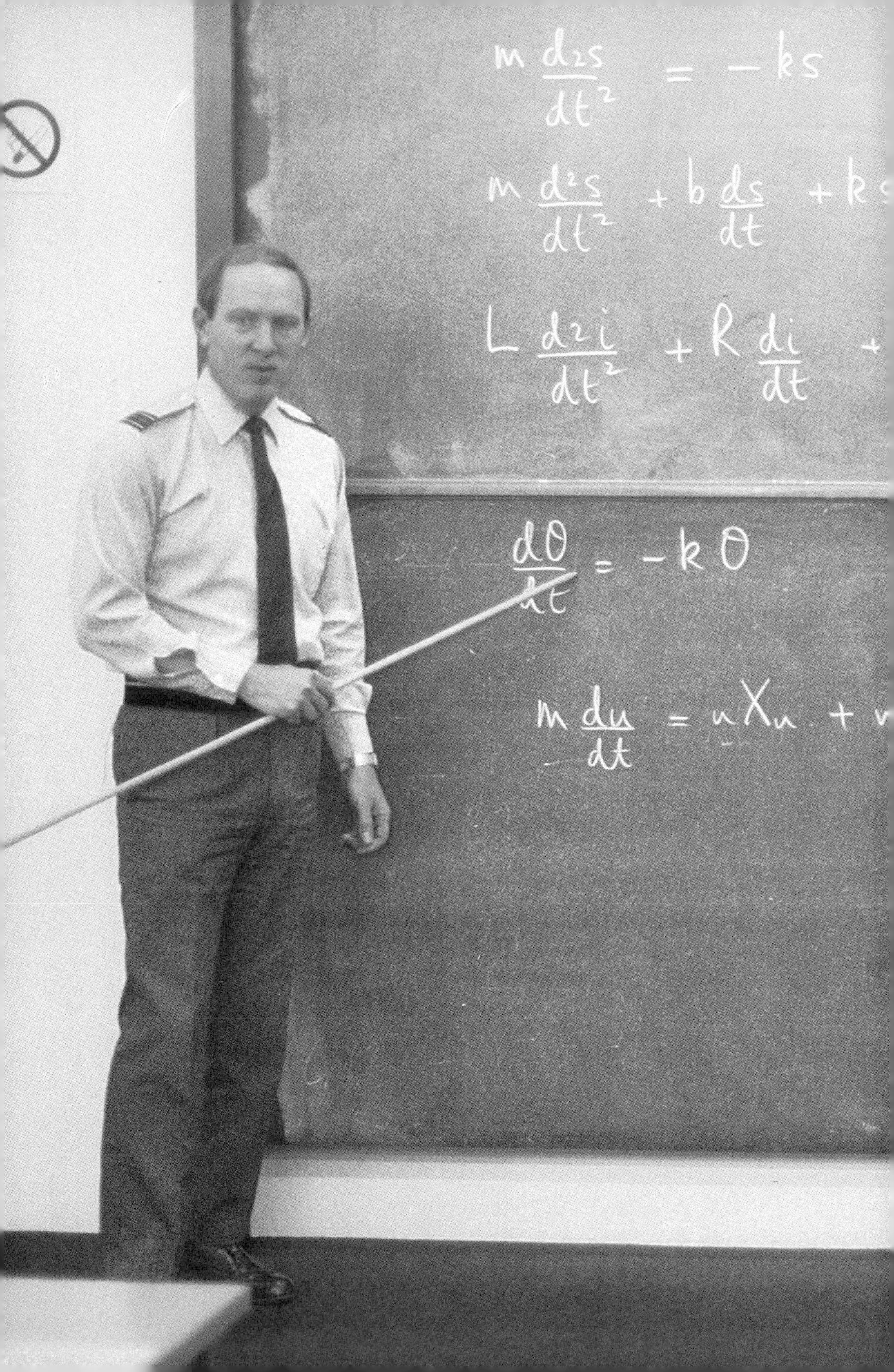
m d2s/dt² = −ks
m d²s/dt² + b ds/dt + k
L d2i/dt² + R di/dt +
dθ/dt = −kθ
m du/dt = uXu +

4 Learn to Test

A test pilot will always walk
round an aircraft twice:
not to double check –
he is looking for the way in.
ANON, *Boscombe Down*

No. 44 ETPS course began like any other at Boscombe Down, in the first week of February. It ran for forty-five weeks divided into three terms, separated by three short leave periods, which as the learning curve built up, started to seem like distant oases in a desert of work. The CO of the School, Wing Commander John Bolton, laid down a list of five main headings which delineate the function of the course:

1 *To Develop a Critical Approach* Whilst the military pilot is trained to compensate for any deficiencies in his aircraft and to use equipment to its best advantage, it is the role of the test pilot to identify problem areas, establish limits and to develop techniques.
2 *To Broaden Experience* This is more important today than ever as most of our students have experience of only one, or at the best two, operational types of aircraft. This type diversification is a most important part of the course and allows our graduate test

opposite, Sqn Ldr Andy Debuse, Principal Ground Tutor, ETPS. The 250 hours of ground instruction include 'This subject dear to your hearts . . .' (*B. Johnson*); *left*, Wg Cdr John Bolton, 'The Boss' (*BBC*)

pilots to approach test programmes on new aircraft with confidence based on experience and good training. It also encourages a broadminded approach to new developments in aircraft and systems.

3 *To Understand Theory* This is necessary so that test pilots may understand the language of the scientists and engineers and discuss problems on a near-equal basis. The course does not try to make them into 'boffins'.

4 *To Learn Test Techniques* Results and interpretations must be understood internationally, which is particularly important in these days of co-operative projects.

5 *To Learn to Report* The success of a test pilot depends as much on the clarity of his written and oral reports, and his ability to select and emphasise essentials, as on his flying skill.

It is interesting to note that, in the above guidelines which govern the philosophy of the ETPS course, the presence of flying skills is assumed. ETPS is not a flying school as such; as the Boscombe Down Superintendent of Flying has put it, ETPS is a post-graduate operational conversion course and, although specialised flying techniques are taught, a high standard of what might be termed normal operational flying is essential. To a casual observer it might seem strange that the number of flying hours that the students acquire while at Boscombe Down is about 150 while the number of hours devoted to ground school lectures is over 260; and that figure is a fraction of the time that all the students will spend on briefings, additional study and report writing.

On Course No. 44/23 (the general lectures are common to both the fixed and rotary wing courses), the first three weeks were devoted to ground school lectures. It would be tedious to detail them all but the titles included: statistics, mechanics, engines,

Rotary Wing student Lt Bob Horton RN found the maths 'a hell of a shock' (*B. Johnson*)

aerodynamics, structures, report writing and mathematics. Of the above (and the list is by no means complete), the last two subjects caused the most apprehension; the first because it would dominate the waking lives of the students, the second because it was there.

The lecturer responsible for the teaching of mathematics at ETPS was the Principal Ground Tutor, Squadron Leader Andy Debuse, a rare combination of a highly qualified scientist and humorist, who conceded the difficulty that many of the students would have in dealing with the subject:

'Maths is quite a hurdle for some people especially if they have only obtained an O level. In about ten hours of instruction we have to take them from that O level qualification right through to approximately first-year degree standard: it is a fairly narrow subject area but it is still a very steep learning curve. Our main problem is that we have students coming on the course with a variety of academic backgrounds; some with just a few O levels, others with university degrees, a few with PhDs, and Masters degrees. It is my job, in the first two or three weeks of the course, to bring them to the same academic standard.'

When making the BBC documentary of the course we recorded a portion of one of Andy Debuse's lectures:

'Good morning. The subject of today's lecture is a subject dear to all your hearts: differential equations. We have an example here on the overhead projector and, as you can see, it is a linear second order homogenous equation, one which you will all have learned to know and love . . .'

At the conclusion of the lecture which, it must be said, produced glazed faces on some of his audience, to lighten the atmosphere a little, Andy Debuse produced a textbook and said:

'I am sure you will all want to do some further reading on this fascinating subject and I can recommend this book, *Mathematics for Engineers* by Dull: it is the sort of book that when you have put it down you cannot pick it up again.'

One of his students, a very experienced helicopter pilot, Bob Horton, would no doubt have agreed with him; he found the mathematics, 'A hell of a shock. A lot of the guys are like myself; all failed A level maths, and that was about twelve years ago at school. Suddenly being confronted with quadratic equations and calculus was really mind blowing. It was very difficult.' Bob found the ground school hard work in general, his reaction being typical: 'It is a lot of reading. The subject matter is not fantastically complicated because we have a good tutor [Andy Debuse] here who can put it over well. The problem is the volume; there is so much of it – the whole aviation subject is absolutely vast. It is going to take me at least another year to reread all the notes.'

Concentration. The lectures are integrated with the flying and inattention could prove disastrous. (*B. Johnson*)

If the course was hard on the students it was also hard on their wives. It might be said that it was even harder on them; the students at least had the satisfaction of the course which, despite the hard work, was absorbingly interesting, particularly when the flying started. Bob Horton: 'Unfortunately my wife and I live at Yeovilton, which is my old base, and it was just impractical to move up here, so I live in the Mess during the week in this little hutch. At the weekends I manage to get home but even then I have got to work as soon as I get there, so I do not see much of my wife.'

Some of the students had their wives and families living in married quarters at Boscombe Down. Married quarters are generally available to all the students, including the ones from overseas, but some wives had good jobs near the bases from which the students came and were unwilling to give them up; additionally, those with children at school tended to stay behind. Even for those with their wives at Boscombe Down, the course always came first. As Bob Horton observed, 'All the wives here have been complaining because the fellows will finish work about five o'clock, go home, walk in through the door, say "Hello Dear", then straight into the study and start writing.'

Officers' wives are intensely loyal to their husbands' service; during the ten months that the BBC was at Boscombe Down, the producer and crew often heard of discontent from that direction, but not one of the wives was prepared to express so much as a hint of it before the cameras, indeed the only wife who consented to be interviewed at all was Mme Serge Aubert.

Concurrent with the ground school lectures, the two courses also began the conversion training to familiarise the students with the school's fleet. The training began in the ground school with

Sqn Ldr Ron Rhodes
AFC, ETPS Fixed Wing
QFI (*BBC*)

lectures on the aircrafts' systems and cockpit assessment. The conversion flying was undertaken by the two Qualified Flying Instructors (QFIs) on the ETPS staff. The fixed wing students were trained by Squadron Leader Ron Rhodes, one of the most experienced instructors in the RAF. Ron does not take kindly to the suggestion that he is the oldest pilot still flying with the Air Force; although there cannot be many left who, like him, flew Spitfires operationally. Squadron Leader Mike Butt was the school's Rotary Wing Instructor. Both the senior instructors served for many years with the Central Flying School and have more flying hours in their logbooks than those of all their students put together. The students were, as a matter of policy, converted to all the school aircraft. This was true of both courses: the helicopter men were given an hour or two on most of the fixed wing machines and the fixed wing pilots were expected to fly the helicopters. The really serious flying was, however, devoted to the aircraft appropriate to the two courses. That said, it should be borne in mind that most of the aircraft were new types to the students, although that statement is more likely to be true of the fixed wing pilots than those who normally flew helicopters, simply because there are far more fixed wing aircraft types in service than rotary wing.

The ability to demonstrate an aptitude for quickly adapting to aircraft of very different types is a major qualification consideration at ETPS. The CO, Wing Commander John Bolton, explained: 'We deliberately expose the students fairly early on in the course to a large number of types to check their adaptability. We do not give them long conversions to the aircraft, we give them the minimum conversion, showing them that they can adapt quickly to different aircraft: that basically they [the aircraft] are all the same and, provided they know the fundamental differences, then they can cope with the sort of flying that is required. [The students] are obviously not flying the aircraft operationally, they are flying them in specific areas doing specific tests . . . Now the problem is that some people are not able to rush from one aircraft to another, and unfortunately those people cannot really be employed as test pilots . . . not all the students pass. We hope that our selection procedure will give us students who are likely to pass the course but one can never be sure.'

(Wing Commander Bolton not only passed his ETPS course, No. 33, he also won the McKenna Trophy that year.)

The students' first encounter with the school aircraft occurred in the third week, on the ground, the exercise being 'cockpit assessment'. This was to evaluate the ergonomic layout of the eight fixed, and the four rotary wing aircraft types which the school operates (see page 272)[1].

For five weeks or so the two courses flew the conversion exercises, which mean just that: all the students were skilled, professional pilots, but some had been with fighter squadrons and had not therefore flown transports such as the Andover; conversely the transport pilots had had little or no experience on high-performance aircraft such as the Jaguars. There are no simulators at Boscombe Down but most students would have had an hour or two on a Jaguar simulator, if available, at an RAF station which

A school Hunter (*above*) and a Hawk (*right*) are prepared for training sorties (*B. Johnson*)

operates the type. (This practice has recently become more difficult since RAF Jaguars have been modified and fitted with new
navigation and weapon-aiming systems. The simulators of the
operational conversion squadrons therefore differ markedly from
the ETPS Jaguars, which retain their original avionic fit.)

The helicopter students converted to the Lynx, Scout and
Gazelle. The amount of time devoted to conversion by both wings
was, as Wing Commander John Bolton has pointed out, intentionally limited, the actual figures being:

Fixed Wing

Andover:
  2 hours dual, 1 hour solo, 1 hour Instrument Rating Test.
Jaguar:
  2 hours dual, 1 hour solo, 1 hour Instrument Rating Test.
Hunter:
  2 hours dual, 1 hour solo.
Hawk:
  2 hours dual, 1 hour solo.
BAC 1–11:
  2 hours dual, 1 hour solo.
(The Andover and BAC 1–11 solo flights are with a student
command pilot and a second student acting as the co-pilot. A staff
flight engineer is carried.)

This BAC 1-11, ZE 432, joined the school fleet during Course No. 44. Apart from the two ex-transport students, none of the remainder had flown anything so large. (*B. Johnson*)

The ETPS maintenance hangar at Boscombe Down in which a Hunter and a Jaguar are being overhauled (*B. Johnson*)

Rotary Wing

Lynx, Scout and Gazelle:

2 hours dual and two separate solo flights of one hour each.

After the conversion training with the QFIs, the students flew the first of many exercises which were investigative and not part of the training given in a normal flying school. The sortie was called Pressure Error Correction (PEC) and was flown on the Hawk. (The Rotary Wing have a similar exercise.) The object of the exercise was the calibrating of the aircraft's pressure instruments, the altimeter and the airspeed indicator (ASI), both of which operate, as their names imply, by air pressure which they measure and display either as altitude or indicated airspeed – both may be subject to errors.

These two instruments are vital to any aircraft, from a microlight to Concorde: the ASI to help the pilot to keep the machine above stalling speed and below the 'Never Exceed' speed (Vne) given by the manufacturer; and the altimeter to help the pilot keep above ground in every sense of the word.[2] The two instruments with which we are here concerned are, when compared with their fellows on the aircraft's instrument panel, extremely simple and pre-date aviation by many decades. The altimeter is really an aneroid barometer calibrated in feet or metres above a given datum instead of 'Stormy–Very Dry'. The principle of the ASI was used by Pitot around 1730 for measuring the flow of rivers and is based on that of a manometer: if a tube which is closed at one end is placed facing the airflow to be measured, the pressure difference between the two ends of the tube will be proportional to the airspeed. The ASI is a sensitive pressure gauge which can measure the differential and display it, usually in analogue form, to the pilot as knots, miles or kilometres per hour.

In practice, the Pitot tube is more complicated. It is not closed at one end but placed so that it compares what is known as static and dynamic pressure, the static pressure being that of the surrounding air and the dynamic pressure being the airflow over the aircraft, which is a function of its speed. Unfortunately, the disruption of the air which the aircraft creates as it flies can affect the pressure being sensed by the Pitot tube, causing what are known as Position Errors. (There are other errors caused by altitude and temperature, in addition to those connected with the instrument itself, but to discuss them is beyond the scope of this volume.) Designers place the Pitot tube in the best position they can, normally near the outer leading edge of the wing or on the aircraft's nose; clear of such obvious error sources as propeller slipstream or jet engine intakes, and as far from the leading edge of the wing as possible to avoid aerodynamic effects. However, residual turbulence from the aircraft's structure remains as it is impractical to extend the Pitot tube far enough away from the unwanted influences to ensure complete accuracy. In fact, the errors caused by dynamic pressures are small, it is the provision of the static pressure which causes the major difficulties.

The problems of the altimeter, which requires only a source of static pressure, are simpler, although the provision of an area of neutral pressure on an aircraft capable of over 700 mph is not all that easy. The static vent, as it is called, is usually to be found on the side of the fuselage. It consists of a plate with a small port in it, to which the static tube is connected: the legend 'Static vent, do not paint' is nearly always stencilled by it. The accuracy demanded from the altimeter is of the order of one millibar, which is equivalent to 30 feet of height. To compensate for the day-to-day changes of atmospheric pressure, provision is made to set the instrument to zero before each flight by adjusting a sub-scale calibrated in either Millibars mb (Europe) or Inches of Mercury Hg (USA).[3]

It is appropriate that calibrating the ASI and altimeter should form the first exercise of both the fixed and rotary wing course at ETPS, since the first duty of a test pilot confronted with a prototype is to do precisely that. There are several methods of calibrating pressure instruments for errors, some of which require calibrated pacer aircraft or the use of radars and lasers. The method used at ETPS is the simplest and the one known as 'Tower Fly Past'. Each student is required to fly at least ten runs at a planned

'Tower Fly Past'. This is a print of an ETPS test run. The Hawk (with wheels down) is precisely over the Boscombe Down tower. The special camera has superimposed a calibration grid to enable the student to reduce the results for his report. (*MoD (PE)/A&AEE*)

indicated airspeed and nominal height. The Hawk makes its runs over the centre line of the main 24/06 runway[4] at Boscombe Down at a height not less than two wingspans of the test aircraft. In the case of the Hawk that is about 50 feet. The speeds range from about 160 to 500 mph. An F24 camera is placed on the roof of the A&AEE HQ building which photographs the runs and superimposes a calibrating grid on the photographs, from which, after data reduction, the true height and speed of each test run can be determined.

An observer, one of the students, is carried in the rear seat of the Hawk, and he records the conditions of each run. When the tests are over, the two students work as a syndicate to reduce the figures which include other factors: the indicated airspeed, height, barometric pressure, temperature and corrections for the height of the recording camera and other elements. The syndicate is required to produce a graphical report of the pressure error corrections for the Hawk within ten days. The ground school has a computer to help in the work. When the students have produced the results they have completed their first exercise as test pilots.

The next task to be flown in the first term was a rather more complex one: Longitudinal Static Stability.

An aircraft in flight is a compromise balancing the five forces which govern its ability to remain airborne. The five forces are: lift from the wings; lift from the tailplane; thrust from the engine(s); aerodynamic drag caused by the passage of the aircraft through the air; and, of course, weight which opposes all flight. The balance of these conflicting forces is not constant; it is, to put it simply, dependent on the attitude and speed of the aircraft at any given moment. The degree to which an aircraft can maintain controlled flight is expressed in terms of its stability. Stability is a house of many mansions, and there are a number of textbooks devoted to the subject; only a simple outline is offered here.

The two major sub-divisions of stability are static and dynamic. The ETPS exercise which we are now discussing is static stability. The classic definition of static stability is the tendency of an aircraft to return to its balanced state, level flight for example, after a pilot has disturbed that equilibrium by making a control input and then releasing the stick. The aircraft is said to possess positive static stability if it returns to its former balanced flight; if on the other hand it departs from equilibrium when the pilot releases the controls, the aircraft is said to have negative static stability. If the aircraft remains in balance when the stick is released then it has neutral static stability.

The simplest way of envisaging the three forms of static stability is the analogy of the ball and basin. If a small ball is placed in a

pudding basin it will always return to the bottom of the basin however much the basin is tilted; that is the analogy for positive static stability. If the basin is inverted (assuming it has not got a flat bottom) the ball will not remain on it for very long; that is negative stability. Neutral stability can be demonstrated by placing the ball on a flat surface.

Good stability is vital when an aircraft, like this ETPS Hawk approaching Boscombe Down in a left-hand turn, is manoeuvring at low altitude (*MoD (PE)/A&AEE*)

An aircraft with longitudinal static stability will fly as if it had two springs attached to the tail of the fuselage; one pulling the aircraft up, the other down, maintaining a state of balance with the machine's centre of gravity (C of G) as the pivot. If a gust disturbs the equilibrium, the springs return it to level flight. The greater the disturbance, the greater the force returning it to balanced flight. Of course, no aircraft has such springs but the balance of the various forces acting on the airframe behave in precisely the same way provided the aircraft has been designed to exhibit longitudinal static stability.

An aircraft which possesses a marked longitudinal stability will tend to oppose the intentional changes to its flight attitude and will not be very manoeuvrable; fine for an airliner but less desirable for an air superiority fighter. Designers have therefore to decide the amount of stability to build, as it were, into their aircraft.

There are many other factors to take into consideration when the question of stability is being considered, the major problem of control systems being one.

The ETPS students, before embarking on the stability exercise, had read the excellent paper on the subject 'Stability and Control' by one of the tutors, Squadron Leader James Giles. This extract puts the problem most succinctly:

> So why do we, as test pilots, need to understand about stability and control to say whether or not an aeroplane is good at its job? The heading of this section [*Flying Quality Testing*] should be a clue, so try a definition:
>
> 'Flying qualities are those stability and control characteristics which govern the ease, precision and safety with which the pilot can fly his aeroplane to perform the tasks necessary to execute the required mission.
>
> 'The mission is determined when a new aeroplane requirement is drawn up: however the mission may be changed during the service life of the aeroplane. The Jaguar is a case in point, where the mission changed from advanced trainer to low-level strike-attack. It is essential, therefore, that the total mission requirements are defined, and clearly understood by all test pilots involved in a flight test programme . . . The tasks for which the most favourable flying qualities are required are the critical tasks within the overall mission. For an aircraft which must perform air-to-air or air-to-ground functions (and the training for those functions), the greatest emphasis must be placed on the flying qualities exhibited while performing the manoeuvres needed to accomplish these critical tasks . . . in all cases, adequate flying qualities must be provided so that take-off, approach and landing manoeuvres can be performed precisely, consistently and safely.'

For the students to experience different flying qualities it would be necessary for the school to have a very large fleet of aircraft, far more than would be a practical proposition. Furthermore, it would be desirable to have access to aircraft which were in fact deficient in handling, to the point of being unsafe, in order to demonstrate deficiencies of control. Apart from the obvious dangers of flying such aircraft, they do not exist, despite the opinion of some pilots; even if one were built it would not be possible to certify it to fly.

At ETPS there is, however, a rather elegant compromise: the Variable Stability System Basset (VSS). This unique aircraft, XS 743, was specially modified for use at ETPS and was delivered as long ago as June 1973; it has been in continuous use at Boscombe Down since that date. The original Beagle Basset was a small, twin-

engined, passenger aircraft; twenty-two were ordered, mainly as VIP transports (one, XS 770, was part of the Royal Flight). The ETPS Basset was the second of the order and is now one of only three remaining in RAF service, and uniquely was fitted with a computer which derives its input from the right-hand-seat flying controls. The left-hand, or command pilot's controls, are normal and original. The right-hand controls, which are the ones used by the student, are only connected to the computer, sending analogue signals which the computer interprets and uses to move the appropriate flying surfaces. The tutor can vary the signals from the controls to simulate various handling and stability problems, hence the generic term for such a system: variable stability. In effect, the VSS Basset is a flying simulator which, by altering a set of potentiometers placed at the side of the tutor's position, can be made to exhibit a number of characteristics which a normal Basset does not possess. What happens is that the computer can overlay the student's given control inputs and add or subtract to the actual, as opposed to the intended, movement of the flying control surfaces to a degree predetermined by the tutor. In this way a number of possible options are available. The Basset, a light twin, can be made to handle like a heavy transport. It can also be made to fly exceedingly badly, to mimic serious design deficiencies, the only inhibiting factor being the structural limits of the Basset's

The cockpit of the VSS Basset. The right-hand controls are only connected to the computer which can interpret the analogue signals from the pilot in a number of different ways; making the aircraft, if required, virtually unflyable. (*B. Johnson*)

The VSS Basset at altitude on an ETPS exercise; all flying via the computer has to be above 3000 feet in case of electronic failure (*B. Johnson*)

airframe. If the student mishandles the aircraft and begins to encroach on the limitations, the computer cuts out and the right-hand control is disconnected, the tutor taking over control. This is the reason for the strict rule that the VSS Basset must never be flown solo to take off or land, or to fly below 3000 ft when the computer is in use.

A typical exercise flown by the VSS Basset is an investigation into a stability problem that is common to a number of aircraft; the so-called Dutch roll, a wallowing motion, noticeable particularly in swept-wing aircraft at high altitude and at low speed, which can make landing approaches difficult in that the pilot finds it hard to fly smoothly and accurately. The following extract is from one such exercise. The tutor was James Giles and the student was Serge Aubert. We take it up when control was handed over to Serge Aubert, once the Basset was level at 3000 feet:

'Right, Serge, you have control of the aircraft and the computer. What we are now going to see is the effect that a Dutch roll has on the flying qualities of the aircraft and the extra workload you will then have to control it. What I want you to do is to put a small rudder doublet in [that is, moving the rudder from left to right twice] then, holding the wings level, with the stick central just have a look at the natural response of the aeroplane as it comes round. As you can now see, it is gradually getting divergent . . . [The Basset began to yaw and roll with increasing amplitude until the safe limits of the Basset were approached: a sideslip angle of 8 degrees,

and the computer cut out with an audible signal.] . . . There, that is the system cutting out saying that probably the aircraft would have crashed had that been allowed to continue. What that means is that in turbulence you would expect a major problem.'

The success of the VSS Basset in demonstrating handling problems to embryo test pilots is such that an updated version, using a

above, Tutor James Giles and his French student Serge Aubert, strap in for a VSS Basset sortie Informality is the keynote of the relations between ETPS staff and students. (*B. Johnson*)

left, The T5 Lightning XS 422, a still from the BBC *Test Pilot* series. The Lightning is the fastest aircraft on the school fleet and is usually the fastest most of the students have ever flown. (*BBC*)

Hawk as the host aircraft, is under development and it will join the ETPS school fleet in the not too distant future. With the great advances that have been made in computer design in the thirteen years since the VSS Basset joined the ETPS fleet, it is hoped that it will be possible to remove some of the limitations which restrict the use of the Basset: landings and take-offs for example, for as Squadron Leader James Giles, who is very much concerned with the development of the new VSS Hawk, pointed out, 'One of the hardest tasks for a test pilot to assess is an aircraft during approach, landing and taking-off. These are critical areas to all aircraft operations and it would be very nice if the student could actually assess different aircraft characteristics in these areas of flight.' There would seem to be little reason why this should not be possible; after all, most modern military aircraft are what is known as 'fly by wire', using computers to interpret the pilot's control inputs.

The VSS Basset is one of only two aircraft on the ETPS fleet which is used solely as a teaching aid. The second aircraft is the BAC Lightning. The one on the ETPS flight line is a two-seat conversion trainer, a T5, XS 422. One of twenty T5s ordered in the mid-1960s, it is still one of the fastest and most powerful aircraft on the RAF's inventory. (The RAF in 1985 still had two operational squadrons of Lightning F6s.)

Powered by two 15,000 lbs thrust Rolls-Royce engines which can accelerate (with afterburners) the Lightning up to around

The dated cockpit of the Lightning XS 422 makes this Mach 2 fighter attractive to the school since students can fly supersonically without the aid of advanced avionic systems which contemporary 'fly by wire' strike aircraft require (*B. Johnson*)

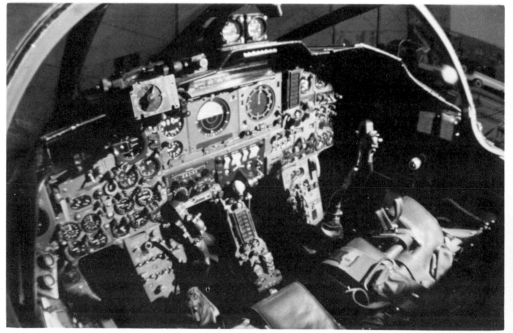

Mach 1.8 or 1400 mph at 40,000 ft (although with, it must be said, very restricted endurance, typically half an hour), the ETPS Lightning is used for demonstrating the effects of transonic flight, for which its dated design makes it ideal. The aircraft is also used in the first term to investigate longitudinal stability. It is always flown dual, because there is insufficient time to convert students from other than fighter backgrounds to this formidable machine.

Not all the fixed wing students can be allowed to fly the Lightning: to his intense disappointment Mirco Zuliani could not. It had nothing to do with his flying ability – he was an F-104 pilot in Italy – Mirco was simply too tall. The cramped cockpit of the T5 leaves little room for the pilot and anyone with long legs is liable to find that his knees will not clear the instrument panel should he have to eject. If this be the case, and as far as Mirco was concerned it was, he is, for obvious safety reasons, debarred.

With the intensification of the flying it should not be thought that the number of lectures diminished; far from it, they continued on a daily basis, starting at 0830 hrs and continuing until 1030 when the day's flying commenced. The character of the lectures changed; no longer devoted to resurrecting half-forgotten school subjects such as mathematics, they now had a direct relevance to the work of the test pilot. For the BBC programme one was filmed which was typical: Squadron Leader James Giles on flight control systems:

'Gentlemen, this morning we are going to start a course on flight control systems. During the course we will be looking at the F-16 in some detail. I shall be using it as an example, not to teach you how to design flight control systems, but to demonstrate to you the complexity of modern designs. Since the Second World War, we have seen a growth in complexity, starting with basic aircraft that flew with a very limited flight control envelope and were able to use simple control systems. We have seen control augmentation systems and stability systems using feedback loops into the basic mechanical controls. Today we have full "fly by wire" authority.

'One might expect that we would have been seeing an increase in the excellence of control systems and the capability of pilots to fly the aircraft; it has not, however, always been the case. For an example one can cite the F-16's first flight, which was not in point of fact meant to be such; it was a high-speed taxiing trial that got out of control with a lateral, pilot-induced oscillation: the pilot simply selected full power, became airborne and fortunately was able to sort things out. Nearer home, one could look at the case of the Tornado which crashed on landing after flying many hundreds of hours, indeed the type was then in service; the pilot was pumping the stick, sampling the pitch attitude, on a landing approach,

Each hour of flying at ETPS generates about twenty hours of writing. Here Serge Aubert toils late at night on his VSS Basset report. For the overseas students who, like Serge, have to write in a foreign language, the already high workload must seem oppressive. (*B. Johnson*)

when through no fault of his and no failure of the control system the aircraft crashed its nosewheel very heavily on to the runway, wrecking the Tornado, because within the software there was a loop which the pilot inadvertently got into. The loop was an augmented response to stick pumping which put pitch acceleration in phase with control stick input, in other words pitch attitude; the attitude of the aircraft became 180 degrees out of phase (this is a basic situation for a pilot), so that as the nose was descending and the pilot attempted to correct by pulling the stick back, it was just causing an increasing oscillation which drove the aircraft steeply into the ground. I could also cite the space shuttle which nearly crashed on its third or fourth landing because it got into a lateral pilot-induced oscillation.

'These are examples of aircraft whose designers thought that there were no problems, yet clearly there were; that is what we are going to try to teach you, to look into those corners of flight envelopes in modern flight control systems where you may find problems . . . we now have aircraft whose dynamics, whose modes of flying, are created by software designers and not, as in the recent past, by airframe designers. Remember you must always look at the flight control systems of aircraft, you must be aware of what is happening and what the engineer has designed in before you can make an assessment. Most important.'

That is a small extract from a series of lectures given by Squadron Leader Giles on the subject of the complex control systems of the F-16 fighter. The amount of paperwork generated by the lectures and the growing volume of report writing increased as the course proceeded and for many, if not all the students, posed a major worry; for the demands of advanced flying, which calls for a fit and wideawake pilot, coincided with the steepening learning curve.

Squadron Leader Vic Lockwood, the Principal Fixed Wing Tutor of No. 44 Course, was well aware of the problems: 'In simplistic terms, all the men who come on the course are professional pilots; this is a post-graduate course. They have already proved themselves in their own fields: they come here and they embark on a new career, a difficult career. They bring with them their flying skills but we have to push them even in that sphere. At the same time they have to cope with academics; there comes a point during the course where students are being driven beyond the flying skills they have had in the past, at the same time as they are being pushed very hard academically . . . the biggest problem from the staff point of view is knowing just how far to push these chaps. [What] tends to happen is that, as the academic side builds up, it puts a great deal of pressure on some of the students who, although they have achieved a high standard of flying, are not necessarily the most natural pilots; they achieve their high standards by hard work. Now their hard work is being redirected into academics and there is therefore less time to concentrate on the flying. The result is a falling off of both flying and academic standards: it is a vicious circle . . . we expect a high standard; if any fail to meet it, I am afraid they must pay the consequences. I think it is fair to say that people who have not done very well on the course in the past have known they were not doing too well and we were able to come to an amicable arrangement about them leaving.'

Vic Lockwood knew well the pressures of completing a course at ETPS; he remembers clearly a morning about half-way through his own course, No. 33: 'It was the morning of my thirtieth birthday; I was having a shave and for the first time that morning I looked into the mirror, and saw to my horror this old man looking back; I had aged about ten years on the course.'

There is little doubt that all the students found the writing of reports onerous, yet it is an essential aspect both of the training and the subsequent work of the test pilot. Since written reports form such an important part of the ETPS course, it is interesting to quote from the relevant chapter 'Report Writing', which is, significantly, Chapter 1 in the ETPS Flying Wing notes.

Introduction

1 The end product of all flight testing is the test pilot's written report on the results of his work in the air. No matter how skilful he is as a pilot, his efforts will be wasted if he is unable to communicate his findings and persuade others of his viewpoint. The art of effective report writing is as important to the test pilot as a sound knowledge of his aircraft or the theory and practice of test flying.

2 Proficiency in report writing can only be acquired through practice and a thorough understanding of the basic principles involved. Reports thus constitute a major part of the ETPS syllabus, the primary aims being to give students such practice and to ascertain whether the test exercise has been properly understood . . . in addition, students will practise verbal presentations for the same reasons; the basic rules of report writing also apply to such presentations.

General Considerations

3 The flight test report follows the basic conventions of good English prose with particular emphasis on the following factors:

ACCURACY Facts and wording must be accurate. Opinions and deductions must be distinguishable from facts. The reader's confidence in your judgement and your report will be undermined if he discovers errors of fact.

BREVITY The reader must be informed in the shortest way consistent with accuracy and clarity. His time is wasted by 'rambling' statements, unnecessary repetition, the inclusion of non-essential information and verbose phrases. Be concise; omit irrelevant information. Careful planning and editing are essential.

RELEVANCE Any irrelevant word, phrase or idea must be excluded. Avoid any tendency to include information outside the terms of reference of the report merely to demonstrate your powers of observation or the comprehensive nature of the flight tests performed.

LOGIC Conclusions, from which costly and time-consuming modifications may be recommended, must be fully supported by the facts obtained in the test. Conclusions should be contained in sentences and paragraphs which follow a logical sequence related directly to the argument.

The Successful Report

If your report is to be effective in convincing the reader of the soundness of your observations, you should ensure that the answer to the following questions is YES before submitting it:

    a Does my report fulfil the purpose for which it is intended?
    b Are my data and observations accurate?
    c Does my writing clearly say what I want to be known?
    d Will the reader be able to understand it?
    e Will the reader enjoy it?

The workload on the staff at ETPS is also high: tutor Sqn Ldr James Giles reading and correcting a student report in his office at Boscombe Down. Academic duties are in addition to the tutor's flying demonstrations. (*B. Johnson*)

Bob Horton, when asked about his reaction to the writing of test reports, said, 'I spend most of my time sitting at a desk, pen in hand, scribbling away, writing up reports on all the flights that I do. After every flight I have got to sit down, analyse all the data that I have taken and try to put it all together in good English so that someone, not necessarily connected with aviation, a scientist perhaps, can understand what I have found in the air.'

The arbiter of the students' reports is the exercise tutor and he can be very critical indeed for, as James Giles pointed out, once the conversion phase of the course is over and the students begin assessment exercises, their reports become more important:

'Reports are important for two reasons; firstly from the teaching standpoint they enable us to make sure that the student has understood the exercise that he has been given, they enable us to make sure that he can analyse the results he gets and that those results are correct, and that correct conclusions have been drawn. The second point is this: a man can be the best pilot in the world but unless he can sell his conclusions to his readers then there is no point in his getting airborne in the first place. [But] some people do have difficulty in communicating their ideas and developing them into convincing arguments. We have to make sure that the student test pilot can understand the relative importance of his findings . . . I look for the development of how he came to his conclusions and read his report as if I was a Project Manager at the Ministry, and the report had come from this Establishment and obviously I am going

The immortal RAF Form 700, which has been signed by generations of pilots. Once the form has been signed the pilot has accepted that the aircraft is airworthy and that he has assumed responsibility for it. (*B. Johnson*)

to be critical. I have a number of priorities: financial priorities, timescales, and other programmes to fit in with this one. So I am looking for really strong arguments to convince me.'

Having read the student's report, the tutor will annotate it and return it to the student. Later, it will be discussed in the same way as an essay at a university tutorial. All the ETPS tutors concede that the workload is very high; the course lasts for ten months, as it has for very many years, the difference is that the complexity of aircraft and the level of technical understanding required has grown to an extent unthinkable in 1943 when the course was founded. However, in the real world outside, the role of the test pilot too has changed and the course has to recognise that fact. James Giles:

'Test pilots today have to have a deeper knowledge of technology. However that same technology also helps the pilot. He is now closely monitored by ground [telemetry] stations; there are computer models, wind tunnels [simulators] and other technology to help. In the early days of test flying it was very much a case of "bolt on the modification, go and fly it and see how it works". So in many ways the job is safer, even though it is more technologically demanding.'

A cynic might point out that the sheer cost of a modern military prototype is such that it will be made as safe as possible to fly from the word go. There is no place in today's atmosphere of tight budget control for the 'kick the tyres and light the fires' attitude, which allegedly prevailed at certain American test centres in the 1950s, where test pilots flew, to quote one source, 'with almost reckless abandon'. This raises the point: are test pilots a race apart, immune to fear, unlike the rest of humanity? One of the most experienced British test pilots, John Farley, had no doubt on that question for, when asked if test pilots frighten themselves, he answered, 'If they don't they should not be test pilots. Fear is a very, very necessary thing . . . if a pilot does not have the greatest respect for any aeroplane that he is flying, not testing, but just flying then he ought not to be an aviator. It is a very unforgiving environment, the air; you must be frightened, you must know your limits, and you must know the aeroplane's limits, and if you come close to either you must be frightened. If you're not, your chances of being successful or avoiding an accident must greatly be reduced.'

John Farley went on to confirm the growing use of technology in test flying:

'Test flying these days is a team effort, the pilot or pilots concerned will be very well backed up by many aids to a successful test flight. Engineers, aerodynamicists, equipment, better knowledge of the weather and the atmosphere, a better knowledge of the aeroplane we are testing, simulators, computers, everything; it is a totally known risk . . . it is not dangerous. That is not a casual comment, it is based on a very good track record. The number of test pilots we have killed in the United Kingdom in the last twenty years is very small indeed.'

To even the most casual of observers it is clear that the standards of the ETPS courses has to be very high indeed to prepare their graduates for the exacting job of military test flying. The standard has to be absolute: an ETPS graduate is a test pilot; there are no grades, the students either pass or fail. As James Giles put it, 'We are not looking at a student in terms of success or failure, our job is to teach him. If he cannot reach the standards of safety in the air and credibility as a test pilot we will not pass him.'

As the first term ended, that fact had become clear to all the students at Boscombe Down, who were by then under no illusions about the work ahead if, in December, they were to be able to add the coveted letters 'tp' after their names on the Air Force List.

5 Test to Learn

*'Very fine aeroplane,
tell the designer chappie.'*
Taken from the radio sketch 'The Test Pilot' in
THE SECRET LIFE OF ANTHONY HANCOCK

On return to Boscombe Down after the short Easter leave, the students were formed into two- or three-man syndicates which operated under a single tutor's supervision. One of the first exercises on which the fixed wing students collectively embarked was a fundamental of all flying: the stall. Like the shark, which must keep swimming all its life, aircraft, once in the air, cannot stop. (Helicopters can hover, but in certain circumstances they too can stall their rotors.) The reason is simply that the flow of air over the wings and tailplane alone generate the lift which keeps the aircraft flying; disrupt the airflow by either flying too slowly, or raising the nose of the aircraft to the extent that the angle of the wing, relative to the airflow over it (the angle of attack), becomes too acute for the flow to be maintained, and the lift generated will cease and the aircraft will stall; the nose drops sharply and the aircraft will fall until the speed builds up to the point where lift is once again generated. Unfortunately for uncounted numbers of ex-pilots, if this happens near the ground – and the nearness is relative to the aircraft type in question – there may not be sufficient height in which to recover. The dangers of inadvertent stalling are increased by the fact that aircraft tend to be flying slowly when near the ground, for example during the approach to the landing.

Like so much else in the consideration of aerodynamics, that basic account of stalling is subject to certain caveats: stalling can be provoked in other ways. For the moment, it is sufficient to appreciate that the determination of the basic stalling speed of a prototype aircraft is one of the first duties of the test pilot. All pilots have to be aware of the nature, speed and stall recovery techniques of any aircraft which they are flying. For private pilots of straight-wing light aircraft this will simply be a minimum speed; the 'stalling

opposite, A student on No. 23 Rotary Wing ETPS course flying the school Scout helicopter. The Rotary and Fixed Wing courses run concurrently with a great deal of interchange. (*B. Johnson*)

speed' of the type. For a Cessna 172 the stall would typically be around 40 KIAS (Knots Indicated Airspeed). Even that simple case is subject to qualification: the stalling speed will be different with the degree of flaps lowered, the loading of the aircraft and the manoeuvres made at the relevant time: a steep turn will raise the stalling speed by a significant margin. It is obvious that a modern high-performance fighter is far more complex than a Cessna and the stalling characteristics are correspondingly more complex, particularly in the case of swept-wing aircraft.

The stalling exercises at ETPS are flown on two types of aircraft: the Hawk and the Hunter T7. The sortie on the Hunter was the final exercise. The students were briefed to suppose that the school's T7 Hunter was a new aircraft; that it was being evaluated as a conversion trainer (which was its original role in the RAF) and that therefore the stalling characteristics must be such that a trainee pilot could reasonably be expected to be able to recover from an inadvertent stall. To achieve the remit the students not only had to undertake the stalling programme, they also had to note the relevant parameters in the air, to enable them to reduce the results to a cogent report. The report had to be handed to the tutor within ten days of the exercise.

The first thing the syndicate did was to read the excellent ETPS précis on the exercise. The introduction to the paper (written by Lieutenant Commander M. A. Baker, USN, an ETPS tutor who left Boscombe Down in 1985 for astronaut training) is well worth quoting in part:

> As the complexity of aeroplanes has increased over the years, testing in the high angle of attack flight regime has progressed from 'seat of the pants' type investigations into well-structured, highly visible test programmes, today's aircraft frequently exhibit unpredictable and disorientating flight characteristics at high angles of attack and therefore require a comprehensive, logical build-up flight test investigation . . . Tactical and training aeroplanes frequently operate near the limits of the flight envelope where the likelihood of inadvertent high angle of attack flight is great; here a thorough investigation will be conducted.

The actual briefing included a dual demonstration flown with the tutor. The purpose of the flight was to acquaint the student with the stall techniques and also the procedures for recovering from an incipient spin which can follow a stall. The profile for the flights was to give the student practice in the use of special instrumentation fitted to the ETPS aircraft as an aid to data recording and spin recovery. Although students carried compact voice recorders which were connected to the aircraft's intercom system, as a precaution against a failure of the recorder, which is far from unknown, students were required to use the time-honoured knee-pad to note the various figures and aspects of the Hunter's behaviour during the sortie. A small strain gauge was fitted to the control stick to measure the hand forces required to control the aircraft during the flight. A number of stalls were made at high and low speed, with and without flaps, from a height of 25,000 feet. A normal one-turn spin and recovery was demonstrated at 40,000 feet.

It might be mentioned that the normal limits which are applied to the Hunter in squadron service do not apply at ETPS, who have special rules; for example, intentional spinning in the Hunter is not permitted at all on squadrons.

The weather has to meet certain minima. The notes are quite clear on that point:

> The exercises must be carried out clear of cloud, with a clear horizon and, if possible, in smooth conditions. The amount of height lost in recovering from unusual attitudes must be borne in mind when assessing the prevailing conditions, and there should be *no* chance of entering cloud, in the event of delayed recovery. Stalling is not to be done over the sea. Because of the possibility of entering a spin inadvertently, stalls are not to be carried out if there is 4/8th cloud or more above 15,000 feet in the exercise area. The time allowed: one dual demonstration flight, two exercise flights are allotted. During the exercise flights, an observer will . . . assist in data recording, look-out and flight safety.

The test techniques are precisely defined.

> In outline, the tests consist of flying the aircraft down to the stall, and recovering. Significant items at each stage should be noted. Although the flying must be done in a planned, controlled way, this is essentially an exercise in observation and reporting. It is all too easy to overlook or ignore symptoms and characteristics because they are already familiar to the pilot. Additionally, the test pilot must ensure that the characteristic which defines stall warning will be unmistakable and well-timed for the pilot in the operational environment. Students should remember that the stalling test is essentially a qualitative exercise.

The exercise begins when the Hunter is at 25,000 feet. For a normal-level flight (1g) stall, which is the first that the student experiences, the aircraft is slowed down by throttle reduction and use of the air brakes to about 20 knots above the 'book' figure for the stalling speed of around 150 knots. The horizon is used as a visual reference and the ASI is monitored to check the speed of

XL 612, one of two
Hunter T-7 trainers used
by the school for
advanced spinning
exercises. The Hunter
has had a replacement
wing fitted; such is
the pressure on the ETPS
fleet it has yet to be
repainted. (*B. Johnson*)

deceleration which should initially be 1 knot per second; the speed
reduction is maintained by the student raising the nose of the
aircraft. As the stall approaches, the student switches on the automatic data recorders and, using the voice recorder, calls out the
airspeed figures and an estimated angle of attack (the angle of the
wings relative to the horizon and level flight). As the angle of pitch-
up increases and the speed drops, the onset of pre-stall airframe
buffet commences; this too is quantified and recorded. (This is
most important since it is the only warning of the onset of an
inadvertent stall, apart from the ASI, which a trainee pilot would
get.) The ETPS student continues to raise the nose of the Hunter,
maintaining a 1g acceleration and a steady rate of deceleration. On
the threshold of the stall the airframe buffeting will be high and
control authority will become marginal. Swept-wing aircraft such
as the Hunter do not exhibit a clean 'g break' stall as do straight-
wing aircraft; the Hunter will adopt a nose-up angle of between 20
and 30 degrees (dependent on weight and the small rigging
anomalies of individual aircraft). The inexperienced pilot might
not predict a stall but in the condition described above the Hunter,

despite the high nose-up attitude, is actually falling at up to 4000
feet per minute. When the speed has dropped to a very low figure
the nose will eventually pitch down, at which point the pilot has to
note the parameters and instigate the recovery action which consists of levelling the wings, if one has dropped, to prevent an
incipient spin (the ailerons can be used on swept wing aircraft, for
the ailerons remain effective after the remainder of the wing has
stalled) pushing forward the control stick and opening up the throttle to regain flying speed. The aircraft is thereby eased out of the
resultant dive which can be very steep relative to the horizon.

One side-effect of the high angle of attack assumed by swept-
wing aircraft in the stall is the very real danger of causing a 'surge'
in the engine which will decrease substantially the thrust being
produced; furthermore, a full compressor stall can occur which
could lead to an engine flame-out. A flame-out is serious enough in
a single-engined aircraft such as the Hunter; in a twin-engined
fighter, the F-14 for example, should an engine surge at the point of
stall, the resultant asymmetric thrust will cause the aircraft to yaw
into a spin. As if this alone were not bad enough, the remaining
engine may well also flame-out, leaving the aircraft in a flat spin
from which recovery is wellnigh impossible. Two F-14s are known
to have been lost in just this way.

The remainder of the ETPS stall sortie was devoted to exploring
the dangers of entering and the techniques of recovering from
inadvertent stalls caused by mishandling, following such

XL 612 taxies out for a
sortie. ETPS Hunters
remain the only
swept-wing aircraft in
the world to be spun
inverted as a matter of
routine. (*B. Johnson*)

Two views of the Rotary Wing's Lynx helicopter, which is used on a number of advanced exercises, just as demanding as any flown by the Fixed Wing students (*B. Johnson*)

manoeuvres as air combat, short landings and take-offs and evading missile attacks. At the end of each part of the exercise the student will have to had noted a Situation Review containing the following information:

1 Stall warning speed and angle of attack.
2 Type and adequacy of stall warning.
3 Stall speed and angle of attack.
4 Stall characteristics.
5 Recovery characteristics.
6 Altitude lost and airspeed acceleration during recovery.

After the flight with the tutor the complete exercise was repeated by the student with an observer, usually the other member of the syndicate.

At the same time as the fixed wing students were flying the stall and stability exercises, the rotary wing students were exploring similar subjects.

The mention of longitudinal stability and manoeuvre stability was enough to produce glazed expressions among most of the fixed wing students. The subject is even more complex when applied to helicopters. The simple fact is that rotary wing aircraft have little or no inherent stability; they are dynamically unstable and nearly all modern service helicopters have stabilising devices and/or auto-pilots. Without such aids, the aircraft would not continue to fly on a stable course for very long once the pilot had released the controls and they would have to be hand-flown all the time they were airborne, even in level flight, in all but perfectly still air.

The fitting of stabilising devices improves handling; such aids range from a simple mechanical system to very sophisticated electronic autostabilisers. The main purpose of autostabilisation is to reduce the pilot workload; in some cases, however, the aerodynamics of a helicopter might be such that a full electronic autostabilisation system is essential for the stability and control of the aircraft.

Helicopters which employ 'fly-by-wire' techniques are known as 'Control Configured Vehicles' (CCVs). In such aircraft, as in many modern fixed wing high performance fighters, the pilot flies the aircraft through a computer with no direct mechanical control of the rotor or control surfaces. Electronic control enables the full performance of a helicopter to be exploited without the designer having to compromise performance by providing natural stability, or having to balance against the agility required in battle.

The ETPS exercises call for one hour dual and two hours solo in a Lynx helicopter. The brief for the exercise is as follows:

1 To evaluate the suitability of the helicopter's longitudinal flying qualities for the designed roles.

2 To explain with quantitative data, qualitative handling problems.

3 To predict problem areas in the helicopter's flight envelope in terms of centre of gravity (C of G) position, airspeed or manoeuvre or in the completion of a specific task.

4 To compare the aircraft's [actual] characteristics with a specification, or set criteria, in quantitative terms.

5 To assist in the design of autopilots and stability augmentation systems.

6 To assist in the design of modifications to alleviate handling deficiencies.

To discharge the brief is clearly a substantial task. The subject is complex and the technicalities are beyond the scope of the present volume. The general reader can, however, gain some idea of the exercise from the following quotations from the ETPS précis.

> The need for stability and control. A pilot needs to be able to fly a helicopter with the minimum of attention and correction under steady, trimmed conditions, and following a disturbance he expects the aircraft to return to approximately the original trimmed condition. Similarly he requires to be able to manoeuvre the helicopter easily, quickly and accurately; for example, to be able to rotate the 'nose' at a given rate of pitch without having to make a large number of corrections. This means that a pilot expects the helicopter to display some positive value of static, manoeuvre and dynamic stability throughout the flight envelope yet possess good agility whilst giving an acceptable ride in turbulence.

The ETPS notes then proceed to discuss the degree of stability required:

> If a helicopter exhibits a comparatively large value of static stability then relatively large stick movements will be required to change attitude and speed, and the response of the helicopter control movements may be sluggish; additionally relatively high control force may be required. The combination of large stick movements and high stick forces, for example, is unlikely to be acceptable for a reconnaissance helicopter operating close to the ground, whereas it may be acceptable for an Anti-Submarine Warfare (ASW) or communications helicopter.

The assessment of static and manoeuvring stability of a helicopter requires the test pilot to make a considered judgement of the handling qualities of the aircraft not only as he personally perceives them in terms of 'good', 'poor', but also in relation to the intended service role of the helicopter when flown on a military sortie by an average squadron pilot. The assessment may well then change to 'ineffective', 'inadequate', or even in an extreme case 'impossible'.

The test pilot's empirical and subjective impression of the aircraft's handling will be backed up by the quantitative data obtained by the special instrumentation and recorders fitted to test aircraft: g loading on the airframe and crew, the pull (or push) forces which the pilot has to apply for a given manoeuvre; the radius of turns, height loss, power settings, air and rotor speeds and other factors. All the test flight manoeuvres will be made with and without autostabilisation (except in the case of advanced helicopters where the stabilisation forms an integral part of the aircrafts' control systems, to the extent that they are, for all practical purposes, unflyable without it; in which case the technique of flight testing is partially to disable the stabilisers – with one or more 'lanes' rendered inoperative – to represent battle damage or partial electronic failure).

This essentially abbreviated account of the ETPS exercise gives some impression of the workload imposed on the test pilots' course; it should be remembered that, in addition to the flying exercises, and the inevitable report writing that was involved after virtually every flight, the ground school lectures and visits to other establishments continued unabated. In the six weeks following the short break for Easter the students had to attend the following lectures:

Fixed Wing
Longitudinal Dynamic Stability.
Longitudinal Stability at High Mach Numbers.
Power Controls.
Subsonic Lateral and Directional Stability and Control.
Roll Performance.

Rotary Wing
Longitudinal Static Stability.
Longitudinal Manoeuvre Stability.
Oscillation Analysis.
Longitudinal Dynamic Stability.
Helicopter Automatic Flight Control Systems (AFCS).

Fixed and Rotary Wings
Displays.
Weapon Aiming.
Navigation Systems.
Flying Wing Vivas.

The above are the lectures which were given in the ground school by the ETPS staff; in addition there were lectures presented by invited speakers. To complete the picture, the six weeks also included visits to The Royal Aeronautical Society for a series of talks by the Test Pilot Group. The rotary wing students attended a two-day symposium on 'Helicopter Simulators' and 'Helicopter Power Plants'. The students of both wings also visited both Rolls-Royce at Bristol and British Aerospace at Woodford. The rotary course went to Westlands at Yeovil, while the fixed wing students made a visit to the Royal Aircraft Establishment at Bedford.

The flying, interspersed with the lectures and visits, included an interesting exercise for the rotary wing course students; a climb to

XZ 936, a Gazelle used, among other exercises, for the climb to assess the service ceiling
(*B. Johnson*)

assess the service ceiling and predict the absolute ceiling of the school's Gazelle helicopter, XZ 936, measuring the rate of climb and noting any aircraft or engine handling difficulties encountered. Since the sortie was to fly the helicopter far beyond its normal service operating envelope, certain limitations were placed on the flight.

The maximum altitude was restricted to 20,000 feet as indicated by the pressure altimeter fitted to the aircraft. Since the sortie involved operating over 10,000 feet, oxygen had to be carried. The climb was to be discontinued if the outside air temperature (OAT) dropped to −30°C; if the rate of climb dropped to 100 feet per minute, or if vibration levels became unacceptable. (The tracking of the rotor, that is the setting of each individual blade, has to be as good as is possible before the exercise can be undertaken; a poorly tracking rotor which produces just acceptable levels of vibration at low height will cause unacceptable vibration at high altitude.)

The cabin heater fitted to the Gazelle had to be serviceable; the extensively glazed cabin of the helicopter would, if unheated, soon mist over once the aircraft had climbed to a significant height. (In round figures the temperature drops 2°C per 1000 feet of altitude.)

Although it was possible to carry automatic recorders to monitor the parameters of the flight, the students (two took part in the exercise, one acting as a flight observer) were required to make written notes. During the long climb the helicopter was flown on a steady

above, XZ 939, another
of the Boscombe Down
Gazelles. It carries
markings from a
previous unit, most of
the ETPS aircraft are
ex-operational; *right*,
XZ 936 flying at its
ceiling of 20,000 feet.
(*both B. Johnson*)

heading and a constant rate of climb maintained. With the aid of a stopwatch the following figures were noted:

Height, using the pressure altimeter set to 1013 mb.

Time.

Indicated airspeed (IAS).

Torque/collective pitch. (The control which is used to select the rate of climb. The throttle control is in the form of a twist grip on the collective lever.)

Rotor speed (N_R) in rpm.

Gas generator (N_G).

Jet pipe temperature (JPT). Power turbine inlet temperature (PTIT).

Fuel flow.

Fuel quantity.

Engine temperatures and pressures.

Control positions.

The determination of the last parameter was interesting as, in contrast to the exotic electronic test equipment used at Boscombe Down, the device for calibrating the amount of movement of the cyclic pitch (the helicopter equivalent of a fixed wing aircraft's control column) was simply a calibrated elastic band. The measure-

A Gazelle landing at Boscombe Down. Gazelles (and the Scout) are used for one of the most demanding exercises on the course: the determination of the avoid curve. (*B. Johnson*)

The cockpit of Gazelle XZ 936. Surmounting the standard panel are the additional instruments carried by most of the ETPS aircraft. These show the actual position of the various control surfaces and, in the case of the helicopters, the rotor pitch demands. (*B. Johnson*)

ment was made at maximum altitude to assess the effect of a given control input, which was very different from that which would have been obtained at lower altitudes. A brief summary of the handling and performance figures obtained during the service ceiling climb is tabled below:

Change in vibration levels.

Comfort and view [the former is relative, *Author*].

Ease of flying the climb schedule.

Changes of handling with altitude.

The adequacy or otherwise of the range of controls.

Engine and rotor governor behaviour; engine and transmission
    temperatures and pressures.

The height at which maximum N_G or JPT/PTIT was reached.
After the sortie the results had to be reduced to a graphical presentation and a full report submitted to the tutor (Squadron Leader Iain Young) within two days.

The first term ended on 20 May. The students and their tutors then went on two weeks of well-earned spring leave. One can say with some confidence that many of the students spent a good proportion of the leave studying and revising their school notes.

6 Mid-Term

What is chiefly needed
Is skill rather than machinery.
WILBUR WRIGHT, 1902

Summer at Boscombe Down. For the members of the 44th ETPS course it meant frustrating days of endless rain and a restricted flying programme which, in the jargon, began to 'slip'. A new aircraft had joined the school fleet; a BAC 1-11, 475 Series, ZE 432, ex-Air Pacific DQ-FBV. This particular airliner was selected because it had a strengthened undercarriage with low-pressure tyres, designed to withstand operating from the rough Second World War airfields that formed its destinations as it flew from island to island in the Pacific.

Overhauled, fitted with service communication and navigation equipment, and resplendent in the high visibility 'Raspberry Ripple' red, white and blue colour scheme of the ETPS fleet, ZE 432 was a welcome addition to the Boscombe Down flight line for, training apart, it could also be used as a transport. One of the first items on the syllabus of the summer term was the BAC 1-11 'Convex' – Conversion Exercise. Here was one aircraft which the giant Italian student Mirco Zuliani *could* get into without difficulty. Mirco and his instructor Ron Rhodes had a short preliminary first conversion flight and then undertook a second, with Mirco in the left hand, captain's seat. This exercise was far more advanced; it included various emergency drills, a stall, and a 'maximum rate descent' to simulate a cabin pressurisation failure. At the conclusion of this second sortie Mirco would be expected to be able to fly the 1-11 as captain, in contrast to commercial airlines where a captain will have spent years as a co-pilot before assuming the left-hand seat. However, the RAF do not carry the general public as fare-paying passengers.

The briefing took place in Ron Rhodes' office which, like those of all of the flying staff, is attached to the ETPS hangar at

opposite, Tutor James Giles 'books out' in the ETPS Operations Room at Boscombe Down prior to an exercise
(*B. Johnson*)

Sqn Ldr Ron Rhodes
briefing his student, the
Italian fighter pilot Mirco
Zuliani, for a training
flight on the BAC 1-11
(*BBC*)

Boscombe Down. (The hangar is one of the originals which was
built in the late 1920s when the airfield was reactivated by the then
slowly expanding RAF.)

Ron began the briefing by telling Mirco that he would be acting
as the captain on this flight, but Mirco had a small worry:

'I did not do the start up yesterday; I don't know how to start it.'
Ron Rhodes told him that it did not matter; even though he would
be acting as captain, he would be helped:

'We will do a normal take-off with 20 degrees of flap and climb
to flight level 240 (24,000 feet), and I want you to use the autopilot
on the climb. It does not matter what manoeuvres you do as you
climb; the idea is to get you to learn to use the autopilot. When we
level off I want you to let the aeroplane accelerate – it accelerates
rather nicely – until we get the maximum speed bell ringing; that
will be at about seven-eight (.78 Mach). Just let it wind up; I want
you to see how fast it will go; nothing exciting happens, a little wind
noise from the front, that is about all. Decelerate with the throttles
closed and then use the airbrakes; if you do it the other way round,
as you open the airbrakes, you will get the configuration warning
bell.'

The briefing continued. Ron Rhodes told Mirco that the exercise
would then proceed to what is known as a 'push stall', which is
when an aircraft is flown down to the threshold of the stall at which
point an automatic safety device actually moves or pushes (hence
the name) the control column forward to dive the aircraft to restore

safe flying speed, avoiding a true stall. The BAC 1-11, in common with some other modern jets, can, if allowed to stall, enter what is known as a 'deep stall' from which recovery could prove to be impossible, since the disturbed air resulting from the stalled wings blanks the elevators mounted on the high 'T' tailplane.

After the push stall, the next part of the exercise would be the 'maximum rate' descent. The 1-11, like all passenger jets, has a pressurised cabin. The pressurisation system maintains the cabin – and its passengers – at an equivalent altitude of 8000 feet, even when the aircraft is flying at a true altitude of 35,000 feet. Should the cabin pressurisation fail, the internal pressure will drop by as much as 7.5 lbs per square inch and the oxygen level fall to a dangerously low figure; even fit young passengers, and the flight-deck crew, would soon be rendered unconscious. In the event of pressurisation failure, oxygen masks automatically drop from the roof above each seat, but it is imperative that the aircraft is dived down to a safe natural oxygen level, 10,000 feet or below, as soon as possible. Hence the need to practise a 'maximum rate descent'.

The drill for the pilots and the flight engineer was discussed during the briefing; the vital action is for the handling pilot – the one who happens to be flying the aircraft at the time – to put his oxygen mask on as soon as possible; as Ron Rhodes put it:

'You put your [oxygen] mask on. The one who is flying can just get his mask on and still do all the actions. His co-pilot fits his own mask on; the oxygen is on all the time so all you have to do is

Mirco flying the BAC 1-11 with oxygen mask as the big airliner dives to 10,000 feet, at maximum rate (*BBC*)

breathe. As soon as I have my mask on I will take control of the aeroplane so that you can fit your mask on properly, so you will not be without oxygen for very long.'

The descent would be made with the throttles closed and with the airbrakes out, to restrict the speed of the dive which would otherwise build up to beyond Vne, the 'never exceed' speed of the aircraft.

Mirco had done his homework; when asked the speed of the descent he replied:

'Mach .77 or 352 mph maximum.'

'Yes, that is right. That is as fast as you can legally go down to flight level 100 (10,000 feet). When we are level there and have sorted everything out, put the oxygen masks away, I am going to ask you to simulate an engine fire or an overheat. I do not need to tell you that there will be a certain surprise element to it. First of all I want you to give me the touch drill. I want you to say "I would move that lever, I would check that . . ."'

'Just touch?'

'Just touch. I don't want your hands flashing round from lever to switch. What I want you to do is to put your hand on the thing and wait for the Flight Engineer to confirm that you have the correct lever. Otherwise you could have a fire in number one and . . .'

'Close down number two?'

'It has happened . . .'

'OK.'

'So once we have sorted that out and we know what the drill is, I will say "Shut down number one or number two engine". You, Mirco, will do the essential shut-down drills and when you have control of the aeroplane and everything is going well, you call up the Engineer and say, "Let's have the shut-down drills for a fire in number one engine". He will start at the top [of the check-list] and work all the way down through the drills. He will do some of the checks and he will ask you to do others. He has got important drills to do; he has to shut down the air conditioning system which is above my head, above your head he has got to switch over the electrics.'

The briefing continued, followed by a visit to the ETPS operations room to file a flight plan and to check the weather and restrictions – a Royal Flight, for example – near their proposed route. Having booked out, Ron Rhodes and Mirco Zuliani walked out to the BAC 1-11. The 1-11 was on the hardstanding ready for the flight. Flight Lieutenant Stuart Elliott, an ETPS staff Flight Engineer, was already on board the jet and had carried out most of the pre-flight checks; the Auxiliary Power Unit (APU) was

above, Mirco and Ron Rhodes walk to the BAC 1-11, ZE 432, for the training exercise; and (*right*) climb aboard the aircraft (*both BBC*)

running, providing all the electrical power required until the two flight engines were started. Two or three ground crew stood round the aircraft wearing ear defenders.

Ron and Mirco entered the surprisingly small flight-deck; Mirco climbed into the captain's left-hand seat, and Ron into the right. Stuart Elliott sat between them, busy with the long check-lists. Despite Mirco's worry, the engines started without difficulty and the chocks were waved away: ZE 432 was ready for taxi and take-off.

'She is all yours, Mirco.'

The tower at Boscombe Down called the 1-11 on the UHF radio: 'Tester 56 [Ron Rhodes' call-sign] clear to taxi.'

'Clear to taxi,' replied Ron Rhodes. 'Mirco, you will need rather a lot of power to get it moving: a surprising amount.'

The take-off and climb went without incident. The push stall, or dive to be strictly accurate, was also unremarkable, the most

The BAC 1-11 held by Mirco just above the stall; a moment later the automatic 'stick pusher' lowered the nose and the 1-11 regained safe flying speed (*BBC*)

exciting aspect being the shrilling of the warning horns and the rattle of the stick shaker to draw the attention of the pilots to the approaching stall. The push dive gave the crew (and the BBC film unit) a brief sample of weightlessness; Mirco quickly recovered the big aircraft and, under Ron Rhodes' guidance, climbed the 1-11 back to 24,000 feet for the maximum rate descent. (The aircraft was cleared to make the maximum rate descent from 35,000 feet but the ETPS exercise was made from the lower altitude simply to save time and fuel that would have been used in climbing back to the higher level after the stall exercise.)

'Right, Mirco, what Mach have you got there?'

'Point seven seven.'

'We will now practise decompression.'

The decompression warning bell rang on the flight-deck as Ron Rhodes counted down:

'Maximum rate descent. 5-4-3-2-1 go!'

Mirco made a wingover diving turn to starboard, shut the throttles, extended the airbrakes and, with the 1-11 descending at 4000 feet per minute at around 350 mph, put on his oxygen mask with the help of his co-pilot, Ron Rhodes. The reason for the spectacular diving turn is simply that it maintains positive gravity or g. This is an important factor for a passenger aircraft; no one can foresee when a pressurisation failure might occur, the passengers might well not be strapped in. If a maximum rate dive were entered by pushing the control column forward (as in the push stall exercise) the passengers could well float (briefly) around the cabin.

The exercise with the 1-11 ended with the jet being recovered at 10,000 feet and level flight resumed. It was quite impressive: the BAC 1-11 shook a little in the dive and the 2½g pull out would have shaken and stirred the martinis had the aircraft been on a scheduled flight.

It might be supposed that pressurisation failure is a very remote eventuality. At one time it was. Unfortunately, in this day of the terrorist hijacker it is not: a single small-calibre bullet from a pistol or automatic weapon, let alone a hand-grenade or bomb, is all that is required to rupture an airliner's thin pressure hull.

On the way back to Boscombe Down, Mirco survived a practice fire drill and shut-down of number one engine; he then made a perfect landing. Ron Rhodes was asked how his F-104 fighter pilot had handled the passenger jet:

'Very well. I would be quite happy to get out of the aeroplane and let him fly it solo, which is the object of the whole exercise.'

Mirco Zuliani too was pleased, he found the flight:

'Marvellous. When you are flying [the 1-11] there is not so much difference in the handling, but it is for me strange to have a crew: I am used to flying on my own. In this aircraft the engineer or co-pilot helps; it is a strange feeling.'

The exercise, or more precisely exercises, which dominate the summer term are the ones devoted to spinning and spin recovery. Spinning or, as the ETPS puts it, 'departure from controlled flight' has, since man first flew, claimed more lives, and resulted in the loss of more aircraft, than any other cause short of enemy action in time of war. According to the latest figures available, the RAF has lost no fewer than twenty-nine aircraft in spinning accidents in the recent past. The figures for the USAF are proportionally similar. A number of light civil aircraft have been lost over the years in 'stall/spin' accidents, although that number has diminished in recent years due to a generation of aircraft coming into service for flying schools and private ownership which are much more spin resistant than the earlier, essentially pre-war designs. (As a consequence, spinning and spin recovery has, regrettably many think, recently been dropped from the civil Private Pilot's Licence (PPL) syllabus.)

All aircraft can be made to spin, but not all aircraft can be recovered. It could be said that no two spins are the same even with the same aircraft. A spinning aircraft is out of control; it has 'departed from controlled flight' and is falling, stalled, seeking a balance of conflicting forces. Darrol Stinton, a test pilot and a visiting lecturer at ETPS (from which he graduated in 1959), in his recent book, *The Design of the Aeroplane*, defined a spin as:

> A self-sustaining (autorotational) spiral motion of an aeroplane about a vertical axis, during which the mean angle of attack of the wings is beyond the stall. A spin follows departures in roll, yaw and pitch from the condition of balanced flight. The developed spin is achieved when there is general (sometimes oscillatory) equilibrium between the predominantly pro-spin moment due to the wings and the generally anti-spin moments due to other parts of the aircraft.

The aerodynamically complex nature of the spin caused it to be the last aircraft manoeuvre to be understood or, more importantly, the last manoeuvre the recovery action from which was understood. As to who actually *did* make that important discovery remains a matter of controversy, although it is generally accepted as being either Lieutenant Wilfred Parkes (Larkhill 1912) or Harry Hawker in his Sopwith. The claims of Lieutenant Parkes are strengthened by the undoubted fact that the spin was, for many years, known as 'Parkes Dive'. It was left to a Farnborough man, Major Frank Gooden, a Royal Aircraft Establishment test pilot, to define a standard recovery technique: to unstall the aircraft by moving the control stick forward and applying opposite rudder to contain the yaw. Although the correct recovery techniques were known as early as 1917, pilots were still killing themselves in spins and have continued to do so to the present day. Why?

The answer is partly because spinning with a yaw rate of 120 degrees per second can be extremely disorientating. Without a turn and slip instrument, a pilot can be uncertain about the direction in which he is spinning; even with the correct recovery techniques, some aircraft can take up to five turns to recover; there can therefore be a strong temptation to try different control combinations with fatal results. The situation is bad enough even when intentionally spinning, as in training. If a pilot enters an inadvertent and unexpected spin, following a stall or a badly executed aerobatic manoeuvre, it can be far worse. In any spin, even in a light aircraft, the height loss will be high, typically 300 feet per turn. A high performance fighter can lose 10,000 feet in a spin.

The next question is the obvious one: why spin at all? As Vic Lockwood pointed out in the ETPS ground school lecture: 'It is a useless manoeuvre which has ceased to have any tactical value since the First World War.'

The answer is simply that it is done not for the actual spin but for the subsequent *recovery* techniques. Since there is no such thing as

top to bottom, A sequence showing the SH-1 Trago-Mills entering an intentional spin. In the first frame the pilot has applied full 'up' elevator to initiate a stall; at the same time full left rudder is yawing the aircraft into the direction of the spin. The control positions are held as the spin develops, and will remain, after four or five turns, until the pilot applies full opposite rudder and 'down' elevator to recover. (*BBC*)

an unspinnable aircraft (there are many aircraft in which spinning is forbidden which is not the same thing), it is essential that aircraft which are either licensed for civil use, or military aircraft placed in service, should have a suitable recovery technique available for recommendation to the pilots. Even if, as is the case with some aircraft, recovery is *not* possible, that too must be known to the pilots flying the type. It follows that a test pilot must be able to investigate the spinning of a given aircraft, be it a prototype or a standard service type which may, or may not, have had its known spin characteristics altered by the addition of external stores or some other modification to its airframe.

Intentional spinning is forbidden in practically all contemporary service aircraft apart from *ab initio* trainers, which means that few squadron pilots will have had any recent spinning experience and none in modern front-line aircraft. (Few pilots on the ETPS course had any real experience of spinning. Harry Fehl was typical: he said he had last spun ten years previously when on his basic flying course.) The fact that an aircraft is not cleared for spinning does not, of course, mean that it will not spin: fighter pilots are not selected for their timidity and it is not unknown for the more aggressive types to lose control of their fighters in mock combat manoeuvres, stalling and 'departing from controlled flight'. The possibility of a spin then developing is high. Most aircraft will, however, offer the pilot the lifeline of the 'incipient' spin; the half-way house between a fully developed spin (from which recovery might well be problematical) and the threshold of such a spin when the aircraft's anti-spin characteristics are not yet overwhelmed by pro-spin forces and recovery is still possible.

Test pilots have to investigate the whole of an aircraft's spinning envelope, including the fully developed spin. In such trials, special precautions to enable the pilot to recover from spins are employed: anti-spin parachutes are shot from the tail of the aircraft with the object of stabilising the spin by causing drag which stops or impedes the rotational moment (small rockets under the wings are also used for this purpose). Telemetry transmitters are usually fitted to aircraft undergoing full spin trials. A ground station displays the control positions and other relevant factors of the airborne sortie to a qualified pilot who, not being disorientated, can calmly analyse the situation to decide if the spin is inverted or erect and advise the spinning pilot on recovery action. Boscombe Down has such a facility which is used to the full by the ETPS.

The spinning exercises at ETPS are divided into three parts: first, erect spins in the Jet Provost with a tutor or instructor; second, a dual demonstration of the spinning techniques in the Hawk, followed by two solo sorties, on which a report is written;

third, a full dual investigation in the Hunter, spinning erect and inverted.

The philosophy of the ETPS spinning test is laid down with great clarity in the relevant chapter of the Flying Wing notes from which the following extract is taken.

Spinning Tests

Introduction

1 The development of sophisticated weapons systems, high speed fighter/attack aircraft and air to air guided missiles has not reduced the need for operational pilots to fly their machines to their perform- ance and handling limits. Although spinning is of no tactical use, experience has shown that inadvertent spins will occur as long as aircraft are 'spinnable' and pilots are required to achieve the max- imum manoeuvring performance from their aircraft. As a result, aircraft which exhibit poor stall, post stall, spin or spin recovery characteristics will not be flown to their maximum capabilities. Pilots will establish their own buffer zone in an effort to allow for the inevitable human errors in handling and judgement. Only pilot con- fidence in the high angle of attack and out-of control characteristics of his aircraft will restore this lost capability, while maintaining acceptable safety margins. It is the responsibility of the test pilot/ engineering team to provide this confidence by thoroughly evaluat- ing all aspects of an aircraft's spin characteristics, if high manoeuvrability is inherent in its role.

2 Until about 1970, this thorough investigation usually centred around the aircraft's characteristics in a fully developed spin and the recovery therefrom. However, recent work has shown that simplified recovery procedures can be utilised if departure from controlled flight is recognised in the early stages of an impending spin. The United States spinning specifications have recently been rewritten to place new emphasis on departure recoveries and to decrease the requirements for prolonged spins in all but training aeroplanes, the latter exception taking into account the need to use the aircraft in a teaching environment. It should be noted, however, there is still a necessity to document all phases of the post stall and spinning regimes in order to provide recovery procedures to the operational pilot whose aircraft, and perhaps life, could depend on the accuracy, clarity and conciseness of the information.

3 Because of the frequently unpredictable and disorientating nature of post stall characteristics, the fact that they do not lend themselves to rigorous aerodynamic analysis, and the inherent risk during out-of-control flight testing, spin testing requires a most comprehensive pre-flight and in-flight build-up programme on the part of both the test pilot and the test engineer.

The ETPS notes proceed to discuss the objectives of a spinning programme on a new or modified aircraft, which include a deter- mination of all control positions, to define the optimum recovery techniques, to investigate the effect of the gyrations during the spin on the operation of the engine(s); also to define the effect on the aircraft's electronic systems and instrumentation, with particular emphasis on gyros. The final task will be to provide the required information on which to base the spin recovery/prevention recommendation in the pilot's notes for the aircraft type.

The above abstract is a précis of the role of the trained test pilot conducting a full spin test programme. The ETPS student had to, because of the limited time available, fly a reduced programme, which is not to say that the ETPS exercises were anything but very demanding indeed.

The ETPS exercise was constructed for the students to assume that they were test pilots with the A&AEE at Boscombe Down, charged with the task of evaluating the Hawk for clearance to allow intentional student solo spinning. The brief began:

> Due to the large number of out-of-control/spin accidents in almost every operational and training environment, a programme is being established by the RAF which will provide pilots with the fundamental knowledge necessary to recognise, prevent and/or recover from out-of-control flight . . . Recommendations concerning operational recovery techniques from out-of-control flight conditions and the adequacy of aircrew manuals are also desired . . . Each syndicate is to act as a test team for this evaluation, but each student is to submit an individual report. As a work up before starting on the Hawk programme, one spin familiarisation sortie will be flown on the Jet Provost. After the Hawk exercise, two spin sorties will be flown on the Hunter . . . Six hours' flying are allowed for the exercise: Jet Provost 1 hour dual; Hawk 1 hour dual, 2 hours solo; Hunter 2 hours dual.

> **Recovery**
> With the exception of the aft stick recovery and reversed controls recovery [where forward stick is applied before opposite rudder], only the pilot's notes standard recovery will be made on the Jet Provost. Standard aircrew manual recoveries will normally be made on the Hawk, but the effect of mishandled controls . . . will also be investigated. Aside from the effect of aileron investigation, only the following three basic recoveries will be used during the exercise on the Hunter:
> 1 The standard recovery is defined as follows: close the throttle, apply full rudder opposite to the turn needle [of the 'turn and slip' instrument], then move the stick progressively forward until the spin stops. As soon as the spin stops, centralise the controls. Keep the ailerons central throughout.
> 2 The departure, i.e. the first indication of loss of control, recovery is defined as follows: close the throttle, positively centralise the rudder and ailerons, then move the stick progressively forward until rotation ceases.

Although the Jet Provost XS 230 was to be used for the first dual demonstration, there had been some doubt that it would ever

emerge from the distant hangar at Boscombe Down where it was undergoing an extensive overhaul; as one of the ETPS tutors put it: 'The only way that thing will every fly again is if it falls off its jacks'. But emerge it did, a tribute to the men who have the difficult task of maintaining the varied ETPS fleet. John Winder, the civilian in charge, conceded that the Jet Provost is typical of the problems of keeping what is in effect an obsolescent aircraft airworthy: 'It's a hybrid, being a mixture of Mk 4 and Mk 5, so it has problems of interchangeability and spares.' That is true of most of the ETPS aircraft. The Hunters XL 564 and 612 are T7s which date from 1958, but they are the only swept-wing aircraft in the world that are routinely spun inverted. To replace them, even with other Hunters, will be difficult for the ETPS aircraft nearly all have special instrumentation fitted which makes them unique in the RAF. Difficulties notwithstanding, the entire fleet, including the BAC Lightning XS 422, is maintained to an extremely high standard.

The Jet Provost has reasonable spin characteristics; however, it is believed that some twelve have been lost in spinning accidents (although as a basic trainer it has, as a type, undergone more intentional spinning with student pilots than most RAF aircraft). The ETPS exercise consisted of a dual demonstration which began with a review of the Provost's emergency drills, including engine surge and simulated 'flame out' landings.

The Provost climbed to 16,000 feet for the first exercise, which was an erect spin from a 'wings level' stall. The aircraft was trimmed with the throttle at idle and the speed reduced at a rate of 1 to 2 knots per second by increasing the nose-up angle. At the onset of

The ETPS Jet Provost XS 230, as it emerged from an extensive overhaul ready for the summer term spinning exercises. The Provost is the first of the school's aircraft which the students spin. (*B. Johnson*)

the stall, with ailerons neutral, full rudder in the desired direction of the spin was applied and the stick pulled fully back. The events that follow are not easy to describe; they should essentially be *experienced*. The orderly relationship between sky and earth was suddenly reversed, but only for a moment as the small agile Provost flipped on to its back; it did not stay there but continued to drop and turn through 360 degrees until it pointed straight down, rotating at what appeared to be a very high rate, judged by the only available datum; the spinning earth directly below, which was getting perceptibly nearer with every revolution. To enable the uninitiated reader to savour the sortie, the entire exercise is reproduced below:

1 A three-turn erect spin in one direction entered from a straight (i.e. wings level) stall with standard recovery initiated after the third turn.

2 An eight-turn erect spin in the opposite direction entered from a straight stall with standard recovery initiated after the eighth turn.

3 An erect spin applying in-spin aileron after the aeroplane is clearly in a steady spin. Held for about one turn and ailerons centralised before executing standard recovery.

4 As in 3 but with the application of out-spin aileron.

5 An erect spin with a reversed controls recovery (stick centralised prior to opposite rudder being applied).

6 An erect spin with an aft stick recovery. Opposite rudder applied but full aft stick maintained until rotation stopped, at which time the stick should be centralised.

Having experienced the above programme of spins entered from 'straight' stalls, the student was next required to undertake spins entered from a 2g decelerating turn: 'At least two three-turn erect spins entered from a 2g level decelerated turn. When unable to maintain 2g, apply and hold full aft stick and "bottom" rudder on one and "top" rudder on the other. Standard recovery after three turns.'

The Jet Provost has many virtues but lightness of its manual controls is not among them. It is interesting that the spinning sortie in the Jet Provost included (3–6) deliberate mishandling of the controls during recovery: the sort of mistakes that a student pilot could well make if disorientated. It is essential that an *ab initio* trainer should be as forgiving as possible. (Forgiving or not, at ETPS it is mandatory to abandon the Jet Provost if recovery from any spin is not completed by 5000 feet: no one has had to bail out . . . so far.)

After completing the inevitable post-flight report (within three hours), the next part of the spin exercise was the far more demanding programmes flown in the Hawk and the Hunter.

The ETPS Jet Provost on a spinning exercise piloted by the German student, Harry Fehl. As with the Trago-Mills light aircraft, full 'up' elevator is applied together with full left rudder. For some reason never satisfactorily explained, nearly all pilots instinctively spin to the left. During the war, German night fighters discovered that nine out of ten RAF bombers broke to the left when attacked. (*BBC*)

However, before the serious spinning was undertaken, the ETPS students were given a lecture in the ground school by the Principal Tutor, Vic Lockwood. The lecture included some remarkable film of modern high-performance aircraft on spinning trials that went wrong. The film opened with an American Buckeye trainer which was to undertake a three-turn spin; it went into an inverted spin from which the US Navy test pilot managed to recover *thirty-three* turns later. No reason for the aircraft's reluctance to recover was ever discovered. An F-4 Phantom was shown in a flat spin from which its pilot, from the Patuxent River Naval Air Test Center, failed to recover; an anti-spin parachute also failed because it had too short a cable – the parachute would not deploy in the turbulent air behind the F-4, which spun on to destruction in Chesapeake Bay after the pilot had ejected. The film contained many other examples of spins which went badly wrong. The object of showing the film was not to concentrate the minds of the students but rather to impress on them the salient fact that, when undertaking spin testing, even if only as part of the ETPS syllabus, it is essential, as Vic Lockwood put it, 'always to expect the unexpected'.

Spinning the Hawk is a different proposition from spinning the Jet Provost; it is a high-performance advanced trainer aircraft, moreover it has to be spun solo. The Hawk is not cleared for inverted spinning even under the extended rules applied to the performance envelope of the ETPS aircraft. To aid any student who might find himself in danger of going inverted in the aircraft, it is fitted with full telemetry transmitted by a UHF radio data link to

For the more advanced spinning exercises in the Hawk and Hunter, telemetry is used. This is the ground receiving equipment at Boscombe Down, with an A&AEE operator adjusting the multiple pen recorder which traces the parameters of each spin. (*BBC*)

the Boscombe Down Telemetry Station. The working of this station had to be understood by all students attending the fixed wing course. Each of the pilots had to do duty as Ground Pilot, and the life of a colleague, to say nothing of a valuable aircraft, could have been in their hands.

The operation of the telemetry system is laid down in the ubiquitous Flying Wing notes. The following checks and duties were to be carried out by the telemetry Ground Pilot:

Before Take-Off

a Brief with the pilot conducting the spinning exercise to ascertain the scope of the spin test to be carried out, and any special requirements.

b Obtain the pilot's call-sign and the serial number of the aircraft.

c Man the telemetry station at least ten minutes prior to take-off.

d Carry out a check of the two-way radio telephone.

e [Check the data link by verifying] sense and calibration of aileron, rudder and elevation positions and yaw rate and engine parameters. [This is done with the aircraft still on the ground.]

After Take-Off

a Establish two-way [voice] communication with the test aircraft.

b Carry out sense and calibration checks of airspeed, altitude and angle of attack (AOA) and roll rate.

During Spins

a Both the Hawks and the Hunters use the same telemetry transmit frequencies. When monitoring more than one of these aircraft ensure that only the appropriate aircraft is transmitting data.

b Monitor the telemetry to ensure that the spin progresses as planned and advise the pilot if any unusual characteristics observed.

c Advise the pilot if improper recovery controls are noted during spin recovery.

d Aid the pilot with advice on correct recovery controls if difficulties arise from improper recovery inputs.

e Advise the pilot of significant altitudes when reached *if the aircraft is not recovering*, i.e.

Hunter		*Hawk*
25,000 feet	Initiate Standard Recovery	15,000 feet
20,000 feet	Jettison Tanks	N/A
10,000 feet	Eject	5000 feet

Both the Hunter and Hawk aircraft used at ETPS have a recorded female voice which automatically advises the pilots over their headsets of the actions they should be taking at the appropriate heights: 'Recover now'; 'Jettison wing tanks'; 'Eject! Eject!' (It is not known if the choice of a female voice is made because the pilots

The telemetry building at Boscombe Down with a steerable Yagi antenna on the roof which tracks the spinning aircraft (*B. Johnson*)

would be more likely to listen, or if she would be less likely to be confused with other radio telephone traffic which tends to be male-dominated.)

The telemetry building is some distance away from the hangars and other activities at Boscombe Down. It has a steerable Yagi UHF antenna on the roof which tracks the aircraft it is receiving. A technician monitors the tracking of the antenna, the tuning of the receiver and the operation of a multiple-pen recorder which traces eight parameters of the flight for later analysis. The Ground Pilot is in an adjacent room, seated in front of a panel which has a cathode-ray tube which continuously displays the position of the stick and rudder of the aircraft being monitored. Other, conventional, instruments show altitude, airspeed, angle of attack, engine temperature, roll and yaw rate.

During the making of the BBC film of ETPS, a typical Hunter spin sortie was filmed and recorded in the telemetry room. Vic Lockwood was the Ground Pilot on that occasion, with Mirco

Sqn Ldr Robin Tydeman, acting as a ground safety pilot in the telemetry building (*BBC*)

Zuliani in the Hunter. An abstract from the transcript with Vic Lockwood speaking gives a good idea of the operation of the Boscombe Down telemetry:

'Right, about ten seconds to spin entry; twenty knots to lose; soon the stick will be coming back. Now the stick is back, left rudder, angle of attack has gone up, airspeed is reducing. The aircraft has now entered the spin, it will settle down with roll and yaw in the direction [it entered the spin], he has [applied] in-spin aileron which is a very powerful recovery aid but [which] will cause the spin to become oscillatory, as can be seen by the angle of attack moving up and down quite rapidly, with the aircraft trying to recover and the airspeed building. The roll and yaw are settling down. The ADD [airstream direction detector: the airstream relative to the attitude of the aircraft] is reduced, the airspeed is building and the aircraft has now recovered from the spin at 28,000 feet.' (No need for advice from the on-board lady here.)

The ETPS Hawk spinning syllabus calls for six four-turn spins with in- and out-spin aileron to demonstrate the effect of control mishandling. The sortie began, as all do at Boscombe Down, with a briefing by the course exercise tutor. In this case the tutor was Vic Lockwood and the student was Steve Moore, the New Zealander. Steve had little previous experience of high-performance jets as he had flown mostly helicopters and Strikemasters (armed and uprated versions of the Jet Provost). The briefing took place in the tutor's office and was informal.

'Sit down, Steve. Before we get into the spinning briefing, we will run over the emergency drills. First of all, as you know, I asked you to look at the [engine] surge drills. Are you happy with those?'

'Yes, I'm quite happy.'

Vic Lockwood briefing the New Zealand student Steve Moore for the spinning exercise in the Hawk which was to go wrong (*B. Johnson*)

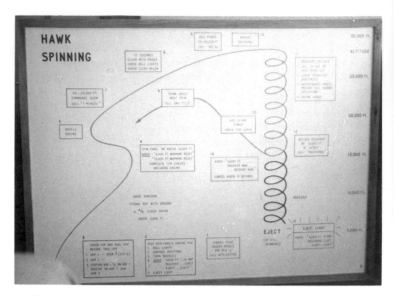

The diagram used by the tutors during the briefing for the Hawk spinning sortie (*B. Johnson*)

'You know the temperatures that we will be looking for, and the actions to take?'

'Yes, 450 and 635 are the magic ones.'

The figures are of the Exhaust Gas Temperatures (EGT). Due to the high angle of attack of the Hawk in certain phases of the spin, there is a possibility of the airflow to the engine compressor being reduced and the compressor stalling; the fuel flowing into the engine is still at the same rate as it was before the stall, consequently the mixture runs rich, causing a dangerous rise in engine temperatures which, if unchecked, could burn out the jet pipe and turbine. The 'magic numbers' quoted by Steve Moore are 635°C which is the maximum safe EGT, and 450°C which is the figure for the Hawk's engine when idling. The aircraft's engine will be set to idle during the spins; the danger is a 'surge' causing a partial compressor stall when the engine is opened up to recover from the resultant dive after spin recovery. Should that happen and the engine overheat, the correct drill is to throttle back to idle until the temperature drops to the lower figure, when the engine can be slowly opened up to normal settings. The possibility of engine surges is another reason for ETPS operating practices demanding a safe altitude for all spin exercises.

Vic Lockwood continued with the brief:

'Right, so throughout the spin we will be aware that there might be engine surge problems?'

'Yes.'

'And watching those temperatures and the actions we need to take. Also I asked you to look at spinning in the aircrew manual under the limitations section; it gives a broadbrush view of spinning in general and the effect of controls . . . I know you have read it. Let's talk about the weather criteria now. We must have less than 4/8ths cloud above 5000 feet; we must not spin over 8/8ths cloud or over water, and we must be able to have a clear view of the ground to remain orientated.'

The briefing continued with Vic Lockwood reminding his student of the need to check that there was no loose equipment in the cockpit; stop-watch, pencils, maps or the inevitable knee-pad. The pilots had to check that their harness was tight and that there were no loose ends which could, in negative conditions, distract the pilot. Another vital check was the adjustment of the controls to suit the individual pilots so that they could easily apply full control movements. It is particularly important that the rudder is capable of a full range of movement since it is a primary control in spin recovery. Having discussed the safety aspects of the sortie, Vic Lockwood turned to the procedures:

'On the taxi out, we will go over to the Ground Pilot and we will check with him. [After take-off] we will head for 25,000 feet which is our base altitude for spinning. Entries to the spins will be made from between 25,000 and 30,000 feet. Steve, you will call London Military [Air Traffic Control section responsible for integrating military aircraft movements with those of civil aircraft in the busy London control zone]; he will clear us on to a heading that will ensure that we will be clear of other traffic.'

Vic Lockwood reminded his student of the special instruments in the Hawk that are fitted as an aid to recovery, including the visual and audio height warnings (the recorded lady).

'Set the throttle to idle, raise the nose of the Hawk and zoom up to above 25,000 feet [looking for 170 knots]. When we are about

The additional instruments fitted to the school aircraft are of particular importance in spinning, for they enable the tutor in the rear seat of this Hawk to see exactly the control positions applied by the student (*B. Johnson*)

fifteen seconds from spin entry, transmit blind [i.e. call telemetry and advise them that the spin will commence in fifteen seconds] and telemetry will start running the recording instrumentation. So, throttle to idle, airspeed 170 knots, wings level, speed down to 150 knots, height above 25,000 feet, call [telemetry] "Entering spin number one, erect to the left". Apply full rudder in the direction of the spin and simultaneously full aft stick with the ailerons neutral, and we will enter the spin.'

'How many turns, Vic?'

'We will, in the main, do four-turn spins but, during any of the spins, should the airspeed build up to 180 knots, or if there are large or even transient side forces, or if you feel large forces on the rudder, or we encounter engine surge, then you must immediately recover. Normal recovery will be by the centralisation of the controls; recovery must be initiated by 15,000 feet. If the aircraft continues to spin, we will continue to take normal recovery action; if we reach 5000 feet and we are still spinning, we must abandon the aircraft. We will have some help with the audio warning, the little lady's voice; she will say, "15,000 feet, recover now!" At 5000 feet she will tell us to eject; if we are still spinning and we have not [been able to regain] positive control over the aeroplane, we will obey her. I will tell you to go and I will quickly follow.'

'OK.'

'Having done the first spin, which will have given us a baseline of Hawk spinning, we will play tunes on the basic spin by using the flying controls. On the next spin we will enter with wings level as for a normal spin, but after one turn you will apply full out-spin aileron and hold it for three turns before making a normal recovery . . . What tends to happen is that the ailerons affect the aerodynamic rolling moment and in this case it will . . . smooth the spin . . . we should see a slightly oscillatory spin, which is normal for the Hawk. When we come to recovery, I want your first action to be the centralisation of the ailerons, followed by normal recovery.'

The next spin that was discussed was one with in-spin aileron which Vic warned would be far more oscillatory, with large variations in the aircraft's angle of attack and attitude during the four turns that have to be made before recovery. Steve Moore had a small worry about that last spin:

'During the spin with the in-spin aileron, is there any danger of the spin becoming inverted?'

'Well, Steve, the spin does get agitated and I suppose of all the spins we do [in the Hawk] that is the one that has a chance of going inverted. I do not know of a Hawk going inverted; however, if the aircraft does enter an inverted spin, I want you to take the normal control positions for an inverted recovery [which is the same as for erect recovery]. However, there is a warning in the aircrew manual that there may be excessive forces on the rudder, so you may have to restrain the rudder pedals to the neutral position.'

The Hawk is not cleared for inverted spinning even under the special rules that ETPS enjoy, so Vic Lockwood's last remark on the subject had a certain significance: '. . . and then I'm afraid we will have to see what happens from then on in.'

'I'll get you to help me with that.'

'I'll do my best,' said Vic.

The weather for the Hawk spinning exercise was ideal: 3/8ths cloud at 22,000 feet; the weather at the two designated diversionary airfields, Brize Norton and Yeovilton, was fine. Diversionary airfields are always nominated in case the runways at Boscombe Down should become blocked by a crash landing while the school sortie is airborne. (The main runway at Boscombe Down is 300 feet wide and 10,500 feet long and one of the longest in the country; it is equipped with arresting gear and a crash barrier. The airfield has a comprehensive range of radar approach aids and full lighting, and is available for any RAF aircraft or civil airliner that might be in trouble and in need of a long runway.)

The Hawk spinning exercise was not just a question of flying the sortie and recovering from the various spins. In fact Steve Moore,

A BBC camera fitted under one of the ETPS Hawks shows the steep angle of approach as the student performs a simulated dead engine landing. This is always done on the dual exercise to prepare the students for the possibility of a 'flamed-out engine' (by no means unknown) on their solo spinning sortie. (*BBC*)

in common with the other fixed wing students, had to note the parameters of the spin as it progressed; the figures noted were then to be used as a basis for a full written report which was required:

> within ten days of completing the Hawk exercise . . . the report should contain a general qualitative description of the aircraft behaviour during the spin entry, the spin and the spin recovery. The spin and recovery characteristics should be evaluated against the aircraft role and specification requirements. The following quantitative data should be included in your report and used to support your qualitative opinion.

1 Entry
a Starting height.
b Engine rpm.
c Trim settings.
d Fuel state.
e Entry technique.
f Entry height and speed.
g Control positions and forces.

2 In the Spin
a Time per turn and overall time from entry to starting recovery.
b Height loss per turn and total height loss from entry to starting recovery.
c Control positions and forces.
d Estimation of roll, pitch, and yaw angles and rates (if possible). Students may check in-flight estimations against telemetry data.
e Airspeed and angle of attack, including any variations.
f Number of turns.
g Aircraft attitude and any apparent variations as the spin develops.
h Wing tilt angle (if possible).
i Engine characteristics.
j Pilot restraint system.

3 Recovery
a Height initiated.
b Time, height loss, and number of turns from start of recovery to stopping of rotation.
c Airspeed (rate of increase and maximum reached).
d Control positions and forces.
e Optimum recovery technique.
f Maximum g during recovery.
g Time and height loss from stop of rotation to level flight.

The list is quite formidable and the students had a difficult time on the initial spins, flying the aircraft and noting the many figures required. Steve Moore had one or two of his spins nearly go out of control, as Vic Lockwood pointed out at the subsequent debrief, using the telemetry traces as evidence.

The telemetry traces, which are used in the debrief of the spinning exercises, record all the information required to reconstruct the entire sortie (*BBC*)

'This is where things started to go wrong. We briefed that the second spin would be a normal entry to the left; after the first turn we would put in out-spin aileron, which is right aileron, which would in theory smooth the spin. Now what actually happened, having looked at the [telemetry] traces, was this: we got into a very strange spin mode, and the reason was that you had put in a quarter aileron, so we had the yawing moment from the rudder to the left, and the aircraft tried to roll to the left, but you had put in a quarter out-spin aileron [to the right] which was preventing the aircraft from rolling . . . instead of completing the first turn you got yourself a little disorientated and at three-quarters of the turn, which we had not quite completed, you put in the rest of the aileron.'

The effect of this error was to produce a markedly oscillatory spin with a high angle of attack. The aircraft rolled to the right but yawed to the left; the rolling to the right against the entry direction of the spin became extreme and the Hawk was on the brink of entering an inverted spin when Vic Lockwood gave Steve Moore the cue to recover, which he did without difficulty. The incident was turned by Vic Lockwood into an illustration of the role of the test pilot when evaluating a prototype trainer:

'Now the whole point of your test spin [in the Hawk] is to see whether this aircraft is suitable for solo spinning by students. Here is a mode, during spin entry, that is very easily influenced by a small application of aileron. The student [in a standard Hawk trainer] will not have the special ETPS aileron position gauge, and he will therefore be uncertain of the position of the ailerons during the spin. You, Steve, made a small deflection of the ailerons and you had the gauge; that is a point to bear in mind when you are making up your mind if this aircraft is suitable for solo spinning by students.'

Steve Moore, in a BBC interview after the spin exercise, acknowledged the value of the sortie:

'There were good learning points for me, especially with the aileron input during the spin which I could not detect myself. It is good to see the [telemetry] traces but, as Vic said, a student would not have had the traces or the special gauges in the cockpit to tell him he had put inadvertent aileron application in, which certainly does make a difference to the [Hawk's] spin characteristics.'

'Is it easy accidently to put in unwanted aileron input?'

'It is. Especially with the stick in the Hawk: it is slightly canted over to the left. I was using two hands on it, which is a

The cranked control stick of the Hawk caused Steve Moore to apply unwanted outspin aileron which nearly caused the aircraft to enter an inverted spin (*B. Johnson*)

habit of mine because of the Strikemaster which has got pretty high elevator forces; to relieve the strain on the arms I used to pull back with both hands; I think I was doing this in the Hawk, as a result, with the canted bit on the top [of the stick] I was centring it [and applying unwanted aileron]. That is my excuse anyway!'

The final word on the subject was this observation by Vic Lockwood:

'I think Steve learned more on that sortie than he will ever admit: I think he felt chastened that his spin entry technique was not consistent, but by the end of the sortie he had overcome the problem and regained his confidence.'

It must be added that Steve Moore completed the entire spinning exercise, including solo spinning in the Hawk and the inverted (intentional!) spins in the Hunter which followed, with distinction.

The Hunter is not normally cleared for *any* intentional spinning. The rule probably dates from the early days of the two-seater Hunter T7 trainers. There were fatal accidents at Chivenor in 1959 when two student pilots, flying solo in T7 Hunters, crashed following failure to recover from spins. There was an intensive investigation into the spinning characteristics of the Hunter two-seaters at Dunsfold (the factory airfield of the old Hawker company) and Boscombe Down, following the Chivenor incidents. It was decided that, while the Hunter as a type did not exhibit any marked vices in the spin, it had a disorientating spin which could, if the pilot mishandled the controls (particularly the ailerons), become inverted. Recovery from an inverted spin, if the pilot is unaware of the fact that he is inverted, can prove impossible. If the pilot is aware of

The Hunter about to be flown on a spinning sortie (*B. Johnson*)

The cockpit of an ETPS Hunter showing the special spin panel fitted on the eyeline of each pilot, giving positive information on the direction of spin. This is required since inverted spinning can be very disorientating, even for an experienced pilot. (*B. Johnson*)

which way up he is, the Hunter can readily be recovered from a spin, erect or inverted, as Bill Bedford, then Chief Test Pilot of Hawkers, so memorably demonstrated at Farnborough in 1960.

Despite the convincing demonstration by Bill Bedford and the tests conducted at Boscombe Down and Dunsfold, the 1959 ban on intentional spinning in RAF Hunters remains in force to this day (there are in fact very few Hunters remaining on RAF charge), with two exceptions: XL 564 and 612. These T7 two-seaters, which first flew in 1958, are both on the strength of the ETPS fixed wing fleet and they are the only swept-wing aircraft in the world that are routinely intentionally spun, inverted and erect. To achieve this unique distinction, they have been fitted with telemetry data transmitters and special head-up spin panels in the two-seater cockpits.

The spin panels (see page 145) show the student and tutor yaw (direction of turn), using a conventional analogue turn and slip instrument, backed up by red and green 'left and right roll' lights; altitude, with a single-needle coarse altimeter calibrated from 40,000 to 10,000 feet, augmented by a 10,000-foot warning light, itself backed by a Hunter version of the recorded lady advising 'Recover now' at 25,000 feet, and 'Eject!' at 10,000 feet.

above, The ETPS Lightning seen from the open cargo door of the school Andover; *left*, The Lightning XS 422. The sheer size of this fighter surprises many who see it for the first time. (*both B. Johnson*)

below, XX 830, one of two Jaguars used by the school for modern strike experience; *opposite above*, Swing-wing Tornados on the flight line at RAF Honington. Two of the students, Steve Moore and the US Navy pilot Tom Koezler, previewed one of these aircraft at Honington; *opposite below*, Vic Lockwood visually checks the pitot tube of XX 343, one of the two ETPS Hawks, prior to take-off. (*all B. Johnson*)

right, *Luftwaffe* pilot Harry Fehl displays a 'g' suit as he walks out to his aircraft. Note the classic knee-pads for in-flight notes. Since the coast is never more than seventy miles from anywhere in Britain, pilots flying high-performance RAF aircraft always wear life-jackets; *opposite above*, Harry Fehl contemplates his forthcoming spinning exercise on the ETPS Provost; *opposite below*, The cockpit of a Jet aircraft, in this case one of the school Hunters XL 564, presents to the lay eye an unbelievably bewildering environment. The duplication of the controls and instruments in this side-by-side trainer makes it appear more complex than it in fact is. (*all B. Johnson*)

top, A school Jaguar taxies in after landing. The pilots have opened the canopies a little to give them fresh air after breathing oxygen through rubber tubes for an hour or so; *above*, A Tornado at Honington taxies out. (*both B. Johnson*)

top, The ETPS HS 748 Andover makes a short field
landing with full flap on the grass runway at Boscombe
Down in the evening. The transport has its navigation
lights on – flying at ETPS is not on a 9 to 5 basis;
above, A school Jaguar on the Boscombe Down
taxiway. The anhedral tailplane is well illustrated.
(*both B. Johnson*)

An F-4 Phantom takes off from RAF Coningsby on an ETPS preview flight, flown by Sqn Ldr Les Evans (*B. Johnson*)

There are three gauges which display the positions of ailerons, rudder and the aircraft's angle of attack. These instruments are mounted on head-up panels which are on the pilot's eyeline and are supplementary to the aircraft's conventional instruments. In addition, telemetry continuously transmits to the Boscombe Down base station data of the Hunter's altitude, airspeed, angle of attack, roll and yaw rate and control positions. There is also a UHF voice communication link between the ground pilot in telemetry and the airborne pilot.

By the time the ETPS students graduated to the Hunters they had completed five spinning sorties on the Jet Provost and the Hawk during the previous week, so that they were adjusted to the (largely unpleasant) physiological sensations of spinning a high-performance aircraft and trained to analyse with detachment any departures from controlled flight.

After a comprehensive briefing by the tutor, the Hunter was taxied out for take-off; as it did so, the UHF radio telephone link to the Ground Pilot in the Boscombe Down telemetry station was checked, as was the yaw and control position data. London Military Radar was advised of the sortie and a flight plan filed with the controllers. During the climb the spin panel, with its warning systems, was checked and the Ground Pilot asked to verify the data transmission of altitude, airspeed, angle of attack and roll rate. The weather minima and the banning of spinning over water were the same as for the Hawk sorties. Normal entry height for the Hunter spin exercise was 40,000 feet; as the aircraft approached that altitude, the Ground Pilot was called and advised of the intention of

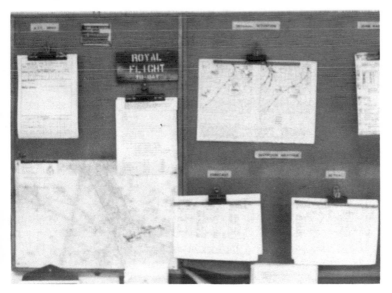

The self-briefing board in the ETPS ops room at Boscombe Down. Even military aircraft have to comply with air traffic rules, and meteorological information is just as important to a Mach 2 fighter as a civil airliner or light aircraft.
(*B. Johnson*)

the Hunter pilot's first spin: type, erect or inverted, number of turns (it might be mentioned in passing that the one parameter that is not available to the Ground Pilot is the number of turns the spinning aircraft has made), control positions (in-spin or out-spin aileron) and the intended mode of recovery. The Ground Pilot noted the information against the spin number on a special form for later reference.

On a normal Hunter spin exercise the amount of fuel carried permits up to seven spins, each from an entry altitude of 40,000 feet. The first spin was an incipient one-turn erect spin. It was followed by several four-turn erect spins, some with intentional control mishandling. The final part of the exercise was an inverted spin with the correct recovery action demonstrated.

As Wing Commander John Bolton, the CO of ETPS, pointed out in a recent authoritative article,[5] the Hunter is a 'spin resistant' aircraft which requires the full application and holding of pro-spin controls to enter and to maintain autorotative flight. The motion of the spin in a Hunter is confusing and the aircraft is very sensitive to any mishandling of the controls, especially the ailerons. The normal technique of entry, as practised at ETPS, is to ensure a clean configuration: flaps and undercarriage up and airbrake retracted; the two 100-gallon tanks on the inboard pylons empty. All Hunter spins are made with idle engine power selected. The pilot allows the airspeed to decay until moderate stall buffet is apparent: this occurs at around 150 KIAS; at entry, a full rudder application in the direction of the spin is made simultaneously with full aft stick with ailerons held neutral.

John Bolton described the resultant spin:

'After entry, the incipient phase lasts one to two turns and is characterised by a slow, tight, horizontal barrel roll with marked roll-rate hesitations; the first turn usually takes six to eight seconds. During the second turn the nose drops to 30 to 40 degrees below the horizon and the yaw rate can be felt to increase as the spin stabilises. Roll-rate hesitations, and even brief reversals, occur at irregular intervals and each subsequent turn takes four to six seconds to complete. In comparison with spins experienced in straight-winged aircraft [the Jet Provost or the Hawk], the Hunter spin is slower but very oscillatory; it can be quite disorientating and physically uncomfortable . . . The recovery actions are "standard" in that full opposite rudder is applied to oppose the yaw, as seen on the turn needle, and the stick is moved progressively and centrally forward until the spin stops. If any significant amount of out-spin aileron is held, the aircraft will not recover.'

Once the Hunter recovered from the spin, the pilot had to ease it out of an 80-degree dive at up to 300 knots at $3\frac{1}{2}$g, during which he

An ETPS Hunter entering a spin (again to the left!). This is an erect spin. After two turns the spin will become oscillatory and disorientating to a pilot, even an experienced one, who is not 'current', that is in recent spinning practice. (*BBC*)

lost some 5000 feet before level flight was gained. The total height loss from a four-turn erect spin entered at 40,000 feet is typically 15,000 feet. For those readers with strong stomachs, here is an extract from the part of John Bolton's article which described the inverted spin in the Hunter:

> There are two entry techniques [to the inverted spin]: out-spin aileron applied at a roll-rate hesitation during an erect spin, and an entry from a full aileron roll. The latter is described here. At about 175 KIAS in level flight, full aileron is applied with a slight forward stick pressure; when a good roll rate has developed (after about 270 degrees), opposite rudder is applied whilst the stick is held in its fully deflected position. At the end of the first roll, pitch/yaw coupling can be felt and by the end of the second roll the spin is usually established. During the second roll the stick is brought to a position slightly aft of neutral and held there with the ailerons central; the rudder is held fully deflected throughout. The inverted spin is less oscillatory than the erect spin but it is faster, with each turn taking three to four seconds. The predominant sensation, apart from the negative −1 to −2g, is of a high yaw rate . . . Perhaps surprisingly, the spin recovery actions are the same as for the erect spin but a more determined effort must be made to apply and hold full rudder, and full forward stick is usually needed before the aircraft recovers.

A secondary effect of the inverted spin in the Hunter is the danger of excessive jet pipe temperatures being generated if the spin is held for more than four turns.

The Hunter is not normally flown on an ETPS spinning exercise solo, but due to unserviceability of the Hawk, some of the students on the course carried out solo erect spins in the Hunter. One of them was Flight Lieutenant Dave Southwood. Dave was asked if the thought of solo spinning in a swept-wing aircraft in any way intimidated him. He replied:

'No, I am looking forward to it very much; I have done the dual sortie [including inverted spinning] and it is a very interesting aeroplane to spin.'

'Does even an experienced fighter pilot like yourself get disorientated in a spin?'

'You can get disorientated in a spin certainly. It is an exercise or a flight regime where you need a fair amount of practice to stay familiar with it, but again that is one of the things we are looking at the aeroplane for: to see how disorientating it is. If it is too disorientating and confusing then there is no way one can let students go off solo to spin it.'

'The Hunter is a really strong aeroplane, isn't it?'

'It is very strong, and for that reason it makes a good spin trainer in that there are very high stresses put on the airframe, but it stands up to it very well. One of the ETPS Hunters has got close to 3000 spins.'

'What about the physical stress on the pilot?'

'You do feel large lateral accelerations as well as normal accelerations but that is all part and parcel of spinning [assessment] and the disorientating effect it might have on the unprepared pilot.'

On the sortie, Dave Southwood carried a voice recorder and calmly recorded his impressions of several spins as they were performed; only the effect of g and the depth of his breathing gave any hint of the considerable effort he must have been making to control the Hunter:

'Spin two. Entry height 40,500 feet. Fuel gone 1890 [lbs] . . . Trim to 170 knots; on course, nose down, dropping level at 40,000 [feet] to enter from the right . . . 150 knots. Hesitation very soon on entry there, there is rolling, two hesitations by the first turn, and that is one turn, 110 knots . . . very steep nose down, two turns, getting about two hesitations per turn, airspeed up to 180 [knots], very fast there. Three turns. Speed is slowing to 140, rudder tramping, four turns. Left rudder, stick coming forward. Aircraft has recovered. Airspeed good; that spin appeared very oscillatory: the first turn got two large oscillations, the speed was about 180 knots . . . spin attitudes tend to go about 70 degrees nose down up to 30 degrees nose down, the wing tilt angle going from zero up to about 15 to 20 degrees as far as could be ascertained.'

Dave Southwood made several spins, one of the most interesting being spin number five:

'Spin five with in-spin aileron . . . entry will be at 40,200 [feet]. Fuel on entry is 2670 lbs gone, and entering. Hesitation again after half a turn, one turn; there's the hesitation, [in-spin] aileron

ETPS student Flt Lt Dave Southwood about to spin the Hunter inverted. He was not as depressed at the prospect as this film still might suggest! (*BBC*)

coming up. Two turns large accelerations, and that is three turns. Very much more pitch oscillation noticed, as well as very violent roll. Rudder forces becoming light, [air]speed the same, and recovering, ailerons neutral. Full right rudder, stick coming forward. Very high rate of roll to the right . . . and stopped suddenly. In that spin there, the pitch oscillations became much more noticeable than before, with a fairly high wing tilt angle, the aircraft being inclined to the right . . . much higher lateral accelerations with the oscillations more violent but occurring about as frequently. The recovery; the rate of roll kept going from probably two to three rolls and it was only by looking at the yaw needle [on the spin panel] that it was possible to ascertain that the controls were applied in the correct sense.'

It is significant that, during his solo spinning sortie, Dave Southwood had at one point to rely on the Hunter's special instrumentation to be able to ascertain the direction of the spin. In the event, he was able to do so and recovered without incident but it poses the question: is intentional spinning, forbidden in most RAF aircraft, a dangerous manoeuvre, even given the ETPS safeguards? The question was put to Squadron Leader Vic Lockwood:

'We tend to shy away from words like "dangerous", because we will not embark on anything unless it is truly thought out. But there is always an area of uncertainty and, in spinning, there is perhaps the highest area of uncertainty; but we prefer to call it "high risk" rather than "dangerous".'

'Is spinning considered high risk because the aircraft are difficult to recover in the aerodynamic sense, or because pilots tend to become disorientated and fail to apply the correct recovery techniques?'

'In general, once an aircraft enters a spin, it is a very disorientating motion and pilots are not normally used to it, which is one of the reasons we train here. The more often you experience a spin, the more likely you are to be able to recognise any problems and recover.'

The ETPS spinning exercise, whether considered as 'dangerous' or just 'high risk', is without doubt the most exacting, in terms of piloting ability, required of the fixed wing course. The rotary wing students, too, have their Everest: Autorotation and the Avoid Curve.

Autorotation and the Avoid Curve

If a single-engined fixed wing aircraft should suffer the misfortune of engine failure, the pilot can glide and with luck make a forced landing, with the likely possibility of his passengers and himself surviving. The pilot of a single-engined helicopter is not so well placed: helicopters do not glide. The only recourse the helicopter pilot has open to him, in the event of total engine failure, is autorotation. Squadron Leader Iain Young, tutor Rotary Wing at ETPS, described autorotation and engine-off landings as 'the most demanding and potentially high-risk areas of helicopter flight testing'.

The two exercises are related but separate. Autorotation is the technique whereby the pilot of a single-engined helicopter suffering engine failure in flight is able to turn his aircraft into an autogyro with the rotor blades acting as unpowered windmills, rather like a sycamore seed, to enable the pilot to control the rate of descent. This rate will, however, be too high for a safe landing; at a critical moment, therefore, the pilot will have to use the energy stored in the rotor to cushion the landing. This is done by altering the pitch of the rotor blades back from the small autorotative angle to the original helicopter setting to produce lift. To achieve this successfully, the pilot's height judgement has to be perfect; there is only one chance; the amount of energy stored in the rotor blades is distinctly limited, just enough to cushion the landing. If the pilot misjudges the rate of descent or the height, the landing will become a crash, probably fatal. It is obvious that the height and speed at which a helicopter pilot can hope to achieve a safe autorotative

If spinning the Hunter inverted is the high (or low) mark of the Fixed Wing course, the Rotary Wing's equivalent is the avoid curve. Here the Principal Rotary Wing tutor, Lt Cdr Mike Swales, is about to supervise an avoid curve sortie on the Scout. *(BBC)*

landing are important factors. The pilot will turn speed into height, for height is of paramount importance: the higher the aircraft is, the longer the pilot has to set up his aircraft for an auto-rotation landing. It follows that there must be finite limits for auto-rotation – if the helicopter is too low the rotors will not have time to windmill up to a safe speed. For each helicopter type, the manu-facturers will produce what is known as the 'avoid curve' as a guide to pilots. Lieutenant Commander Mike Swales RN, Principal Tutor, Rotary Wing, ETPS, defined the avoid curve as:

'An area of the aircraft's flight envelope which the pilot must avoid staying in continuously if in the circumstance of his suffering a sudden engine failure he is going to manage to land the aircraft safely. It is usually defined by a height and speed combination. There are two major areas. First of all there is the area of airspeed from the hover to about 65 knots, and height, typically 800 feet [the figures refer to the school Scout]. The second area is low-level high-speed area from about 60 knots to the aircraft's maximum and up to a height of 50 feet. If a pilot should have engine failure within those areas, the chances of his getting away with a safe landing are remote.'

The best way to sum up the avoid curve is simply as a graphical curve of height and speed combinations to avoid. Autorotational landings are those which can be performed, in the event of engine failure, providing the pilot has remained on the right side of the avoid curve.

The object of the ETPS exercise was to define the avoid curve. Before flying on that high-risk sortie, however, the students had to perform, with their tutor, a number of autorotational landings.

Generally, autorotation is only considered a necessary exercise for single-engined helicopters; however, as Iain Young pointed out,[6] a recent incident involving a civil twin-engined helicopter on duty in the North Sea which suffered a double flame-out, might well cause a rethink. The ETPS rotary wing flight notes, 'Autoro-tation and Engine-Off Landing Assessment', written by Mike Swales, cover the subject in detail.

The introduction to the paper gives the background to the ETPS exercise:

> You are to assume that the helicopter has been developed up to pre-production standard by a manufacturer, and has been allocated to your test team at a test establishment for a handling assessment of its qualities during autorotative and engine-off landing phases of flight. You are to assume also that the helicopter has been built to fulfil anti-submarine and search and rescue and training roles.

(All the roles require the helicopter to fly within the avoid curve.)

The autorotation and avoid curve sorties required that the student pilot was in current practice on the type of helicopter on which the tests were flown; the nature of the exercises was high risk and the ETPS précis warned that: 'It is necessary during some of these tests to use techniques which leave little or no margin for errors.' Although a tutor was sitting in the co-pilot's left-hand seat, the time for remedial action, in the event of the student making an error of judgement or mistake in an autorotative landing, was so short that by the time the tutor realised that a mistake had been made it would have been too late to do much about it. Before the flights the students were instructed in the theory of autorotational descents, recovery techniques and engine-off landings. Service helicopter pilots would have had such instruction during their training but that may have been some years earlier and on different helicopter types; furthermore, the limits that apply to squadron pilots are much extended on ETPS rotary wing exercises, as with the fixed wing.

Although total power failure on a modern helicopter is a rare occurrence, it is not unknown. In any event, the possibility of enemy action must always be considered with military aircraft. There are three main cases when a single-engined helicopter can suffer total engine failure in flight:

1 Hovering near the Ground

If a helicopter is hovering near the ground at the time of engine failure, the pilot has few options open to him other than to raise the collective pitch lever to increase the pitch of the rotor blades, to use such energy remaining in their rotation to cushion the inevitable contact with the ground. The main factor in the success or otherwise of the landing in this situation is the strength of the undercarriage.

2 Hovering away from the Ground

An engine failure at a reasonable height offers the pilot that most vital commodity: time. The correct recovery technique is for the pilot to lower the collective lever as far as it will go to maintain rotor speed. (It is normal practice for helicopter manufacturers to arrange the controls so that fully lowering the collective lever will set the rotor blades to the optimum pitch setting for autorotational flight.) By lowering the collective lever, the fine pitch setting of the rotors will produce less lift and therefore will unload the now unpowered rotor until the downward movement of the aircraft maintains rotor speed by simple windmill action. To control the descent, the pilot should simultaneously ease forward the cyclic pitch control (the one which is the equivalent of a fixed wing aircraft's stick) to increase forward speed, even if this initially increases the rate of descent. As the helicopter descends, the windmilling rotors will generate sufficient lift for the pilot to control the descent to the moment of landing, when the pilot has to 'flare' the helicopter by pulling back on the cyclic pitch control, raising the aircraft's nose to absorb the forward speed and, at the same time, raising the collective lever which increases the rotor's pitch to turn the energy in the rotating blades to lift, cushioning the landing. Perfectly judged, the landing will be smooth and the landing run short; imperfectly judged, it can range from a heavy landing to total disaster. It might be mentioned that the pilot has very little time to react to engine failure in a helicopter, even under the most favourable conditions. The critical figure is the rotor rpm (NR), if the pilot is slow in appreciating and reacting to the loss of power and the rotor speed decays to a certain figure, it will not be possible to restore it. Tests have shown that the average time taken by pilots to *begin* to react to engine failure is 0.75 seconds. Helicopter designers have provided a margin of two seconds before the rotor speed decays to a dangerously low level. Not a very large margin one may think. (About the time it takes to read aloud those last eight words.)

3 Forward Flight

If a helicopter has engine failure in normal cruising forward flight, the pilot has a number of options open to him. If he has sufficient height he can use his forward speed to maintain rotor speed, or to attain the optimum autorotational attitude. If he considers that he is a little low at the moment of power loss, he can turn his forward speed into altitude.

The ETPS syllabus allowed for two dual demonstration flights with a tutor. The flights enabled the student to assess the techniques for rapid entries into autorotative descent and engine-off landings. The student then had four hours allocated for the exercises, culminating in an avoid curve sortie.

The initial exercises consisted of both slow and fast entries into autorotation made from level and climbing flight, at various airspeeds from zero (that is, when hovering) to maximum level speed. The collective lever was lowered at progressively higher rates to simulate sudden power loss. No matter how quickly a pilot reacts to sudden power failure by depressing the collective lever, it is almost certain that the rotor rpm will fall below normal speed. An important part of the exercise was for the student to assess the handling of the helicopter at low rotor speeds when in autorotative flight. Control response and the onset of blade stalling was observed.

The next stage of the exercise was the recovery to powered flight. As the tests continued, the students were required to investigate flare techniques to arrest the downward and forward motion of the helicopter. The tests allowed recoveries from autorotative flight leading to power-off landings.

The first solo engine-off landing that the student performed was made under optimum conditions. The penultimate test in the series was to observe the effect of entry into autorotative flight with delayed lever lowering. This test determined the limits, in terms of aircraft handling and rotor rpm, resulting from a pilot reacting slowly to sudden engine failure. In essence it was to confirm the mandatory two seconds' lever lowering delay which all helicopters are supposed to offer. It was critical testing and the ETPS flying wing précis warned that:

> This is your first experience of 'critical testing'. Approach all test points incrementally, using the build-up technique. Do not exceed limits; either yours or the aircraft's. If at any time you are unhappy with the way the tests are progressing, land and discuss the problem with your tutor.

The autorotative landings, difficult and in the ETPS critical testing category though they may be, were but a preparation – a mere qualifying round – for the final test: the establishment of the avoid curve, the most dangerous in the syllabus of the rotary wing course.

The helicopter used for the flying test is the Scout XP 849. The ETPS Flying Wing notes, as usual, gave the student a clear idea of the brief:

> You are to assume that the helicopter has been developed up to pre-production standard, and has been allocated to your test team to determine the validity of the contractor-furnished avoid curve diagram. The aircraft is being procured as a light observation/basic trainer.
>
> The aims of the tests are to determine the . . . operational avoid curve, considering the roles and normal capabilities of the majority of operational/student pilots, and boundaries for inclusion in the aircrew manual.

The importance of the avoid curve exercise was such that, in common with the fixed wing spinning sorties, it merited a lecture of its own. The speaker was the Rotary Wing tutor, Iain Young. The lecture was, as might be expected, very technical and it included a film compilation, shot in America, of a series of avoid curve tests which went wrong; one of them a total disaster in which a Huey was written off (fortunately without fatal casualties). Iain concluded with a warning which was hardly needed:

Sqn Ldr Iain Young
lecturing to the Rotary
Wing course on the
techniques for flying the
avoid curve on the school
Scout (*BBC*)

Sqn Ldr Iain Young lecturing to the Rotary Wing course on the techniques for flying the avoid curve on the school Scout (*BBC*)

'An avoid curve is an area which you will not have flown before. At least at some stage throughout your operational flying you will have carried out engine-off landings, but you will never have looked at landings on the edges of the avoid curve, and you will certainly not have tested some of the more critical areas of the avoid curve. So it is important that you must have the detailed knowledge which you have now attained, and very important that you are in excellent flying practice.'

For the BBC Television series, the following briefing for the avoid curve was recorded between Mike Swales, the Principal Rotary Wing Tutor, and Bob Horton, the ETPS student who was to fly the exercise in the Scout. Mike Swales spoke first:

Lt Bob Horton asks about lowering the collective lever (*BBC*)

'Firstly it is critical testing.'

'Awkward this one, isn't it?'

'It is the ultimate test . . . so if you are in doubt at any stage during this exercise, shout out and we will stop, consider what we are doing and if you are not happy for any reason we will simply come back and think about it for another day.'

'OK.'

'Right. Let us see how we are going to evaluate this avoid curve. This is the one you are familiar with from the Scout aircrew manual: standard conditions, with no wind and with the aircraft at the maximum weight of 5000 lbs . . .'

'This is assuming no lever-lowering delay on entry?'

'No. As far as the manufacturer is concerned he has assumed a normal pilot reaction time above the height of 200 feet.'

The briefing continued with the details of the sortie discussed, including the question of the 15-knot wind, which was a little on the high side but fortunately blowing straight down the light aircraft grass runway at Boscombe Down. (In point of fact the wind made the avoid curve exercise marginally less demanding since it reduced the forward speed at touchdown.)

The really critical area in the avoid curve testing is, without doubt, the judgement of the height at which to 'flare' (raise the nose of the aircraft) and select the pitch to convert the stored energy in the autorotating rotors. It is critical because if it is misjudged there is no possibility of correcting any mistakes. The ETPS notes cautioned the student to set his altimeter to read zero on the selected touchdown point and not to rely on the 'QFE' for the day. QFE is the barometric pressure to be set on the altimeter's sub-scale in millibars to enable it to read zero on the airfield. However, one millibar is equivalent to 30 feet of height which would be a large margin of error for the avoid curve tests. As the notes put it: 'Do not be satisfied if you are not *exactly* on airspeed or altitude: 5 knots slow and 50 feet low could really make your eyes water!'

It should be realised that the avoid curve *is* a curve and has to be plotted: it is not merely a case of making a couple of autorotational descents and writing down the 'numbers'. The ETPS exercise called for no fewer than nineteen test points.

Due to the nature of the testing, the time available and the relative inexperience of the student test pilots, the exercise was confined to confirming the makers' figures although, because of such variables as weather, pilot reaction times, individual helicopters' loading and small rigging anomalies, it remained a difficult and searching sortie which was found to press students to the very limit of their flying skills and ability to observe, for later analysis, the many facts and figures fleetingly presented. The actual avoid curve for the Scout has nineteen entry points ranging from the hover at 5 feet (No. 1), the hover at 800 feet (No. 7), to 60 knots at 30 feet (No. 19).

Mike Swales went through the points with his student, Bob Horton:

'Let's just go through each point. . . and see the sort of problems that we are likely to encounter. We will start off right at the bottom of the avoid curve [No. 1]: engine failure in the hover. Bob, what are the factors that are going to affect the pilot's ability to carry out a safe landing?'

'How heavy the helicopter is. It is all a function of how rapidly your NR [rotor RPM] decays and how much stress the under-carriage can take.'

'Yes. It is really taken out of the hands of the pilot; it is very much up to how the manufacturers designed the machine in the first place. From 10 feet in the hover, if a pilot has engine failure, all he is going to be able to do is to correct the yaw [the yaw is caused by the sudden cessation of the engine's torque, which is still being compensated for by the tail rotor being permanently geared to the main shaft]; he will see himself descending towards the ground and he will pull the collective [lever] to cushion the touchdown. It will be an instinctive reaction and, as you say, the strength of the under-carriage is probably the deciding factor as to how high the hover can be for the pilot to be able to hope to get away with it. The height that we are looking at, point 1, is 5 feet in the Scout.'

'Right.'

'We will start off with a practice forced landing with power on so that we can assess the wind conditions and see what the flare effect is like today . . . having done that we will work our way back to the avoid curve. OK, Bob, let's just go over what we are going to do on this test. First of all, establish that this is a critical test; there is a certain amount of risk involved. There is nothing equivalent to this particular exercise on the fixed wing side: they [on forced landing exercises] always have the chance of opening the throttle on an overshoot; once you have closed the throttle in the Scout, you are committed to a landing, so it has got to be right. The purpose of this test is to bring the Scout back in one piece with no damage whatsoever.'

'Right. Bit of chinagraph on the tail-skid?'

'That's right! We will mark the tail-skid just to make sure we haven't touched it, and I'm sure we won't have done.'

The discussion turned to specific figures and techniques at the various entry points for defining the avoid curve for the Scout. Mike Swales then told his student that 'HQRs', Handling Quality Ratings (see page 279), would be required for each point of the test, right down to touchdown.

'Bob, if I were to ask you to break down the engine-off landing manoeuvre during any of the test points, what sort of areas would you be particularly looking at?'

'I think I would divide it up into four areas, consisting of the entry, the autorotation, the flare and then the landing. On the low ones the areas are going to be combined into one quick movement but on the higher ones we can quite easily divide this exercise up into four . . . I think what we ought to do is to try to identify which of those four sub-tasks is the most difficult and then perhaps assign the HQR to it.'

'Yes. Let's take a few of those points and see if we can predict what is going to be the most difficult sub-task. Take the hover at 700 feet [No. 8].'

'Right. Well in that situation we are going to have a lot of power on because we are in the hover. At the moment we close the throttle you have to get the [collective] lever down pretty quickly and you will be pulling zero g, and going to be coming out of the seat at the time. You have got to recover your NR because it will have dropped quite a long way . . . so it is going to be a large push forward [of the cyclic control] to get the nose down in order to get the speed up. At the same time, of course, we do not want to do that too fast, or we may start bunting[7] forward and that will drop the NR even more.'

'So the entry is the critical phase?'

'Yes. The entry is going to be the critical phase. I think you might get a lot of yaw as the engine fails and I don't know what the pitch changes are going to be like, but there will probably be some of that going on as well.'

'Good, Bob. I think we are agreed that once you have got your airspeed back and you have the aircraft in a level nose [up] attitude, then it is really an academic engine-off landing.'

'You are at 60 knots going down. Super! The entry is the critical part.'

'OK. Let's take a lower one; point 13: 100 feet, at 65 knots. What do you think is the critical sub-task in that one?'

The collective lever on the Scout which, when flying the avoid curve, the pilot must smartly lower, at the same time closing the spring-loaded throttle which is a twist grip on the lever. That, as Bob Horton pointed out, could be awkward. (BBC)

'On that one, Mike, I would say the landing, because at point 13 you are going to go straight into the flare. So the moment the lever goes down you can go into the flare. As to whether you are going to get the lever all the way down or not I don't know, you may at that height. I think that is something we will have to take a look at; the NR will have dropped quite a long way by that stage, so directional control is going to be difficult on the landing and I may run out of lever at the bottom [of the landing flare]. We are going down at 65 knots, and a lot depends on how much speed I'm going to get off in the flare. So I think the landing is the major task there.'

'Yes, I agree, and remember you are always trying to get below 50 knots for the touchdown if possible. What about point 18: 90 knots and 50 feet?'

'On this one you are co-ordinating lowering the collective with the flare, so you want to maintain 50 feet, zoom very slightly if you can; I don't know if the Scout is capable of zooming.'

'It won't zoom at all, no. So really it's the flare, isn't it?'

'It is a co-ordinated flare; a 'quick stop' manoeuvre, followed by allowing the aircraft to descend in the flaring attitude, check level, and then run on [to the touchdown]. I may have a high-speed run on the ground: I will have to look at that one.'

'Good, Bob. I think you have a good idea of what we are looking for. Bear in mind that although we are trying to predict what is going to be happening to the aircraft at each point, always keep an open mind. Be prepared for something a little bit different.'

Bob Horton replied that with the Scout helicopter that was always a distinct possibility. Mike Swales pointed out the cardinal rule for all test pilots:

'When you are assigning the Handling Quality Ratings, I would like you to assign them as you perceived them at the time, so we can look at how difficult a particular task is going to be for the average pilot in a squadron. It is for him that the avoid curve was constructed in the first place.'

Bob was assured by his tutor that the flight would be the most rewarding he would make on the ETPS course. As Bob Horton, Falkland War pilot, was getting into the Scout for the avoid curve flight, he was interviewed for the BBC:

'I gather that this exercise is called "critical testing", Bob?'

'Well, that is to use the official phrase, yes. Personally I think it's bloody dangerous: if you did this exercise on a squadron, for example, you would be in for a court martial: quite looking forward to it really.'

From the ground the test looked impressive: the Scout, hovering at 700 feet, suddenly appeared to drop like a stone at a steep angle, then the nose was raised and, with the rotors creating a good deal of

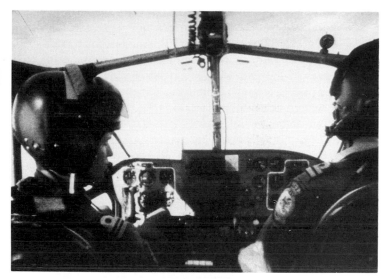

left, Mike Swales and
Bob Horton count down
to the avoid curve dive;
middle left, The Scout
autorotates at a high rate
of sink; *middle right*,
At precisely the correct
height Bob Horton flares
the Scout and, using the
kinetic energy stored in
the whirling blades,
makes a perfect landing
(*bottom*) (*BBC*)

noise, the small helicopter seemed to slow down almost to a stop and, as the nose rose even further, the Scout gently touched down to run for a very short distance on the Boscombe Down grass strip. In the helicopter the test was even more impressive; as the collective lever was lowered, the ground seemed to be directly below and coming up fast, very fast indeed, but the calm voices on the intercom were reassuring:

'OK, Bob. Ready?'

'Ready. 3–2–1 . . . lot of left boot in . . . nose going right forward . . . airspeed coming back, NR recovering very slowly . . . airspeed 50 knots . . . selecting a level attitude, watching the NR there . . . a little bit more, and there we are.'

Bob Horton and Mike Swales carried out the entire avoid curve exercise without a hitch. After the final landing Bob was asked how it had gone.

'Well, different, I can tell you. I am still alive anyway so it obviously did not go too badly . . . very enjoyable and I learned a lot from it.'

The avoid curve exercise marked the apogee of the rotary wing training in terms of aircraft handling although they would later fly familiarisation exercises on fixed wing aircraft, including the VSS Bassett and the HS 748 Andover. Most helicopter pilots have had some experience on fixed wing aircraft but this was usually confined to trainers. The fixed wing students, on the other hand, had for the most part had no previous experience of the joys of flying helicopters. At the Boscombe Down school they flew both the Scout and the Gazelle up to the autorotation exercise.

The students of both flying wings proved their ability to fly a variety of aircraft, performing advanced exercises on most of them; exercises that were well outside the limits permitted on operational squadrons. The result of the training at this point was a confidence in their ability to fly aircraft almost as a reflex action, rather like riding a bicycle. That is, of course, an over-simplification: piloting a modern service aircraft can never be that simple, nevertheless their skills were such that they could, as it were, set aside the distraction of flying a given aircraft and concentrate on evaluating and assessing the performance of a specific area of the flight envelope. The next major exercise in the fixed wing syllabus illustrated this point admirably. No fewer than five weeks of the summer term were devoted to it.

Systems Assessment Displays and NAVWASS

This complex exercise, flown on the Jaguar, was undertaken by three-man syndicates. 'B' syndicate was the one filmed by the BBC and its members were Squadron Leader Les Evans, RAF;

Commandant Serge Aubert, French Air Force, and the Australian, Flight Lieutenant Nick Coulson, RAAF. The tutor was Squadron Leader James Giles.

Nick Coulson, RAAF (*left*) has his 'cards' (the notes he will carry in flight) checked by his tutor, James Giles, before their dual first flight on the NAVWASS exercise (*BBC*)

The exercise, like all others on the ETPS course, began with a briefing in the tutor's office at the side of the Boscombe Down hangar 104. James Giles came straight to the point:

'What we are going to do on this exercise is to assess the Jaguar inertial system and we are going to assess it for its operational aspects. That is what you have got to start thinking: "This is an operational aircraft, its job is to go to war." Your job is to assess the aircraft; how well can an operational pilot fly it, how well can he use it, how well does it [the inertial system] help him find small targets and to attack them? That is the game we are in today.'

The syndicate was told to assume it was a team that was to assess a new 'NAVWASS' (navigation and weapon-aiming sub-system). It had been given a specification and the task was to test fly the system and evaluate it against the official specification to check the accuracy and, further, to operate it in the same environment as an operational pilot would have to. As James Giles put it to the syndicate:

'Does it actually perform all the roles the maker claims it does? Do all the small refinements, if you like, of the navigation system work? You have to test them all to ensure they do. You must also look at the accuracy, because accuracy is important. Bear in mind that this system is designed to take men into a battlefield environment, possibly in Germany where the weather is going to be marginal a lot of the time – industrial haze, low cloud – it has got to be able to take a pilot there. He may not have visual cues, he may not be able to see navigational features; he is going to be relying on this system to guide him, so it has got to be accurate. You have got to make it work. That means you have got to manage it. The workload level has got to be low enough so that you can still fly the aeroplane at 200 feet; at a speed in excess of 400 knots, you must still be keeping a look-out for threats; you may have a formation to fly with; you have electronic warfare information coming in to you. The system has got to be simple to manage, it cannot be a high workload otherwise it just won't be used. Possibly most important from both the training and the test pilot's view is the interface; how you react to the system. How well is the information displayed? How easily can you programme it? It is basically a computer so you have to tell it what output you want; what we are looking for is how well an operational pilot can be expected to relate to this system. Go and fly an operational profile, assess the system and come out with a good brief at the end.'

That last remark by James Giles was pertinent for at the end of the NAVWASS exercise each syndicate had to make a presentation to an audience of ETPS staff. Each of the three syndicates took part and marks were awarded. The staff looked for accuracy in the technical presentation, which was expected to include recommendations to rectify any operational or functional shortcomings in the system. The staff asked searching questions about the findings which the members of the syndicate had to defend. Apart from the technical and operational assessment made by the students, which earned or lost most of the marks, the staff also marked the presentation itself: the use of visual aids, the quality of the arguments and the degree of assurance displayed. A failure in that department could lead to failure of the whole exercise, the reason being the oft-repeated one at ETPS: 'It does not matter how brilliant a test pilot you are or how well you may conduct a task; if you cannot convey your findings to others in a clear, concise and persuasive way, you are wasting your own and everybody else's time.'

James Giles continued his brief:

'Let us come to the sortie; how are we going to fly it? Firstly, remember that the difficult task is to do it in bad weather, so right from the beginning you have to put yourself in the place of the operational pilot. How quickly can you become airborne? How fast is the [NAVWASS] system to align [from switch-on]; how quick and easy is it to put all the data you require in? The information we are talking about is the [exercise] route brief here; it has eight way-points [precise geographical locations *en route*], each is a three-dimensional fix: latitude, longitude and height. Northings, eastings, bearing and range: a lot of information to get in there. Time it, set out actually to time how long it takes to put all that data in. Time how long it takes you to align it, and then sit back and think, "Well, how long has the operational pilot got before he is airborne?" See if your findings are tenable. Once you get airborne, navigation, look-out and map reading are the primary things. You have got a moving map and you also have a head-up display to give you information. How easy or otherwise is it to switch between the modes? What sort of errors are you getting? How well can you use the system? How confident are you that it will get you from A to B? Bear in mind, however, that on this first exercise you are not aiming to pin-point targets; you are going for turning-points. Flying is going to be done at 250 feet, in excess of 400 knots. In other words, an operational environment. Remember, this is not an exercise to see how well you can fly the Jaguar at low-level, it is an exercise for you to assess how well the inertial system will aid the operational pilot.'

The main problem with this exercise was the old one of simulating operational conditions as a peacetime training exercise. To assess the inertial system, the student test pilots had to simulate operational work levels while observing the safety levels required of a peacetime training exercise. James Giles was aware of the difficulty:

'By all means pull up to a safe height if you want to change switches; if you are not happy about anything, if you are not feeling confident, pull up to a safe height. You will have a co-pilot for all the sorties; the pilot in the front seat is the assessing pilot; the man in the back will act as the safety pilot. When you are in the back seat, bear in mind that there are other aircraft around, hilly terrain, power cables, birds, you must help the man in front without unloading him from the operational task of using the inertial system.

'There will be two sorties. On the first we will be looking at the navigational aspects. The second will be the weapon-aiming aspect. Try to assess the navigational accuracy of the system, then concentrate on the weapon aiming.'

The ultimate object of the entire NAVWASS system is to take an aircraft to a precise target and accurately to aim bombs, rockets or guns against it. To that end the students were urged to:

'Make sure you can use all the switches correctly, and can assess the modes of operation, looking at the display and information offered, looking at how well you can control that information to get you to the target, bearing in mind that the target will be defended and the weather might well be bad. You are going to be manoeuvring as you come to the target, pulling 3 to 4g, "jinking", and that is the sort of environment in which you have to assess the kit. It is no good making a straight pass. Operationally you would be making a single first pass attack. It is no good seeing the target, missing it and coming back to reattack, because it is not worth it; the risk levels of a second pass are too high. This kit should give you the capability for a first operational pass, and that is what you are assessing.

'Right, you have had the brief, what I want you to do now is to go away and plan the sortie. Plan tasks. Remember that what you are trying to do is to put yourself in the mind of the operational pilot. Work out what he is going to do first, plan the mission that the aircraft is going to fly; split it into specific tasks; see how the inertial system is actually going to affect the ability of the pilot to do his job. Plan the tasks to get quantitative data, that is to get the "numbers", to get accuracy measurements, and qualitative assessments. Make sure you know how the kit works in all its aspects; make sure you know the way-points to look for, because at 250 feet, and 450 knots you are not going to have much time for going back and rethinking. You must be absolutely clear in your own mind exactly what you are looking for. Any questions?'

Serge Aubert wanted to know what was the time factor they should aim for from the moment of being briefed on the target and take-off.

'Well, I cannot give you a straight answer to that; it depends on the complexity of the sortie, the amount of planning required, but assume fifteen minutes as an absolute minimum from leaving the ops room to taxiing, and less if you can make it. Time wasted preparing the kit is time wasted on the target. So you have to be quick.'

Les Evans asked:

'James, can we organise some 16mm [cine] cameras to help us on the test runs [of the low-level sortie] to film the head-up display?'

'Yes, Les, we can, is the simple answer to that, but I warn you on past experience that when people have gone up with cameras they have never switched them on because of the workload; so don't rely on them for information is all I would say. Rely on the [voice recorder] tape by all means, but not on a head-up camera.'

There were no further questions and the members of the syndicate left the tutor's office to plan the first of several flights over the low-level course. The first flight was an hour solo exercise on the Jaguar, to familiarise the students with the head-up display, and the general functioning of the inertial equipment. When all three of the syndicate had flown the initial sortie they discussed the exercise and prepared for the dual low-level navigation flight with the tutor. On this exercise the student was expected to demonstrate a working knowledge of the navigational aspects of the inertial system, whilst flying the Jaguar at low-level accurately. Before the dual flight there was, it goes without saying, a detailed briefing. Here is part of a transcript of the pre-flight discussion between James Giles and a member of 'B' syndicate, the Australian, Nick Coulson:

'Right Nick, Nav. 1 dual; very different from anything that you have done before, and I know you are not familiar with the environment; therefore the way I propose to play it is that I will do a lot of the flying for you: I will actually fly the aeroplane to let you operate the system. So are you happy with the switches? Are you happy with what the system is going to do for you? Good. The first thing is alignment.'

It was decided that Nick would do a 'rapid align' which means that the equipment can accept a less detailed programme of navigational information, at the cost of degraded accuracy. The weather was good and James Giles pointed out that, when he returned with another of the syndicate earlier that morning, the

The NAVWASS exercise involves flying at 250 feet, at 450 knots; there is little margin for error (*BBC*)

A 'Scout' cockpit (Sopwith Pup) of the First World War. The simple instruments are, *left to right*, watch, altimeter, compass and airspeed. (*B. Johnson*)

accuracy of a similar rapid align was within half a mile after an hour's flight. As Nick began the alignment, James put a watch on him to time the preliminaries from planning to taxi.

It would be interesting to point to a revealing set of figures that show just how the workload of the operational fighter pilot has risen over the years; the figures are approximate, differing with sub-types.

A typical Allied fighter of the First World War, the French Spad of 1916, had about five separate display surfaces; by 1940, the pilots flying the Battle of Britain Spitfires and Hurricanes, or for that matter the Me 109s, had to keep an eye on about twenty-five instruments. In the 1960s, the pilots of the RAF's fastest fighter, the Lightning, were expected to cope with the information offered from no fewer than fifty separate display surfaces (at Mach 1.8!); the Jaguar betters that figure by a substantial margin, weighing in with sixty-five.

The number of switch or lever functions to be operated by a pilot shows a similar escalation (the aircraft are slightly different); 1916 Spad, say three; 1944 P-51 Mustang, about sixty; 1960 Lightning, 160; the current American F-15 fighter, in excess of 300. Those figures suggest the extent of the workload confronting an operational pilot of the mid-1980s.

The briefing at Boscombe Down had progressed:

'Right Nick, head-up display. Throughout the NAV exercise I will be going through the head-up display with you. I know what you want to see; the switchery and the NAV mode symbols, so we will look at all that.'

The discussion then turned to the projected map display. This device, which any light aircraft private pilot would give a great deal

The cockpit of a German Bf 109 E-3 fighter *circa* 1940, note the reflector gunsight. This Messerschmitt was captured and bore the RAF serial AE 479. It was photographed at Boscombe Down in May 1940; in the background is the present-day ETPS hangar. (*A&AEE/MoD*)

Forty-five years on: the cockpit of one of the school's Hawks. Future cockpits may become simpler as analogue instruments give way to electronic displays and fully automated systems. (*B. Johnson*)

for, consists of a standard 'half million' (1/500,000) RAF military map, route sections of which are copied on to film and projected to a reasonable-sized image, bright enough to be usable in daylight and constantly driven by the inertial system to show the exact position of the aircraft within the accuracy limitations of the system; the degree of accuracy, or otherwise, to be assessed by the students when on the Nav.1 part of the exercise.

At this point it might be helpful to note the general principles of an inertial system. (The precise nature of the equipment in the Jaguar is classified.) The bedrock of the instrument is the ability of gyroscopes to stabilise a platform so that it can, within certain limits, remain level despite the aircraft's movements. The stabilised platform – the inertial platform as it is termed – has accelerometers which can detect angular movement with respect to the platform. The accelerometers are arranged in order to quantify movement; north/south, east/west, up/down, or, by integration, any combination of these, for example, a climbing turn to the east. To be able to turn the arrangement into a coherent navigation system is a most complex undertaking. A computer is required, and one of considerable power. In practice, the inertial system fitted to the Jaguar works as follows: when it is first switched on, the platform and its attendant gyroscopes are heated to a certain figure to stablise the temperature, and therefore the precise mass of the platform and the gyroscopes. The next move, and this is automatic, is to align the system. This means in effect that it finds the approximate direction of true north by reference to a magnetic compass. Magnetic deviation and variation are taken into account by the on-board computer which then refines the heading by zeroing the east/west velocity of the platform. Once the system is aligned, any movement of the aircraft will be detected with respect to true north and the co-ordinates in latitude and longitude and height above sea-level of the starting place; in the case of the Boscombe Down ETPS flight line: 5109.8N, 00144.9W and 407 feet AMSL (Above Mean Sea-Level). Once that information is programmed into the computer, the system will continuously indicate the position of the aircraft to a very high degree of accuracy; it is not absolute but accurate enough to relieve the pilot/navigator of the need to observe and calculate the aircraft's position on a continuous basis.

The accuracy is not as high as in some modern radio and radar-based aids but these are not passive: they can either be jammed by an enemy, as the wartime 'Oboe', or give away the position of the aircraft by transmitting radar pulses, as did H_2S: a wartime system which was still in service use until relatively recently. The great feature of the inertial system is that it is confined to the aircraft and

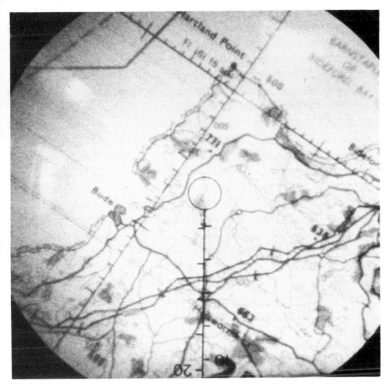

A television still of the projected map display showing the aircraft to be over a lake between Bude and Hartland Point (*BBC*)

is independent of any ground station; it emits no electronic signals which can be detected by normal methods. The position and other information is displayed in several ways, two obvious ones being a digital read-out of latitude and longitude, and as a position in the centre of the projected map display. Other information available is distance to or from a given point, heading and ground speed. The equipment can also guide an aircraft along a designated track.

There are other facilities, one of which is the regress store. If a pilot sees a 'Target of opportunity' when *en route* for another, designated one, he can store the co-ordinates of the new target with the press of a single button, attack the original one, then ask the inertial system to take him to the later target. The projected map display will constantly be showing the present position of the aircraft. The map area stored is extensive: typically the whole of Europe, including the British Isles. Although the true scale of the map presentation is, as already stated, 1:500,000, or 10 nautical miles to the inch, the pilot has also the option of selecting an enlarged mode equal to the scale (but not the detail) of a 1:250,000 (quarter million) map: the same scale as a popular British Ordnance Survey series. The inertial system is a most important aid to the accurate aiming of ordnance.

The above outline of the NAVWASS airborne system is far from definitive: it cannot be, as some details are still restricted, in particular the weapon-aiming facility. The general reader should, however, now be able to follow more easily the remainder of the account of the assessment exercise.

The precise and detailed briefing for the first Nav. I dual exercise to be flown by Nick Coulson and the syndicate tutor, James Giles, continued:

'The projected map display again, we will have a look at the map on alignment to see where it is [that is to compare the known position of the aircraft on the ETPS flight line at Boscombe Down with the position indicated, without correction, on the projected map display in the aircraft's cockpit]. As I said, earlier this morning the error was half a mile to the north. That is within the accuracy of the map [owing to physical stretching of the film from which the map is projected], just as you have it on your card, so follow the map as we fly round the route.

'When we get to this area around Exeter [James indicated on a map],we will fly by map reading just using the projected map display. I would also like you to do a "random fix".'

A random fix is to update the inertial position by moving the projected map display so that the datum relates exactly to a recognised geographical feature: a bridge, lake or hilltop, as the aircraft flies overhead. An update at a pre-planned feature, a way-point, is

The final stage of the NAVWASS briefing; James Giles is pointing out one of the way-points, the lake with a dam, to his Australian student Nick Coulson (*BBC*)

termed a 'planned fix'. Nick Coulson had already decided to make
a random fix as part of the assessment test:

'I planned to do a random fix on the lakes between way-points
two and three.'

'Yes.'

'These lakes here.' Nick indicated the lakes on the chart.

'OK, but there are a number of them, so make sure that you get
the correct lakes.'

'Yes, all right.'

'So once you go over them, over way-point two, which is a
planned fix, get the data to see how accurate the inertial system is,
and then compare that to the accuracy you can achieve by doing a
random fix.'

The briefing discussed other methods of checking the accuracy
of the projected map display including deliberately putting it four
or five miles off course to assess the resetting accuracy. The
briefing then turned to the question of the height and speed to be
flown on the sortie:

'Now I want you to stay low-level: I know it's unfamiliar terri-
tory but I would like you to try to get a feel for the workload
throughout the exercise. I will be monitoring you from the rear
seat, so there is no need to worry about potential terrain avoidance;
so try for 250 feet, if you are more comfortable, four, five hundred
feet, that is fine, but do try for 250. Try to keep the speed up to 400
knots plus . . . if you want me to take over I will, so that you can
look at the system to see how it is operating; if you have any queries
let's clear them up in the air.'

'OK.'

'Good. Now we will go and take a look at the photographs of the
way-points and the map in the briefing room.'

The briefing room had a large display on one wall showing the
track of the sorties, with photographs taken from 200 feet showing
the way-points as they were to appear to the pilot. James Giles
pointed out some of the salient features of the course:

'The lake here, that is the one we are going for, the one with the
dam. There is a small lake just to the south, but we want the concrete dam on the main one. It is actually way-point five.'

'OK. I've got that one.'

'Yes, the lakes stand out very well but it is the dam we are going
for. The other way-points all have vertical extent. Way-point one,
the monument, stands out very well, it's on the side of a hill but it is
a tricky one because, as you can see, it is in an avenue of trees and
there is a single tall tree just to the left of the monument; twice I
have gone after the single tree before picking up the monument. So
that is a tricky one. Alf's Tower [a folly] is on the top of a ridge and

again stands out very well; some are a bit more difficult to find; this one, way-point three, the trig. point, for example.'

James Giles pointed to a photograph of the feature: it was simply a pile of rocks on a hillside and the photograph was helpfully annotated, 'Here folks!'

'We just fly over that one. So those are some of the way-points we are going for. Right we will sign out.'

Nick Coulson is a most experienced pilot who trained first on helicopters then did a tour as a Qualified Flying Instructor (QFI) and then another as the Captain of an HS 748 Andover. He had, at the time of the exercise, over 4000 hours in his logbook (about twice the average for the ETPS students). Asked, just after the briefing, how he felt about flying the low-level exercise over strange country in weather which was far from crystal clear, he replied:

'Well, that is what I am wondering about; normally in Australia you can see things from miles away, so I'm not so sure what I will find.'

The Jaguar XX 145 took off and the exercise began. At 250 feet and a speed of 450 knots there was little time for map reading of a conventional 'looking out of the window' sort. The ETPS Flying Wing notes for the exercise cautioned that: 'Birds are an ever present hazard at low-level, particularly when crossing the coast, so keep a good look-out, know your bird strike drill and *fly with your vizor down at all times*. Data insertion should not be carried out at heights below 1000 feet when flying solo. *Always* go round or climb to avoid built-up areas.'

Nick Coulson taking off from Boscombe Down; the undercarriage doors are just closing as the Jaguar sets course for the first way-point (*BBC*)

The flight track was almost due west (264° True) from Boscombe Down to the first feature, the folly Alf's Tower, then, still flying west, to way-point one, the monument surrounded by an avenue of trees. The next way-point of the nine that comprise the exercise was not difficult to find, being a major flyover on the M5 near Tiverton. Way-point three, the trig. point, was flown over; in contrast to eight, this small inconspicuous target would have been wellnigh impossible to locate by contact navigation, certainly at such a low height and high speed. At way-point four, a conspicuous chimney south-west of Tavistock, the Jaguar turned to the north and was navigated to the next way-point, number five, the lakes and dam, using the projected map display alone. The track is over Exmoor and is not an easy section: the ground is featureless and high; the visibility on the moors notoriously unreliable. Nick Coulson decided on the course as recommended in the notes: west of Launceston, east of Holsworthy. On that demanding section Nick was also assessing the quality of the navigation aid: the presentation of the map, the information on drift, the ease or otherwise of maintaining track accurately to the next way-point, five, the lakes and concrete dam. Over the lakes the aircraft was turned east (095° True) and, passing the remaining way-points, flown back to Boscombe Down. Nick Coulson touched down just fifty minutes after take-off. The debrief was in James Giles' office:

'Right. Well done, Nick, that was excellent. I hope you got all the points from it; I put in as much as I thought you could take. Let's go over some of the points we have got. First, I have all the

En route, the Jaguar is flying at 450 knots and is down to 250 feet as it heads for the lake, way-point five (*BBC*)

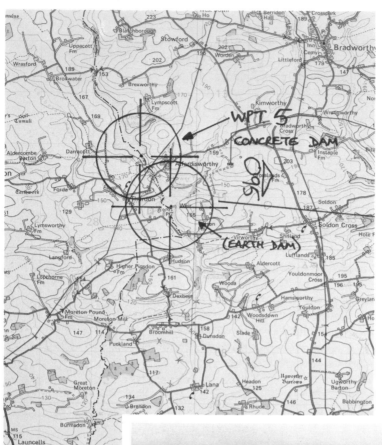

The map and photograph from the briefing room. This is how it should appear to Nick Coulson provided the navigation system is working correctly.

(Map reproduced from the Ordnance Survey 1:250 000 map with the permission of The Controller of Her Majesty's Stationery Office. Crown copyright reserved. Photograph A&AEE/MoD)

Right on track, the
Jaguar speeds over the
dam at 450 knots and
zero error (*BBC*)

timing data for the alignment and that was good. As far as accuracy
goes, as you saw, it is absolutely super. I wouldn't say it is unusual,
but for the inertial systems around here, rapid align and only half a
mile error after fifty minutes is great. And the random fix, 400
yards. That is the sort of accuracy that could take you to a target.
To sum up: we have looked at head-up display, random fix, the
projected map display. On the random fix, we flew over the little
lake, we came round over a wood, and from there we regained [the
planned track]. What did you think of it, Nick?'

'It was good to fly, I liked the thing: it does everything it's
supposed to do within reason. There are a few points on the projected map display as we discussed in the air: I think an operational
pilot would like a better map than the one they have put in the
display.'

'Well, it's simply a photograph of the standard RAF map like
this one. Going over there [Exmoor] it is fairly featureless on the
map, I agree. What do you think about the cockpit environment at
low level; operating the switches, operating the system?'

'It was not too much different from what I had expected, but the
NCU [Navigational Control Unit] is a bit of a pain. [This is the
fitting which displays the latitude and longitude co-ordinates and
which also has the control switches for selecting the various modes
of operation. It is mounted between the pilot's knees.] Having to
look down there when you are at low level going reasonably fast, I
found when we were changing destinations we ended up with the
wrong indication in there. You could end up looking in there
worrying what's gone wrong.'

Nick Coulson after the first dual NAVWASS exercise; he has just been asked by James Giles how he feels about flying the sortie solo (*BBC*)

'I agree, one of the major deficiencies is the fact that you have to spend so much time in the cockpit.'

'That is true, James, but generally, on the cockpit environment, I found the WAMS panel [Weapons-Aiming Mode Selector], once you got used to it, was quite good. I used my fingers, but you can use your thumb. If you know where all the switches are it makes it easier. But you still have to look inside [the cockpit] to change the way-points, and that is not a very good idea.'

'Considering all that, are you happy to go solo?' Nick Coulson thought for a second or two and grinned. '. . . Bear in mind there's a guy in the back, use him to take data, use him as a look-out, there are two of you as I briefed. Make sure he is helping you. All right? Good.'

All three members of 'B' syndicate flew the exercise with the tutor, and then with each other. They then flew the second part of the exercise: attacking a target on the bombing range at Pembrey in Wales. The 'attack' was such only in name; no bombs were dropped but the aircraft were flown as if they had bombs right to the release point. It is an interesting comment on the effectiveness of modern 'smart' bombs that the accuracy of the ordnance itself could be taken for granted. (The controversial attack on Libya by the United States Air Force proved that. It also proved that no matter how good the equipment, if it is not used correctly by the aircrew, some bombs will fall wide of the intended targets.)

A film taken through the head-up display (HUD) on one of the ETPS NAVWASS bombing runs at Pembrey which was shown on the BBC series, depicted the system working on what is termed a

CCIP: Continuously Computed Impact Point, which means that the HUD will display throughout the run-up to the target the predicted impact point of the ordnance, should it be released at any particular moment. The HUD will constantly display target acquisition, airspeed, height, from either a radio or barometric altimeter (RADALT or BAROALT), in addition to aircraft attitude and other information. The point of the head-up display is, of course, that all this information is superimposed on the pilot's view, whilst approaching the target, through the cockpit windscreen. Hence the term head-up, which means that he can simultaneously fly the aircraft both visually and on instruments and, apart from the vital task of keeping the target in sight, he can also keep a look-out for threats.

The method of achieving this goes back to an elegant Victorian music-hall turn, 'Pepper's Ghost'. If a sheet of plate glass is suspended at an angle of 45 degrees and an image is projected on to it, an observer looking at the scene through the glass will see the projected image apparently superimposed on the scene. Pepper used the effect to produce a convincing 'ghost'. The head-up display uses the same method: the information is projected (as a mirror image) to the glass from a cathode-ray tube. Wartime reflector gunsights worked in the same way, the sight, range and deflection scales being projected on to the glass of the sight.

left, The HUD in the Jaguar: the speed is shown as 443 knots and a RADALT of 715 feet. The aircraft is flying wings level but slightly nose down. (*BBC*)

right, The 45-degree 'mirror' of the HUD. Compare this with the reflector gunsight on p. 145; the 1940 sight worked in the same way. (*BBC*)

'B' syndicate, Nick Coulson, Les Evans and Serge Aubert, meet to prepare their joint presentation on the Jaguar NAVWASS exercise (*B. Johnson*)

After all the sorties, including the solos, had been flown on the NAVWASS exercise, the next task was in some ways the hardest: the paperwork and the preparation for the presentation. The Flying Wing notes were uncompromising:

> A post-flight report is required for each of your solo flights . . . each syndicate is required to give a thirty-minute oral presentation ten days after the last flight by the syndicate pilots. Each pilot must make a complete individual assessment in his two post-flight reports. You must then combine your verdicts for the presentation. Remember throughout the exercise what you are doing, which is making a primarily qualitative assessment of the effectiveness of the Jaguar's NAVWASS. The final question must be, 'Does it improve accuracy without increasing your workload so much that safety or operational effectiveness are reduced?'

The syndicate met to discuss their collective findings; contrary to the 'ten days' quoted in the notes, they found that, due to bad weather upsetting the school's timetable, they had only three days when the trio could get together to finalise the presentation. The discussions were very technical and, without background knowledge, meaningless, but for the television series the members were asked about the relevance and importance of the exercise in general:

Les Evans: 'It was a very important exercise. It also has relevance to what we will be doing in the future, simply because we will inevitably be dealing with systems; and most of the work of test pilots is assessing systems to find out if they actually are of use to an operational pilot or simply increase his workload.'

'Is the modern fighter pilot becoming more and more a systems manager?'

Les Evans: 'Yes he is, there is no doubt about that: fighter aircraft are absolutely jam-packed full of systems which the pilot has to monitor, and he is spending a lot of his time analysing what is going on in the cockpit rather than flying the aeroplane in the old-fashioned stick and rudder way.'

'Is this true of the French Air Force, Serge?'

Serge Aubert: 'Yes. The same thing, and even the name is being changed to Weapons Systems Manager or Weapons System Officer, it depends on the country. I know that in France pilots are not happy to be called anything but pilots.'

Nick Coulson, fresh from his exercise, did not agree that the role of the pilot had been diminished at all:

'I think that the modern role may not be the traditional one but it is much more exciting in certain areas and a great deal more is happening . . . it is quite an experience to see the equipment at work.'

(It is interesting to note the agreement of the two fighter pilots, Les Evans and Serge Aubert, who were used to flying solo, and the differing view of Nick Coulson who, as an ex-transport pilot, had done his flying with a co-pilot and engineer and therefore had a lower cockpit workload with ample time to operate any systems that his aircraft may have had fitted.)

Les Evans was asked about flying at low height and at high speed:

'It is a little exciting certainly. There is no doubt that the lower you fly the more you are aware of the ground and the more rapidly things seem to happen. But you must get used to that, because if you're not you certainly fall behind the aeroplane very quickly. Further to the question of the systems being a substitute for the pilot, that is not entirely the case: obviously the pilot still has to monitor it all and still fly the aeroplane and, if the system controls are not in the right place, if they require him to look inside the cockpit or to use three hands to operate the system, it is not to his benefit. That is one of the major points of our exercise, to see if the workload is increased by the use of this particular kit.'

The syndicate was then asked about the recommendations they would be thinking of incorporating into their presentation.

Nick Coulson: 'We found the WAMS panel [the Weapons-Aiming Mode Selector] over on the left-hand side [of the cockpit combing] a little hard to operate because of the size of the buttons. We found that with one finger you still had to look at the panel to

Nick Coulson sees the lighter side of the presentation preparation (*B. Johnson*)

make sure you had pressed the correct one. It is easy to press the wrong button [all pilots wear gloves] as the labels are not very good and with a high workload it was easy to make mistakes.'

Serge Aubert had a complaint about the head-up display; he considered that the field of view it imposed was too narrow. The syndicate was then asked if the shortcomings that it had found (there were others to do with the weapons systems) would have been complained of by Jaguar squadron pilots. Or was the specialised training that the syndicate had received at Boscombe Down such that it now looked at aircraft and systems in a different and rather critical way? Nick Coulson thought not:

'I don't think that the operational pilot would be unaware of the drawbacks [of this system] in his aircraft: he probably is more aware of them than we are because he flies the aircraft every day; he can operate them, but he would probably like to have them in a different place if he could.'

Les Evans pointed out that he had no doubt that all Jaguar pilots found, as the syndicate had, the Navigational Control Unit box too low for easy operating at low level; there was nothing particularly original about that but:

'I think that what we are being taught to do is not just to say that the panel is in the wrong place, but to explain exactly why it is in the wrong place and to explain exactly what aspect of that panel is used in [low-level] flight, so that subsequently people can say "Well, we won't necessarily move the whole panel, but we will move these switches from it". That is the sort of analysis that we are being taught here. I think the course teaches you to see the arguments that there are going to be over moving things; it teaches you therefore to look for evidence that supports your case.'

The syndicate then met in each other's houses to write the script for the presentation to be given in the large lecture theatre in the Ground School building near the main gate at Boscombe Down.

The date of the presentation was 8 August. The audience included Wing Commander John Bolton, OC of the School; the Principal Tutor, Fixed Wing course, Squadron Leader Vic Lockwood; the exercise tutor, Squadron Leader James Giles; tutor Fixed Wing course, Squadron Leader Tim Allen; the principal ground instructor, Squadron Leader Andy Debuse; and the school statistician and systems tutor, Squadron Leader Paul Ashmore. A number of students also attended (it was unclear whether they had come to pick up pointers for their own presentations or simply to enjoy the fun).

The members of 'B' syndicate had put a great deal of hard work into this important occasion; it has been said of the ETPS course that every hour of flying generates some twenty hours of paperwork in the form of preparation notes, notes taken at briefings and debriefings and the writing of final reports on all the exercises. The presentation, which was to assess the workload on pilots using that system, caused a high workload in its own right.

'B' syndicate faces the audience of staff for the NAVWASS presentation. They were – with justification, as it was to turn out – far from confident. (*B. Johnson*)

The syndicate had had photographs taken of the Jaguar's airborne NAVWASS equipment to help them to argue their case and several graphics were also prepared. Les Evans began the presentation:

'Good morning, gentlemen. The Jaguar NAVWASS was assessed in the principal attack modes with regard to its effectiveness

(a) in leading the pilot to the target in planned attack mode

(b) in providing a useful weapon-aiming solution and

(c) in producing a pilot workload commensurate with a tactical low-level mission.'

The presentation then became highly technical and the content is, to some extent, restricted. The summary of the assessment which prefaced the syndicate's written report reads as follows:

> The Jaguar T MK2 aircraft was flown to assess its Navigation and Weapon Aiming Sub-System (NAVWASS) for the low-level retard bombing role. Specifically, the primary navigation modes, the primary weapon-aiming modes and the use of the head-up display (HUD) were evaluated during low-level VMC [Visual Meteorological Conditions] flight. A total of twelve sorties were flown at heights down to 250 feet MSD [Mean-Sea Datum] and speeds of up to 450 KIAS [Knots Indicated Airspeed]. The route was over the southwest of England and included varying types of terrain and simulated targets. The navigation facilities provided by the system were found to be reasonably accurate and the information displayed to the pilot was of a generally concise and usable form. The main problem with the system was found to be the position of the cockpit controls and displays which led to difficulty with the system operation and management. Large amounts of time were spent looking inside the cockpit to operate and update the system. This was considered to be unacceptable for high speed, low-level, wartime environment.
>
> The weapon-aiming functions of the system were evaluated during planned automatic attacks, automatic target of opportunity attacks and manual release Continuously Computed Impact Point (CCIP) attacks. Target-ranging information for these attacks was provided by radar altimeter or barometric pressure altitude. Inertial measurement in this situation was found to be satisfactory; however, certain display functions, specifically the lack of navigation information when in the CCIP mode for free fire zone operations, was found to be unacceptable.

The presentation did not go well. The time for the preparation had not been sufficient; there had been time for only one dress rehearsal in the lecture theatre and the visual aids had as a consequence suffered, since the vital cueing was less than slick. The result was long pauses in the proceedings as Nick Coulson, who was operating the overhead projector, struggled to get the graphics in the correct order. It wasn't all bad; the main arguments about the shortcomings of the NAVWASS system were correct. All three

left, Lack of rehearsal (the syndicate had only three days' preparation) caused delays in the cueing of the visual aids during the presentation; *below*, The trio face the audience for questions (*both B. Johnson*)

of the syndicate spoke. There was some sympathy for Serge Aubert; to lecture, for that is in effect what he was doing, on a complex technical subject in a foreign language must have been difficult and, with the short preparation time at the syndicate's disposal, doubly so. It could doubtless be argued that in the real world, a presentation might well have to be given with a similar lack of preparation time. Les Evans came to the end of the main argument and listed the recommendations thought by the syndicate to be essential or desirable if the system were to be released to Service. Nick Coulson then addressed the audience:

'There are a number of further recommendations included in the report [each member of the audience had been given a copy].

Thank you, gentlemen. That concludes our presentation and I would like to invite questions, if you could direct them through me please.'

The first question was put by James Giles:

'A fair amount of the [presentation] time was given to the question of the function switches on the Navigational Control Unit; you said that a number of them were placed in an unacceptable location, and [as a consequence] you wanted the position of the NCU changed. Would you like to say why you find the position of the panel unacceptable when you were using it while flying at 300 feet, plus or minus 50 feet, and able to maintain those limits?'

Nick Coulson: 'Yes . . . In fact we found that because of its position, the whole panel [of the NCU] was hidden by the control column. Now, we found that only one or two of these switches were in constant use during the flight, so we felt that those switches could be moved into the pilot's field of view. However the panel is down there, and there are other switches which have to be used, though not so frequently as the first mentioned. If the NCU panel as a whole could be moved into a more acceptable position within the pilot's field of view we considered that it would be an improvement.'

The questioning continued on an increasingly technical level as the three members of 'B' syndicate were rigorously examined on their findings on the low-level NAVWASS exercise. Eventually, to their relief one suspects, the questioning came to an end and they left the lecture room for the far more agreeable environment of the ETPS crew room by the big hangar, to reflect that on the test pilots' course the flying, advanced though it may be, is to a large extent the easy bit. Their exit did not signal the end of the presentation, far from it; they still had to face debriefs with the CO and the syndicate tutor, James Giles. There was a little respite however, since the four tutors in the audience had yet to mark the presentation. This began as soon as the three students left. The marks referred to are out of ten.

James Giles: 'Right, start from the top. Timing: I made it two minutes over, so we will give them eight for that. The visual aids: relevance and quality, what do we think of those?'

Vic Lockwood: 'I thought that some of them were put up rather quickly and at one point, when Nick was trying to point out switches, he was waving the [light] pen about so that I wasn't sure whether *he* knew where they were . . . some of the visual aids were excellent – the photographs, for example – but they often made poor use of them.'

James Giles: 'Well, there was one of the field of view which I thought was terrible: busy slides and no pointing; and the way they

The audience was
unimpressed by 'B'
syndicate's presentation
(*B. Johnson*)

were brought in, there were large gaps just when we needed them.'

Tim Allen: 'On the other hand, they were the first syndicate to make use of photographs with the Jaguar cockpit from the pilot's eye position; so for the first time we saw the NCU panel completely concealed by the control column.'

There was some further discussion about the visual aids and the printed 'hand-out' prepared by the syndicate, which was also criticised. The staff marked the visual aids section six out of ten. The question of content was then considered:

James Giles: 'They had most of the conclusions right, although I thought that they overstated some . . .'

Paul Ashmore: '. . . But you see it was too hesitant; it lacked punch; there was no conviction about their conclusions at all . . . just a question and they were a bit dry . . .'

James Giles: 'The questioning did show a lack of depth and, as you say, conviction.'

Tim Allen: 'I thought that they were good on the weapons side, when you dragged it out of them, but it did not come over clearly.'

Vic Lockwood: 'If you look at the hand-out they gave us, there is nothing about Rapid Alignment . . .'

Tim Allen: 'That betrayed their lack of understanding: the fact that they did not look at the alignment at the start [of the flight] and tie [the alignment errors] to the overall accuracy.'

Vic Lockwood: 'Yes. They didn't know what their basis [of accuracy] was to start with.

James Giles: 'Six again?'

Vic Lockwood: 'Difficult. I would say five myself; I don't think they displayed, to me, an overall knowledge of the [NAVWASS] system.'

James Giles: 'Presentation. I'm afraid I thought it was the worst of the three [syndicates] we have had so far. It wasn't at all strong.'

Tim Allen: 'And vague throughout: no clear direction, discussion.'

Paul Ashmore: 'Nick's problem was that he didn't have a script. He tried to do it informally with eye contact, but then ran out of words. When he looked down he hadn't got his notes to drag him back on to the subject again. I think he fell into the trap of trying to be too informal.'

Vic Lockwood: 'He was slow . . . and the voice faded when he ran out of ideas. Serge was quiet, very quiet; I could hardly hear him and he went off at a high rate and was difficult to understand at times. Les read from a script, which is what I would expect; but he didn't know his script, which meant there was no eye contact with the audience: it was fortunate that we could take our eyes from him to look at slides, otherwise we could have had somebody reading it from a book in the corner.'

James Giles: 'They didn't put things into context; they didn't explain why. Then suddenly they came up with a conclusion. There was no lead in, no build up.'

Vic Lockwood: 'I think my mark is a generous five.'

James Giles: 'I certainly had a five. The way they handled the questions. Well, we were fairly firm with them; on the other hand they left a lot of gaps in the presentation that we could get into. They handled the questions quite well, but we did find weaknesses: it really came to weaknesses of understanding. The syndicate hadn't thought out what they were going to say so they had differences of opinion when we came to question time.'

Paul Ashmore: 'They didn't pull together as a syndicate did they?'

Vic Lockwood: 'The other thing was that Nick had said, "Ask the questions through me." I know we did break that down by

'I have a number of points that came from the staff.' James Giles begins his debrief of the NAVWASS presentation which the syndicate passed . . . just. (*B. Johnson*)

asking questions directly. Nick was then quite happy to sit back and allow anyone to answer, because he lacked any deep knowledge of the system.'

Tim Allen: 'They were no worse than the others [syndicates] from that point of view, I think, in failing to direct questions.'

James Giles: 'It was not as good as the others we have seen so far. It was just satisfactory and they have a lot to learn from it; if they use it as a learning exercise, then they can improve.'

The final marking gave 'B' syndicate a pass . . . just.

The debrief confirmed what had been discussed by the staff, although the three students were given an opportunity to argue their case. One felt, however, that in their heart of hearts they agreed with the staff's findings. Here is part of James Giles' opening to the debrief, taken from the BBC transcript:

'Right. What we are going to do now is debrief that presentation. I have a number of points that came from all of the staff. If you want to come back at me, then do so please; let's make this two-sided. To start off let's say it was satisfactory, but there is a lot you can learn from that presentation; a lot of improvements you can make, there really are. It starts right back at the planning stage: when you plan an exercise or a sortie, think what is required at the end. You all knew what you had to do as aircrew on the exercise flights, but the main object was the presentation; therefore, what data did you need to get, what information did you want to put across? Make sure that you do everything that you need to do to be able to get the right data for that information. That is the first priority, then work as a team. Your presentation did not come across as teamwork. It was three individuals giving their own ideas of what they thought of the inertial system. It did not seem that there was a coherent and cohesive line through your presentation. Now you cannot cover everything in forty minutes; you have got to say, right, here are the most important points and forget the rest, otherwise it all gets confusing and important facts tend to get glossed over and critical areas are missed out; the areas that the audience most want to know about. What they want to know are the good things and the bad.'

The discussions went on for some time. At the end of the debrief the members of the syndicate were asked for their reactions to the presentation:

'It would, I think, be fair to say that your presentation opened to mixed notices. On the whole, did you think the assessment was fair?'

Les Evans: 'I think their assessment of the presentation was fairly accurate; the comment basically was that, although our deductions were correct and our recommendations were in line with what they were expecting, we had not co-ordinated our efforts sufficiently well in the presentation, and there were some anomalies where the three of us had similar ideas about the recommendations we were making, but they were not necessarily exactly the same: we needed to get our act together.'

'How long did it take to prepare that presentation?'

Les Evans: 'That presentation in fact was quite rushed; we only really had three days when all of us could get together and those days were fairly busy days; we were flying, so I think you could say that we actually prepared that presentation on about two or three nights, which is part of the reason why it was a bit of a shambles and things were not as well co-ordinated as they should have been . . . we sat around in each other's houses and discussed what we individually thought was wrong with the aircraft, so we had a discussion about what the faults were; we then had a discussion about how we would organise our presentation. We allocated tasks in the preparation of the slides and we allocated areas we would each talk about. Then we came back together again, having prepared the slides and having prepared our scripts, we then went through it.'

It may appear that the findings of the staff on 'B' syndicate's presentation were unduly harsh but military test pilots who, by the nature of their job are in the main young, and of relatively junior rank, become the principal witnesses for the prosecution in the eyes of the men from the Ministry. These men will be concerned about the unbelievable cost of even such an apparently trifling matter as moving the switches on the Jaguar's NCU panel, when considered for a fleet of hundreds of aircraft, let alone a major modification or redesign. The manufacturers, facing cuts and the threat of cancellations of their product in favour of 'off the shelf' alternatives marked 'Made in USA', will fight their corner with great tenacity. There will be others too: politicians, for example, worried about jobs in their constituencies, who will oppose any implied criticism of the products of local factories. It follows, therefore, that any reports of the test teams of the Experimental Establishments – Farnborough, Bedford and Boscombe Down – have to be convincing, utterly watertight, and strong enough to withstand the rigorous cross-examination to which they will certainly be exposed. The treatment of 'B' syndicate by the staff of ETPS gave the three members only a mere hint of the nature of the reception their future presentations will have in the real world. In truth, the flying *is* the easy part of the test pilot's job.

The NAVWASS presentation was in many ways the most taxing assignment that the students of the fixed wing course had to undertake in the crowded summer term but there were other exercises to follow. One of these, flying an Army Air Corps Beaver at Middle Wallop, gained in popularity when the students discovered that, uniquely, a report was not to be required at the end of the sortie; simply a discussion.

The Beaver Exercise

The DHC-2 Beaver is a large high-wing eight-seater monoplane produced by de Havilland, Canada. It is powered by a single 450 hp Pratt & Whitney air-cooled radial engine. Although the RAF no longer use the type, the survivors of the original thirty-six are used by the Army as transports both for personnel and supplies to forward areas; a role that is increasingly performed by helicopters. The Beaver carried out sterling work in places such as Aden, and the type is still used in Northern Ireland. The performance of the aircraft is hardly electrifying (its maximum speed is around 160 mph) but it has certain features that make it attractive to the tutors at ETPS. The long, thin, high-aspect ratio wing and the deep, slab-sided fuselage pose certain handling problems at low speed. Since the Army's Beavers spend a good deal of their operational life flying in and out of small fields, the deficiencies are relevant. Because the Beaver used at ETPS is owned by the Army which, not unreasonably, is keen to conserve the hours flown by its aircraft, it could only be lent to the school for a limited time. As a consequence, there was no time to convert the students to the type as there was for most of the other aircraft which they flew. However, two of the tutors, Vic Lockwood and James Giles, were current on

An Army Beaver lifts off from Middle Wallop's grass runway, flown by James Giles and Tom Koelzer on an ETPS handling exercise (*BBC*)

the Beaver so they flew the machine as command pilots with the students flying dual from the right-hand seat.

The introduction to the Beaver exercise always amuses the jet-trained students: pulling the big radial through compression, the propeller is turned over for several revolutions by the students. The reason for this is historic: when radial engines were commonplace, as on many wartime bombers such as the Fortress and Wellington, it was possible for engines which had been stationary for some time to have oil from the crankcase drain past the piston rings of the lower cylinders into the cylinder heads, causing hydraulic locks; if an engine was started with such a lock, the compressed oil would have blown off the cylinder heads or bent the connecting rods. By turning the engine manually a sufficient number of revolutions to ensure that all the lower cylinders had been 'pulled through compression', the danger of starting a 'locked' engine was avoided. As the ETPS instructors always point out, when clearing an engine in that way it is as well to make certain that the magnetos are 'off' and the throttle and mixture controls are set to 'idle cut-off': that is, firmly shut.

The object of the Beaver exercise was to demonstrate the handling characteristics of a high-wing monoplane with a high-aspect wing and the large flaps of an aeroplane designed for 'STOL' (Short Take-off and Landing) operations. The sortie filmed for the

The crew room at ETPS, Boscombe Down, where
members of the staff take their lunch. *Left to right*, Ron
Rhodes, Colin Wilcock and James Giles. (*B. Johnson*)

above, The control tower at RAF Honington. Members of the WRAF are often employed as controllers; their voices tend to be audible when the radio links are faint or suffering from interference (*B. Johnson*); *opposite above*, The ETPS VSS Basset, flown by James Giles and Nick Coulson. The black and white stripes on the propellers are to draw attention to them – in this jet age they tend to be overlooked by ground staff (*B. Johnson*); *opposite below*, The S-3 Viking taxiing out at Patuxent River.(*Colin Jones*)

Bob Horton seems
unhappy with the engine
of the Scout (*B. Johnson*)

The ETPS Scout about
to make a landing during
Bob Horton's avoid
curve exercise
(*B. Johnson*)

One of the school's Gazelles in flight (*B. Johnson*)

174

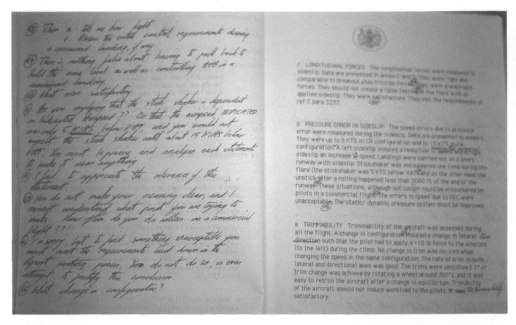

top, A page from a student's report which the tutor (James Giles) has annotated in red ink. In this instance the tutor is lucky: the report has been typed – most are in longhand; *above*, One of the ETPS Hawks, XX 342, undergoing maintenance. The brick piers and iron trusses of this Boscombe Down hangar date it to the 1920s: it must have housed many generations of RAF aircraft. (*both B. Johnson*)

opposite above, Bob Horton (*left*) and the Principal Rotary Wing tutor, Mike Swales, discuss the avoid curve exercise prior to flying; *opposite below*, Writing dominates the lives of the ETPS students: lecture notes, flying briefing notes and endless reports. It is often said by the students that the flying is the easy part of the course. The student burning the midnight oil is Serge Aubert. (*both B. Johnson*)

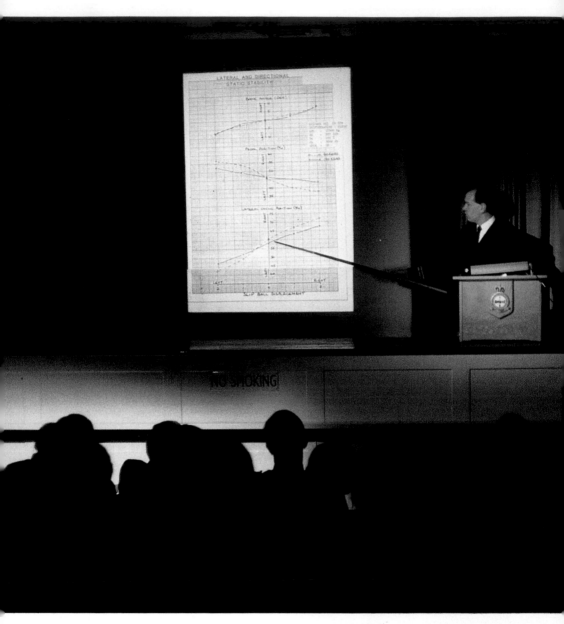

The culmination of the course is the preview
presentation. Here Al Howden is delivering his,
backed by technical facts on the Chinook helicopter.
(*B. Johnson*)

BBC programme was flown by James Giles with the American Navy pilot, Lieutenant Tom Koelzer.

James Giles performed the take-off from the grass Army Air Corps training airfield of Middle Wallop and climbed the Beaver away to level out at 3000 feet. The aircraft was then handed over to Tom for him to assess the stall. With its big wing and large flaps (the ailerons can also be made to droop to increase the flap area), the g break, or moment when the Beaver's nose drops, would clearly be at a very low indicated airspeed: a STOL aircraft must be capable of very slow flight in order to be able to land in confined spaces. Full flap was selected, as for a short landing, and the engine throttled back.

James Giles: 'Sixty-five knots is a good final approach speed so we will leave the power set and come into the stall from here . . . The speed is dropping down now; you talk us through it, Tom.'

'OK. We are down to 55 knots now . . . speed is still dropping. Ailerons are very light and I am starting to use a little rudder to maintain directional control. Forty knots . . . ease the nose up. A little buffeting . . .'

'Keep the speed coming back, Tom, keep it coming back . . . 35 knots . . .'

With the airspeed indicator hovering around 35 knots, the big monoplane suddenly stalled, dropping its nose and starboard wing.

James Giles: 'There's the stall; down and to the right.'

Tom Koelzer: 'Stick forward to lower the nose [to build up the airspeed to unstall the wings]. Open up the engine and bring the nose back . . . speed 65 knots and climb away.'

'OK, Tom, so you can see that – careful, you are going to stall it again – you can see that it is a very slow speed aeroplane but it does tend to drop a wing on the stall.'

Many aeroplanes tend to drop a wing when stalled. The reason is simply that one wing stalls before the other. This can be due to several factors; the pilot may have had a little yaw on at the moment of the stall which would mean that the forward yawing wing had a fractionally higher airspeed and consequently stalled later, or one wing may have slight dents or rigging errors making it marginally less efficient aerodynamically than the other. With a piston-engined aircraft, such as the Beaver, engine torque and propeller slipstream can also be factors. With all straight-wing aircraft, should a wing drop in the stall, it is essential for the pilot to pick the wing up with the rudder. The use of ailerons at the stall, which is instinctive, is incorrect since with the wings stalled the ailerons cannot influence the lift of either wing (which is the desired effect) but only cause drag, delaying recovery from the stall. (Using ailerons to pick up a dropped wing in the stall while on the General Flying Test for a Private Pilot's Licence is to court instant failure.)

To return to the Beaver and James Giles and Tom Koelzer; having recovered from the stall exercise, the Beaver was trimmed for level flight for the next phase of the handling sortie:

'Right, Tom. Settle it down at 90 knots and set the throttle for cruising rpm. What we are going to look at now is a steady heading side-slip.[8] You will remember that steady heading side-slip is simply a test technique to quantify the aileron and rudder inputs required to generate a balanced side-slip.'

Side-slipping is a condition of flight in which the controls are normally crossed; that is right rudder, say, and left aileron. The effect is for the aircraft to head right while actually moving left,

The Basset acting as a camera chase aircraft filming the Army Beaver as it executes a steady heading side-slip towards the Basset. The standard of flying by ETPS staff on air-to-air filming for the BBC series was exceptionally high. (*B. Johnson*)

with a high angle of bank, with the low wing in the direction of travel. It is a manoeuvre which is not much used these days when most aircraft have large and effective wing flaps, since the turbulent air from the flaps can reduce the authority of the rudder, which in contemporary light aircraft is often reduced in area anyway. In earlier days when aircraft, particularly biplanes – the Tiger Moth is a classic example – had no flaps but rudders of generous area, a skilled pilot could side-slip down to a landing with a very low airspeed, due to the drag of the sideways-facing fuselage, using the rudder at the moment of touchdown to straighten the aircraft, simultaneously removing the bank by returning the ailerons to neutral; the result – in skilled hands – was a very short landing. Another use of the side-slip on aircraft without flaps is when landing in a cross-wind: the aircraft is side-slipped to counteract the cross-wind component, so that it approaches aligned with the runway while actually flying crabwise into the wind. Again at the moment of touchdown, the side-slip is removed as described before. That description of the, largely historical, use of the side-slip is for background information only for, as James Giles said, the purpose of side-slipping the Beaver, which has efficient flaps, is to use the manoeuvre for test purposes. The steady heading side-slip is a classic test technique which looks at the interaction between the yaw and roll axes of an aircraft in one manoeuvre. The Beaver flight continued with James Giles explaining that:

'We can see how linear the relationship is between right rudder pedal, right side-slip angle and left aileron requirements. We will look at the angle of bank which will give us a figure of the side force generated and we will look at the PECs [pressure error corrections of the airspeed indicator, due to the angle of the wing relative to the airflow]. So, Tom, if you would like to go into a steady heading side-slip and go all the way to full rudder deflection.'

'OK, left aileron and right rudder . . .'

'Right, Tom, we see immediately that right rudder is generating right side-slip and a lot of left aileron is required: almost full left aileron . . . we are sitting on our side now with a 35-degree angle of bank. Kick off the drift now [by centralising the rudder], and we will see the angle of side-slip. It was from a heading of 110 degrees to 085: a side-slip angle of 25 degrees.'

From these and further figures it was possible to reduce the results to form an assessment of the natural stability of the Beaver.

The flight continued with James Giles pointing out that one aspect of the Beaver's control characteristics was immediately apparent; the handling defect known as 'adverse yaw'. This is common on slow-speed aircraft which have high-aspect wings, that is wings which are long in relation to their chord: a glider wing is typical. If a pilot wishes to roll an aircraft with such a wing and simply applies aileron in the direction of the desired turn, he will find that the aircraft, instead of turning as required, yaws in the opposite direction: hence the name 'adverse yaw'. The cause is aileron drag. Ailerons are designed to move up or down relative to a line drawn through the chord of the wing to which they are attached: they move in opposition; as one goes up the other goes down. The downward aileron acts as a wing flap and increases the lift of the section of wing ahead of the aileron; since the ailerons are mounted on the outer section of the wings, the increased lift causes the whole wing to lift. The opposite aileron, however, is raised, which reduces the lift, lowering the wing; the result is a roll which

top, The Beaver about to stall on the ETPS exercise; *right*, At around 35 knots the big Army monoplane did stall (*both B. Johnson*)

will continue until the pilot centralises the controls. In practice, the up and down movement of ailerons is differential: typically by 5 degrees. For example, an aileron which has a 15-degree upward movement will have only a 10-degree downward deflection, one reason for the arrangement being that ailerons are more effective at increasing lift (downward deflection) than decreasing it. A second reason is that the drag caused by the downward aileron is greater than that of the upward one; it is this 'aileron drag' which causes the adverse yaw. Most aircraft have relatively short-span, broad-chord wings and strong natural directional, or weathercock stability. Therefore the aileron drag effect is small enough to be ignored, and ignored it is, resulting in a generation of pilots to whom the rudder is no longer a primary control. In turns, the rudder is used (if at all) simply to balance the turn. In the case of a glider or a powered aircraft such as the Beaver with long narrow-chord wings, the situation is different because the long wing confers a greater moment to the ailerons, causing their effect – wanted or otherwise – to be much more pronounced. The drag caused by the down aileron is sufficient to overpower the effectiveness of the fin and rudder and to yaw the aircraft into a side-slip in the opposite direction. Glider pilots are trained from the outset to recognise adverse yaw and always make their turns with a bootful of rudder, which overpowers the adverse yaw of the ailerons, the rudder becoming the primary turn control.

Tom Koelzer, not being a glider pilot, discovered adverse yaw empirically when asked by James Giles to look at the rolling property of the Beaver:

'Right, Tom, a 60-degree banked turn; so start with a half deflection [of the ailerons] and then come to full.'

Tom Koelzer: 'OK.'

James Giles: 'We will see what we think of it . . .'

Tom Koelzer: 'Three, two, one, Mark.'

As Tom Koelzer applied the aileron input to roll the Beaver to the left, the big aircraft lurched right. Tom instinctively tried to correct the unwanted yaw by applying still more left aileron:

James Giles: 'Look at the roll rate! Easy, Tiger, hang on; use your feet [apply rudder]! This is a good aeroplane, don't do that to it!'

Tom Koelzer: 'OK, I am now doing that [applying left rudder].'

James Giles: 'Good. You must use your feet to control [the adverse yaw]; if you increase the ailerons all you are going to do is put more adverse yaw on; you must use the rudder to control it.'

Tom Koelzer: 'That was a good demonstration there.'

James Giles: 'OK. Let's try again, using a reduced aileron input.'

Tom Koelzer: 'A 30-degree banked turn, with pure aileron . . .'

Again, the Beaver yawed in the wrong direction but, owing to the lower aileron input, to much less marked extent. James Giles pointed out that the aircraft would not meet the turning specification required without the application of rudder to minimise the yaw and side-slip. Tom Koelzer then applied rudder and found that the aircraft behaved in a controlled way, making a satisfactory banked turn without the adverse yaw effect. James Giles pointed out that to land such an aircraft in turbulence, the pilot would have to be aware of the adverse yaw; to discover it near the ground, if the pilot were not prepared for it, could lead to a crash. Tom wondered if interconnecting the rudder and ailerons would solve the problem. (This has, in the past, been tried on light aircraft without much success.) James Giles' reply was to the point:

'Yes, it would help, but it would still leave the problem, in gusty conditions, of maintaining the angle of bank, [and] you are not going to get them to spend £200,000 on an aeroplane like this; anyway it would take away all the character.'

Tom Koelzer: 'Well, there is one thing to be said about this type of aeroplane; the harder they are to fly, the more personality they have.'

After the Beaver exercises were over the fixed wing students who had taken part gathered in an ETPS office to debrief. The consensus was that it had been a very useful experience in directional control and that the Beaver would, to say the least, be 'interesting' to fly on instruments while making a precision radar approach (PRA) in turbulent conditions.

Manoeuvre Boundaries

The next and last big exercise of the summer term on aircraft handling was the one called Manoeuvre Boundaries: a far more complex subject than the title might suggest, and one which shares its origins with that of military aviation.

The Great War of 1914–18 was the first major conflict in which aircraft fought each other. At first the frail biplanes were used solely for reconnaissance to photograph enemy troop movements and dispositions; bombing followed as a not very accurate form of long-range artillery. If opposing aircraft came across each other, their officer pilots might exchange a few token pot-shots with their revolvers. Later, machine-guns manned by the observers were used but the tricky deflection shooting required made it very difficult to achieve telling damage. An aircraft attacked in this way would have little trouble in evading its opponent's fire. The light biplanes then in use were very agile and the main risk lay in over-stressing the fragile airframes even with the low power then avail-

able. What would now be termed Manoeuvre Boundaries would, in those far-off days, have consisted of a squadron commander warning his young and ill-trained pilots: 'Don't dive it above 150, old boy, or you'll pull the bloody wings off.'

As the effectiveness of military aircraft improved, the Scout, a small, fast single-seater, appeared: the first dedicated fighter. The function of the Scout was to find and destroy other aircraft, to prevent bombing and reconnaissance flights. Before long, fighters fought fighters to protect the bombers. The armament was still the hand-trained machine-gun with all the problems of deflection shooting; then in March 1915 a French pilot named Roland Garros devised the concept of the modern fighter which was to remain valid through the remainder of the Great War and the Second World War, right up to the advent of the guided missile.

What Garros did was to fit steel deflector plates to the wooden propeller of his single-seater Morane-Saulnier 'N' Scout monoplane, to enable him to sight a machine-gun mounted on the forward part of the aircraft's fuselage, simply by flying his Morane at an enemy aircraft. At a stroke, as someone once said, the problems of deflection shooting, although not entirely removed, had become a good deal less demanding, since the pilot was now in effect flying a machine-gun. The bullets from the gun passed through the airscrew arc; obviously a proportion struck the blades but the steel deflectors protected the propeller and the arrangement was very successful to the exent that when Garros was forced down with engine trouble behind the enemy lines in April 1915, the Germans, or more accurately their Dutch aircraft designer and constructor, Antony Fokker, immediately saw the rationale behind the idea.

A Sopwith Pup, one of the most successful Allied fighters of the First World War. This one, N5160, is preserved and flown regularly by the Shuttleworth Trust at Old Warden. The single synchronised Vickers machine-gun is clearly visible. (*B. Johnson*)

right, The Fokker E1 fighter, the first to go into action with a synchronised machine-gun firing through the propeller arc (*RAF Museum*); *below*, The Fokker DVII of 1918 (*B. Johnson*)

above right, Roland Garros's Morane had steel deflector plates to protect the wooden propeller. The infantry Lewis gun is under the pilot's windscreen (*IWM*); *above left*, The concept developed. The Fokker DVII; its twin German infantry Parabellum *maschinengewehr*, their water-cooled jackets fretted to allow for air-cooling, were aimed by flying the aircraft at the enemy. (*B. Johnson*)

Tests at Fokker's Schwerin works proved that the original crude Garros system was not practical since, unlike the French, who used copper-jacketed lead bullets, the thorough Germans used far harder chrome-jacketed ammunition which shattered the wooden propellers despite the steel deflectors. Fokker and his staff designed a far more elegant system: a synchronising gear which allowed the gun(s) to fire only when the propeller blades were clear. The interrupter gear, as it was accurately called, enabled the Germans to dominate the skies over the Western Front to the extent that, by early 1916, the popular press in England was reporting a 'Fokker Scourge'.

The Allies soon adopted the idea, setting the seal on the concept of the fighter aircraft. It also placed a premium on the manoeuvrability of fighters as each tried to get into the most effective firing

position – on the opponent's tail. By 1917, a generation of classic fighter aircraft had evolved as a result: the Sopwith Pup and Camel, the SE5a, from Britain; the French Spad and Nieuports. From Germany came perhaps the greatest of them all, the Fokker D VII. All of those single-seater fighters had well-harmonised controls and, with the growing confidence of their designers, sufficient structural integrity to withstand the stresses of aerial combat, as whole squadrons wheeled and turned in the colourful (though strategically pointless) 'dog fights' which took place high above the squalor of the trenches.

A good deal of the stressing and aerodynamics of the early fighters was achieved – often at the cost of many pilots' lives – by trial and error; mostly the latter. When the war ended and design offices had the time to review the findings of that first war in the air, it became clear that a fighter needed more than mere agility, which is only one factor in a good fighter aircraft. (This was a fact overlooked in Whitehall, causing the RAF to retain biplanes long after they should have done.) In the war, the maximum level speed of the best fighters was around 120 mph and once an opponent got on an enemy's tail, a few rounds of rifle calibre ammunition was often sufficient to kill or incapacitate the pilot, set the unprotected fuel tanks alight or cause the lightly-built, fabric-covered wooden aircraft to suffer structural failure. The most successful pilots, the 'aces' of that war, were not only outstanding pilots, they were also crack shots, skilled in the very difficult art of deflection shooting, which was still required to make allowance for the finite time that the shots took to reach the target when that target was an enemy aircraft turning across the line of fire. Apart from the considerable judgement required, a stable aircraft was essential to provide a good gun platform.

With the development, during the mid-1930s, of the stressed-skin monoplane and the higher speeds it offered, it was clear that the agility of fighters was reduced; no longer was it sufficient just to get on your opponent's tail for a second or two with any hope of shooting him down; the new metal aircraft were far stronger, fuel tanks were now made less vulnerable and pilots had armour-plate protection. All things being equal, however, the fighter that could out-turn another and still offer its pilot a stable gun platform won the day. During the Battle of Britain, some marks of Spitfire were slightly slower than the German Me109s but the Spitfire could always out-turn the enemy fighter. The limits imposed on the turning circle of a fighter are governed by several factors: the power available from the engine(s) to maintain a rate of turn and overcome the increased drag from the airframe: the thrust boundary, and the ability of the aerodynamics of the airframe to continue to support stable flight without stalling: the lift boundary. In practice, the onset of pre-stall airframe buffet limits the effective manoeuvrability of a fighter as a gun platform, the tracking boundary, to less

top, The Supermarine S6, N248, at Calshot during the 1929 Schneider contest, R. J. Mitchell's 350+ mph design that would lead to his Spitfire (*via B. Johnson*); *right*, A Hawker Fury II, of 1932, one of the fastest RAF biplanes. It could achieve 223 mph at 16,400 feet. Its designer, Sydney Camm, evolved the monoplane Hurricane from it. (*Hawker*)

than the actual lift boundary, due to buffeting making accurate gun tracking difficult or even impossible: the buffet boundary. If the turn is tightened beyond the buffet boundary, a point is reached when the g loading of the aircraft, generated by centrifugal force, will exceed the lift generated by the wings. As this limit is approached, the aircraft will begin to drop its nose at an ever increasing rate as the turn is tightened, until the aircraft will cease to fly, stall and possibly spin: that point is defined as the lift boundary. This is, however, not a fixed limit: it is a combination of speed and loading: a far tighter turn can be made at a low speed than at a higher speed. For example, an F-4 Phantom pulling 3g at 600 knots has half the turn rate and four times the turn radius as the same aircraft pulling 3g at 300 knots. In combat it is likely that turns will be made at near the maximum speed of which the fighter is capable, but for any given speed there will be a limit to the tightness of the turn; when the lift is exceeded by the g forces, the lift boundary is reached. It should be pointed out that the lift boundary may never be reached at higher speeds: it could well be beyond the structural limits of the airframe. (The speed at which the airframe can generate the maximum g level for which it has been stressed is known as the 'corner speed'.)

The present generation of 'fly-by-wire' fighters have their on-board computers programmed to limit the applied airframe g so that the g limit cannot be exceeded, even if the pilot demands it with his stick and throttle inputs, and the aircraft is flying fast enough to generate it. This fact enables designers to limit the structural strength, and therefore the weight of the airframe, secure in the knowledge that it can never be exceeded by the most zealous pilot. Previous designers had to rely on the 'never exceed' limits in the pilot's notes being observed and on providing a margin, because they knew that most fighter pilots would invariably go beyond them in the heat of combat. Hence the First World War Squadron Commander's warning to his pilots: what he was in effect doing – although at that time the term would have been meaningless – was to set 150 mph as the 'corner speed' of the aircraft; below that figure the airframe's structural limits would not be exceeded.

Those are the basic elements which comprise Manoeuvre Boundaries. There is, of course, another: the limits of the most complex bit of equipment in the aircraft, its pilot.

The fighter pilots of the Second World War dressed casually: usually Allied pilots wore battledress and a sheepskin jacket with a leather helmet. They sat upright in their cockpits and, as anyone who has read the accounts of the great air battles will know, fighter pilots were subject to 'blacking out' in tight turns. Blacking out is a

Naval Seafire pilots aboard a Carrier of the British Pacific Fleet in 1944. Apart from their oxygen masks and 'Mae West' life-jackets they flew in standard tropical khaki drill. (*IWM*)

personal manoeuvre boundary; what happens is that the g forces generated by the turn cause the blood to flow from the brain at a rate which the heart cannot overcome; the result is a loss of vision and hearing which, although temporary (full sight and hearing are restored the moment the g is reduced), puts one at a disadvantage when flying an aeroplane in combat. The onset of blacking out was when the pilot was subjected to about $4\frac{1}{2}$g for 30 seconds or so. The same pilot, however, could sustain up to 10g for a second or two without blacking out (although the figures are subject to variation with individuals, they are typical for a fit young man). It was discovered during the war that pilots did, to some extent, build up a tolerance of g if subjected to it at frequent enough intervals. It was fortunate that the personal manoeuvre boundary of the wartime fighter pilots was slightly lower than the manoeuvre limits of the fighters they flew, so that it was uncommon for the limits to be exceeded with undamaged aircraft. The important boundary of the wartime fighters that were armed with conventional machine-gun or cannon, aimed visually by the pilot, was the tracking boundary: the provision of a stable gun platform. A fighter which could out-turn its opponent and still accurately bring its guns to bear was the ideal.

With the arrival of the developed air superiority jet fighter, the situation changed. Although the fighter is still armed with conventional cannon, this armament is often secondary; the guided missile has become the primary weapon. Thus the once paramount tracking boundary became, like the cannon it served, a secondary consideration. Unlike the guns it has displaced, the guided missile of the modern 'fire and forget' generation is independent of the attitude of the aircraft at the moment of firing so long as it has 'seen' the target and the guidance system has acquired it. The missile armed fighter has simply to be able to out-turn its target and fire; the missile is indifferent to whether the aircraft it has just left is on the point of stall, or indeed has stalled and is spinning, so long as the target is locked on. In the quest for tighter and tighter turns with the minimum turn radius, Manoeuvre Boundaries have assumed overriding importance.

The pilot is no longer the limiting factor as his personal boundary has been raised to between 7 and 8g by the universal use of the g suit. This is a garment in two basic forms, one being worn under the pilot's flying overalls, the other over them. In either case the suit consists of a pair of special trousers which have air spaces in them. A pipe is connected to the aircraft which supplies air at a pressure which is varied with the applied g; the effect is to compress the pilot's lower limbs and torso to restrict the blood flow in them. Thus, when blood is forced from the brain by the application of centrifugal forces generated by the manoeuvring of the aircraft, it cannot flow far since it has nowhere to go, the lower body's arteries being restricted.

By placing the pilot in a prone position, his g tolerance is further increased, but although experiments have been made in this direction it is not really a practical proposition for piloted aircraft. (It is employed in space vehicles, however.) In many modern fighters, of which the F-16 is typical, a compromise is reached by giving the pilot a reclined seat.

With the pilots able to withstand around 9g in sustained level turns as a matter of routine, the relevance of defining the Manoeuvre Boundaries of military aircraft becomes clear. The

In contrast, Tim Allen and Jim Ludford walk to an ETPS Hawk in their standard RAF issue fire-resistant overalls and 'g' suits (*B. Johnson*)

limits are a complex integration of the designed airframe g limit and the airframe angle of attack (AOA) limit (which will be at a g level below the airframe limit, and at all airspeeds less than the 'corner speed') at which the aircraft becomes uncontrollable through a dynamic departure or an accelerated stall. The setting of these latter limits is, of course, the province of the test pilots at Boscombe Down and similar Establishments in other countries, who have to ascertain them for the writers of the aircrew manuals. The ETPS students are required to establish the boundaries for either the Hawk or the T7 Hunter, the assumption being that they are prototype aircraft undergoing preview tests. (A preview is the acceptance test of a new military aircraft type prior to its being placed in production and released to service. The tests are conducted to specified requirements as laid down in an official document known as 'Defence Standard 00–970'.)

The aircraft tested was the Hawk, the tutor was Squadron Leader Tim Allen, the student was Flight Lieutenant Jim Ludford, an experienced fighter pilot with over 1000 hours on Harriers. The following is an abstract from the BBC transcript of the briefing:

'Right, Jim. This exercise is being flown on a military aircraft and the role for which I want you to test the aircraft is a tactical training role [the Hawk's actual RAF role] so Defence Standard 00–970 will apply. Right, I would like now to discuss the thrust boundaries. We will use the Rylands technique [a standard developed by H. D. Rylands] which is an accelerated level run, followed by the decelerating level turn method of establishing a non-dimensional thrust and lift boundary of the aircraft . . . We are flying this test in the Hawk at 24,000 feet but for equivalent altitudes of 15,000 feet and 5000 feet. Now, by putting our results in non-dimensional form we are able to interpret the results for 24,000 feet down to 5000 feet by putting into your non-dimensional results the real figures of relative [barometric] pressure and temperature which apply to 5000 feet. So although your results at 24,000 feet will be much less than you could get at 5000 feet, for example, the amount of sustained g you can pull at 24,000 feet [the thrust boundary] will be much less, because the thrust is less. Nevertheless, when you insert the real figures for 5000 feet you will be amazed to discover that they are actually a very good fit indeed. So by flying at 24,000 feet and establishing the non-dimensional thrust boundary you can, in fact, extrapolate that to any other altitude.

'We now come to the last element of this exercise, which is establishing the lift boundaries of the Hawk. You may say that there is only one lift boundary; where the aircraft stalls; well we are going to do more than that, we are going to assess the lift boundaries with the wind-up turns technique . . . what we are going to do is to try to establish useful boundaries which we can give to operational pilots to help them in their task, and it is not just the lift boundary. Take the Hunter as a good example: if you go into a wind-up turn in the Hunter, keeping a constant speed, the g will increase and keep on increasing [as the turn tightens]. The first thing that will happen to tell us that we are reaching a high angle of attack will be the onset of [pre-stall] buffet. I would like you to establish a buffet boundary because that is something which a pilot can feel; they can be looking over their shoulder as in combat, not concentrating on the aircraft, and if they feel the onset of buffet that is an extremely useful warning . . . if you go beyond the buffet boundary it might be that the aircraft starts to oscillate in all three axes, such that you can no longer use it as a gun-firing platform [the tracking boundary]. If, however, we are on the wrong side of the guns of a hostile fighter, we might still want to go beyond the tracking boundary, to the lift boundary which is the maximum lift you can get [for a given speed and turn rate].

'We have described three boundaries, but in fact that is not universal; it does not apply to all aircraft. For example, you have flown the Jaguar and you will be aware that the Jaguar does not have the same characteristics as the Hunter when you pull it to its maximum performance in a turn. An aircraft may not have a buffet onset, or you may find that there is no tracking boundary as such and you may find that the lift boundary is determined by some artificial means, like an audio stall warning or, as in civil aircraft, stick shakers and stick pushers; you will be familiar with those from the BAC 1-11.

'Although I am saying test to tracking, buffet and lift [boundaries], that may not be applicable to all types of aircraft which you are going to fly and, of course, the modern aircraft will limit you

XX 342, a Hawk of the school fleet, taxies out for a manoeuvre boundary exercise with tutor Tim Allen and student Jim Ludford on board (*B. Johnson*)

anyway. In the Tornado you have a SPILS system [Spin Prevention and Incidence Limiting System] to prevent a departure of the aircraft at its maximum angle of attack, so the pilot no longer has to worry about pulling to high angles of attack, because the aircraft is self-limiting.

'Right, the test technique which we are going to use is the wind-up turn: the most difficult of all test pilot exercises.'

Tim Allen went on to detail the ETPS exercise. Jim Ludford was to fly the Hawk up to 25,000 feet, a height that had to be accurately maintained, for as Tim Allen explained:

'The accuracy I want for this test should be plus or minus 1000 feet of the test altitude because there is a marked number of effects which change with altitude . . . so we are testing at a particular height. I want you to use maximum continuous power at the test airspeed; ultimate [military] maximum power isn't particularly important in assessing the lift boundary; it may give .1g but that is probably within the accuracy of our results anyway. So use maximum continuous [power] to conserve engine life. Stabilise the aircraft at your test speed as it climbs up through the test altitude, in the case of the Hawk through 25,000 feet, and then start the wind-up turn at 26,000 feet, winding the aircraft in, gradually increasing the g at a slow, steady rate – no faster than half a g per second . . . you keep the speed by altering the pitch attitude of the aircraft with the angle of bank. It is actually very difficult to do and takes some practice. Well, you are going to get a dual flight so practise during the dual and refine your technique until you can do it perfectly on your solos.'

Jim Ludford had a question: 'On the lift boundary part of the exercise, when we are defining the tracking boundary, are we going to let the aeroplane continue its oscillations, or are we to put little [control] inputs in to try and track through it as we would do in real life?'

Tim Allen: 'Well, I think what we have got to look at first of all is the requirement that we are testing the aircraft for. The Hawk is a tactical trainer for operational manoeuvres. So you are preparing information to give to OCUs [Operational Conversion Units] as to how to use the aircraft; how are squadron pilots going to fly it? Now, if the aircraft starts giving uncommanded oscillations [on the tracking boundary], the average pilot will react against that and try to control it. So you are going to establish a reasonable level of control activity to counteract the uncommanded motions of the aircraft; you will have to assess what you think is a reasonable level of control activity, such as a squadron pilot would do.'

With that, tutor and student prepared to fly the exercise. The ETPS précis notes laid down the ideal test techniques for the whole of the Manoeuvre Boundary sortie. The first part was the Accelerated Level test.

> a) Level off at your test height at a speed clear of pre-stall buffet and at a speed at which the aircraft will just accelerate in level flight at the test power setting. Switch on the instrumentation [this includes a trace recorder which will automatically record all the 'numbers' of the flight]. If the power is difficult to set and the aircraft starts accelerating rapidly, start slightly below the test height and allow the aircraft to climb at the starting speed while the throttle is being set. Airbrake may also be used to delay acceleration if necessary. Be smooth. Altitude excursions will be accounted for in energy height calculations but g excursions will not.
> b) During the acceleration, the aircraft's attitude should be slowly altered to maintain the desired height; all control movements must be made very smoothly. Unless the control forces are very high and continuous trimming is necessary, it is best to establish a mean trim setting and then hold the slight out of trim forces during the run.
> c) Adjust the rpm as necessary to hold the correct value. If the JPT [Jet Pipe Temperature] is seen to be on limits on the practice run, a lower rpm should be used for the test. Continue the acceleration until the speed is nearly stabilised, noting the altitude, IAS [Indicated Airspeed] and fuel state. The practical maximum level flight speed may be said to have been achieved when the rate of acceleration is <2 kts/min.

The next part of the test was the determination of the Hawk's thrust boundary in a decelerated turn, which the ETPS précis noted as being '*very* difficult to fly'. The student had to set the required engine rpm then note the airspeed, Mach number indication and the fuel quantity. When the indicated airspeed had settled down at its maximum value, the Hawk (or Hunter) was rolled into a level turn; the g was then gradually increased by tightening the turn until the airspeed began slowly to decrease. As the speed for the thrust boundary was approached, the centrifugal force, the g generated by the turn, had to be increased by a still tighter turn. At a certain point the speed began to drop rapidly for a given value of g – in practice the maximum recorded during the run – and the turn reduced to lessen the g. That point was the threshold of the thrust boundary, when the g forces were just balanced by the thrust of the engine. The run was completed when the aircraft had slowed down to the minimum airspeed for 1g wings level flight, which is just above the stall.

The decelerated turn was only one of a number of techniques for the determination of the thrust boundary; further tests had to be performed, including straight stalls, steady and wind-up turns, which involved the pilot in observing, while in very tight turns, the amount of airframe buffeting and the response of the controls and general handling. The school notes gave some hint of what it must be like for the pilot, in that, when suggesting that full use should be made of the voice recorder, the notes warned: 'Tape operation may be impaired at the higher g levels.' The other boundary to be assessed was the lift boundary, when the g forces in a turn became greater than the lift generated by the aircraft's wing and tailplane; the technique was similar to the determination of the thrust boundary, but the speeds and the figures were different. The definition of the lift boundary is given as: 'The maximum usable lift and therefore load factor that can be achieved at a given speed, altitude and weight. The maximum load factor may be limited by pre-stall buffeting, wing rock, yaw or pitching . . . structural limits and pilot physiology.' The definition of the thrust boundary is: 'The maximum g that can be sustained in a level turn at a given speed, altitude, weight and thrust setting [engine power]; it is a function of the excess thrust available over that required in a 1g flight under similar conditions.'

It might appear to the general reader that the Manoeuvre Boundary series of exercises is far removed from the havoc of a shooting war but this is not the case: the term 'Air Superiority Fighter' is used to define an aircraft which can wrest domination from its opponents. This cannot be achieved, contrary to popular opinion, by speed alone: air battles are not fought in straight lines. Indeed, current thinking is towards fighters which can sustain higher and higher g levels at lower and lower airspeeds to enable them to fly very tight, small radius turns, in order to allow 'fire and forget' missiles to acquire and lock on to the enemy fighter. In a sense the wheel has turned, for that was precisely the object of the 'dog-fighting' biplanes of the First World War. True, they did not have 'smart' missiles but, then as now, the man who could out-turn the enemy, get him in his sights and fire first, was usually the victor.

It is interesting that some of the greatest fighters in the short history of aerial warfare were by no means the fastest of their generation. The first was probably the Fokker E-1 of 1916, followed by the Sopwith Pup. The Spitfire of 1940 and the A6M5 Zero-Sen were certainly others, as were the Harriers in the Falklands. All could better their opponents not by superior speed but by superior flying qualities, of which manoeuvring ability is cardinal, for it gives the pilot that indefinable assurance that his aircraft can be safely flown to the very edge of its ultimate limits; that is a great psychological advantage in battle.

The ETPS students had just ten days to submit their report on Manoeuvre Boundaries. It was in some ways a watershed, for it marked the end of the summer term and also the end of their apprenticeship. When they returned from leave they would be

The Staff v. the Students cricket match which marks the end of the summer term. Harry Fehl is out for a duck, as Vic Lockwood explains. It was Harry's first, and almost certainly last, game of cricket. (*BBC*)

journeymen and as such would be expected to be able to test, not just one facet of an aircraft's performance, but to assess the total capabilities of a range of aircraft, from light trainers to contemporary warplanes. There remained however one final test: the annual tragedy known as the Staff v. the Students cricket match.

It would, one thinks, be true to say that if the men who invented cricket on that revered village green at Hambledon could have foreseen what would be perpetrated on the playing fields of Boscombe Down, they would, without hesitation, have burned their curly bats on the spot and baseball would have become our national sport. Mercifully, they could not.

The scores of the ETPS match are irrelevant. The staff won; the staff have won every game since the fixture was established in the late 1940s; this is due in part to the fact that many of the overseas students have never even seen a game of cricket and do not therefore know the rules, and those who do have a suspicion that anyone getting into double figures is placing his continued presence on the course in grave jeopardy.

It would be pleasant to report that the term ended to the crack of leather on willow, with polite applause rustling on the still evening air of a perfect summer's day. In reality, it was a bitingly cold August day with, as the students batted out their hopeless innings, a thunderstorm of quite exceptional violence.

7 Finals

To err is human;
To forgive is not
Air Force Policy
OPS ROOM, RAF CONINGSBY

Summer leave was for three weeks; most of the students spent a good deal of it revising and rereading the several volumes of notes that they had written in the previous terms . . . that is what they said; some probably did. The BBC film unit returned to Boscombe Down as the third and final term began on 2 September. James Giles was asked what his impression was of the course to date.

'Well, it is like all ETPS courses; there are one or two who are good; very good indeed. They are showing a lot of imagination in the air; they are planning well and really on top of it. At the other end of the scale there are one or two who are having problems with adapting to flying as test pilots. They can fly perfectly well; they are safe but they are having to work very hard at being test pilots . . . It is a high workload; we expect the students to spend a lot of their own time producing reports: it is very much self-pressure. It is up to the individual how much time he puts in. Some put in much more than others.'

'Would it be true to say that the nature of the course is changing as it enters the last term?'

'Yes. The emphasis is changing; the students are now putting their learning into practice; they are about to do the Pilot Assessment exercise.'

The Pilot Assessment was the first opportunity the ETPS students had to bring together all their hard-won new skills and learning, to assess the handling qualities of an aeroplane – not just a defined sector of the flight envelope, for example the stall, or spin recovery – but the general fitness of purpose of the test aircraft.

Three light aircraft were to be assessed. The reason for this was time; light aircraft are simple machines with manual controls and electronics limited to radio telephone and basic navigation aids.

opposite, The Rotary Wing attends a lecture in the Boscombe Down Ground School (*B. Johnson*)

The students need therefore spend only an hour sitting in the cockpit with a copy of the pilot's notes before taking off for the test. All aircraft climb when the stick is pulled back and dive when it is pushed forward; for an experienced pilot, what takes a good deal of time in converting to a complex military aircraft is understanding the systems, which typically could take up to four hours of dual flight. As James Giles put it:

'On a short course like this we cannot give them three or four hours' practice on every aircraft they fly. If they go on to an aircraft like the Chipmunk, they can get into it and fly it within a few minutes. It soon becomes second nature and they can get on with the testing, as opposed to learning to fly it.'

The three aircraft selected for the assessment tests were a Chipmunk *ab initio* trainer, an Edgley Optica (this flight was made in the wake of a recent fatal accident to an Optica), and a brand-new light trainer, the one and only Trago-Mills SAH-1. All three are piston-engined aircraft which, in these days of 'Through Jet' training, can be a novelty to Service pilots.

The Chipmunk was the RAF's standard trainer for many years, replacing the immortal Tiger Moth. It was designed by the Canadian branch of the old de Havilland company and first flew in 1946. The ones to be assessed by the ETPS (lent by the Army Air Corps who still use the type in its original role) were a little younger; they were nevertheless older than the students.

The remaining two aircraft differed from the Chipmunk in that they were both genuine prototypes, the Trago-Mills being the first, and at the time only, example in existence. The Optica to be tested was also a pre-production prototype.

Of the students filmed on their Pilot Assessment exercise for the BBC series, Robin Tydeman went to the Army Air Corps training base at Middle Wallop to fly a Chipmunk; *Luftwaffe* pilot Harry Fehl tested the Optica at Old Sarum, interestingly claimed to be the oldest recognised airfield in the world, while Dave Southwood stayed at Boscombe Down to assess the Trago-Mills.

In all cases the students had been told that they were assessing the aircraft as possible primary trainers for the RAF. The time allowed was minimal: just a single one-hour flight.

The Trago-Mills Exercise

As with all of the ETPS exercises, a briefing with a tutor preceded the assessment flight; since the flight was essentially solo, the tutor's brief was the only advice the students had to guide them. Dave Southwood's tutor for the sortie was Tim Allen:

'Dave, the thing you have got to remember overall on this exercise is that it is tying together everything that you have learned so

The SH-1 Trago-Mills
light aircraft prototype
during flying on the
ETPS Pilot Assessment
exercise (*BBC*)

far on this course, and you have a very short time in which to do it.
You are assessing the aircraft from the very moment that you start
walking out towards it; virtually when you first look at it you are
starting your assessment of it. Every single aspect of the aircraft,
everything you touch, everything you handle, everything to do
with it, you are assessing. Bear in mind throughout [the test] that it
is relating to the role of the aircraft. I know it is a prototype and it is
a civilian aircraft but we are assessing it for a [possible] role as a
primary trainer, like the Chipmunk or the Bulldog.'

Dave assented and produced his 'cards', a series of handwritten
proformas for the results of the tests he was proposing to undertake. The actual cards are a standard size cut to fit into the knee-
pads – the plastic-covered pockets sewn into legs of standard RAF
flying overalls.

Tim Allen: 'Let's have a look. OK, cockpit entry and exit, space
for comments on pre-start, post-start checks. Good to remember
the manufacturer's check-list because if you do not like the checks
or if they are awkward or confusing to the student . . . you have got
to comment on that. Yes, ground manoeuvrability – the minimum
ground radius – I know the manufacturer gives an estimate for the
turning radius but you have to find it for yourself. Stability tests:
this aircraft has got a down spring on the elevator circuit, so it is
probably worthwhile having a careful look at the "stick fixed" and
"stick free" static stability, because the stick fixed may not actually be there, which is why they have the spring there in the first

The Trago-Mills on the
ETPS flight line at
Boscombe Down
(*B. Johnson*)

place. Have a careful look at that. Have you got a tape-measure, or are you going to use a finger resting on your knee?'

'No, I've got a tape-measure.'

What Tim Allen was concerned about was the Trago-Mills' 'static stability', that is its ability to return to stable, level flight after being disturbed by a gust, or the pilot having disturbed the controls, usually by putting in a small 'up' input. Slow-flying aircraft such as the Trago-Mills and others, including many gliders, have a spring to impart a small downwards deflection of the elevators to increase the lift of the tailplane, which allows a slightly aft centre of gravity to be permitted, balancing the spring and positively loading the elevator; that in turn improves the pilot's perception of the aircraft's handling: it is then capable of flying 'hands off', or with little conscious effort on the part of the pilot, when the aircraft is correctly trimmed. Any aircraft with poor static manoeuvrability would have to be continuously hand-flown, which would be very exhausting at any time and virtually impossible in gusty conditions, or when on instruments.

The briefing continued with Tim Allen discussing the climb and the question of the power settings required from the engine:

'Note the trim change from take-off to climb . . . The cruising speed: it will spend a lot of its time with a primary student who is just learning how to handle the aircraft at 100 knots, so you will need to look at the cruise thoroughly. Stalling: the stall performance is a very important aspect for a primary trainer, so again have a careful look. The last time you did stalling you had two flights of an hour each: today you will have about two minutes.'

Tim Allen stressed the importance of assessing the handling at low speed, as in turning on to finals for an approach to a landing which is a high-risk manoeuvre for the inexperienced trainee pilot flying solo since there is usually insufficient height available to correct any misjudgement or error:

'He may totally lose track of the airspeed whilst concentrating on something else. So [you need] a good warning of an impending stall and a good recovery from it. Most of the training aircraft which we have had in the RAF have suffered losses [by stalling and spinning], not because they have been irrecoverable from spins but because the aircraft had confused an already confused [and frightened] pilot. Most pilots are near to their maximum confusion in the spin and if the aircraft does something which tips them over the edge then they are likely to lose the aircraft. If you look back at the Jet Provost and Bulldog spinning accident [reports] that has usually been the case. So look very carefully, in addition to the aircraft recovering from a spin, which it is bound to do, it has a CAA [Civil Aviation Authority] clearance for spinning, but look for any signs of it doing anything which could be confusing to the pupil pilot, for example, the spin [temporarily] becoming worse as you take recovery action.'

The amount of work expected of Dave Southwood in an hour's flight mounted and included aerobatics and stick force per g, that is the amount of pull or push required as the airframe is loaded by centrifugal force in aerobatics, a typical light aircraft figure being not less than 3 lbs per g. (To measure the stick forces, test pilots use a small calibrated gauge which can be attached to the control column.) The brief continued with Dave listing his proposed tests of the light aircraft beginning with a GCA (Ground Controlled Approach) which is a radar-controlled blind landing approach to test the responsiveness and accuracy of the controls. On a GCA landing the aircraft has to be flown very precisely, on instruments, to the instructions of a ground-based radar operator, who may well require the pilot to make height adjustments of the order of a few feet or directional corrections measured in as little as two degrees. To achieve that sort of accuracy, an aircraft must have crisp and well-co-ordinated controls, and a good natural longitudinal and directional stability.

After the GCA, Dave planned to do a roller which is a touch and go landing to simulate a common situation for students (and not only students): an overshoot, when a pilot has misjudged his approach and has elected to 'go round again'. One of the many points which Dave had to look at is the behaviour of the aircraft in the overshoot since that is often a critical area: an aircraft landing will be likely to have full flap selected and be trimmed for the final approach, and with little throttle set. If the pilot has to abandon the landing and climb away he may find that the aircraft will not climb at all, or will climb only very slowly, with full flap. If the flaps are raised it will climb but the trim change and loss of lift could be excessive.

The high workload was to some extent to be relieved by the fact that, although the exercise is ostensibly a solo sortie and no one at ETPS doubted Dave Southwood's ability to fly it safely, the aircraft is civil and a unique prototype at that, so to comply with the terms of the aircraft's insurance the 'owner' of the Trago-Mills was to fly in the right-hand seat as an observer. In point of fact Dave could not have had a more competent passenger for he was a graduate of ETPS, a test pilot and former Commandant of the A&AEE at Boscombe Down, Air Marshal Jeff Caines, tp, RAF Rtd.

Tim Allen concluded the pre-flight briefing:

'Overall this is a very intensive sortie because, as I said at the outset, it is tying together absolutely everything we have done on the course so far, but in a much compressed form and all in an hour and twenty minutes. It is a handling assessment; do not get carried away with taking the numbers so that at the end [of the test flight] you won't know what the aircraft felt like: if someone asked you, "How did it feel?" you would have to say, "I don't know, I was taking down data all the time." So get the handling aspects of the aeroplane and ask, "Was it enjoyable, was it easy to fly?" And if it wasn't, you can use the "numbers" you have taken to back up your impressions . . . but your feelings are the most important thing. It is after all a new prototype aircraft – it is the only one in the world – so there may be deficiencies with it which you could find. If you do, you will have the numbers to back up what you think. Above all, it is handling and your assessment. Happy?'

Dave Southwood said he was and left the tutor's office to walk to the small low-wing monoplane, which was parked on the ETPS

Dave Southwood about to fly his Pilot Assessment on the SH-1 (*B. Johnson*)

flight line. Air Marshal Jeff Caines climbed in and pointed out the controls:

'You will want to adjust the rudder pedal first, before you strap in. Round the cockpit quickly. That is the trimmer, it is set for take-off, on zero. This is the flap lever, you had better try it to make sure you have got it. The fuel cock points to the tank in use. We have two-thirds fuel. The battery master switch, the ignition and starter switch. The brakes, throttle, mixture, throttle friction. Standard flight panel, three warning lights: stall warning, alternator, starter engaged. Clock, ammeter, and suction for the [gyro] instruments.'

The aircraft was fitted with a simple VHF radio with VOR (VHF Omni Range, a VHF navigation aid) supplemented by an ADF (Automatic Direction Finder) operating on long wave; when compared with the aircraft which Dave Southwood had previously flown on the course, it was all positively spartan.

The engine was started without difficulty and the small blue monoplane taxied out to the Boscombe Down runway, passing the school Lightning which was standing close by, presenting a pictorial alpha and omega of the ETPS range of experience.

Dave had a voice recorder with him on the test flight and the impressions he brought back give a good idea of the way his test flight was conducted. First the engine was run up and the magnetos tested:

'Full power, 2350 rpm . . . and into idle at 800 rpm.'

The aircraft was then taxied to the short runway and clearance for take-off given. Dave began his flight recording:

'Fuel at take-off: about 41-41 litres [figures refer to left- and right-hand wing tanks]. Full power, very light rudder required [to counter engine torque and propeller slipstream effect]; 2380 rpm, 40 knots, airborne. Field of view very good, climbing at 75 knots, 200 feet, flaps coming up; very slight nose-up pitch, about 5 lbs push force [on the stick] and stick coming slightly forwards.

'Now we are at 500 feet, turning left; very slight rudder forces, very pleasant. I am taking the speed back to 70 knots so that I can recommence the climb and time it . . . very difficult to lose speed [the Trago-Mills has a very clean airframe]. The initial impression is that the ailerons are the heaviest of all the controls. Seventy-five knot climb, 500 feet, fuel as at take-off. Climb indicating is 800 feet per minute. Very light rudder forces, it is difficult to tell what rudder force is required . . . 1000 feet in 38 seconds; 1500 feet, one minute 15 seconds; 2500 rpm.'

Dave Southwood tested the controls for free play and 'un-stick' friction and forces required in the climb; he found them satisfactory with good centring after they were displaced. At 3000 feet he

Army Chipmunk
trainers at Middle
Wallop. ETPS 'borrow'
two of them for Pilot
Assessment exercises.
(*B. Johnson*)

left the initial stability tests to evaluate the aircraft flying straight
and level, at an altitude a primary trainer would seldom exceed.

'Level at 3000 feet and 100 knots, 1013 . . . [this is the setting of
the pressure altimeter in millibars[9]] Trim position is about a
quarter nose down. Rpm is 2500, fuel is 39–40. Ninety-five knots,
right reducing by 10 knots . . . 85 knots at a [stick] pull force of
around 3 lbs. Increasing [the speed] to 105, and a push force of
4 lbs.'

The next test which Dave undertook was the longitudinal stability commencing with phugoids. That is the term used to define an
oscillatory motion, rather like a small boat heading into a long,
heavy swell. If an aircraft is deliberately displaced from straight
and level trimmed flight by the application of a down stick input,
and the stick is then released, the aircraft will perform the long
period oscillation over 20 to 40 seconds, which is the characteristic
known as phugoids. An aircraft which is both statically and dynamically stable will return to level flight after a certain number of
cycles of phugoid oscillation. On the other hand, an aircraft which
lacks dynamic stability will continue to oscillate until the pilot
recovers the aircraft with corrective control inputs. Since the
period of the phugoids is difficult to assess visually from within the
aircraft, Dave Southwood measured the Trago-Mills oscillation by
logging the indicated airspeed against a stopwatch, as he recorded
in the air:

'We will have a go at the phugoid now: I think that will be the
[stick] releasing speed; 95, reducing to 85 and then release. Releasing now, trim, 6 seconds, [speed] 121 [knots] after 15 seconds, trim
at 25 seconds, 90 at 29 seconds. Trim at 34 seconds. One hundred
and fifteen knots at 42, trim at 52. Level at 85 after 59 seconds.

Regain control. Let's get the height back. There is Boscombe. Right, steady side-slip; I'll fly half-rudder first . . . 95 knots, fairly heavy side-slip, half-rudder; force about 30 lbs, about 5 lbs [stick force] on the right aileron, 2 lbs pull force on the elevator, and that was about 8 degrees of side-slip with no noticeable PEC [Pressure Error Correction].'

Dave tried a half-rudder side-slip in the other direction and obtained substantially the same results, except for a slightly lighter rudder force, due possibly to engine torque. The next test was a side-slip with full rudder deflection:

'Full left rudder, about 60 lbs force; aileron, about 10 mm [of stick movement] to the right. Eight lbs force. Pull force 5 lbs . . . about 25 degrees of side-slip and no PEC. That's fine.'

Next, Dave decided to see how the aircraft responded in aileron turns:

'Rolling out on the heading of two-five zero and back . . . very little adverse yaw, nose tends to swing when you roll out [of the turn].'

The handling of the new aircraft with the flaps down was the next item on Dave's test card. The handling of a training aircraft with full flap selected is very important, since that is the condition in which a student pilot will fly the machine when it is most vulnerable: flying at low speed near the ground on the landing approach:

'Lowering the flaps at 85 knots, very slight nose-down pitch; you can hold the [attitude] change with about 5 lbs pull force. Going down to 65 knots. Retrimming [to equalise the 5-lb stick force required to correct the nose-down moment], 30 [degrees of flap], more nose-down pitch, and about 8-lb pull force [that is the force required on the stick to correct nose-down pitch].'

Dave then examined a side-slip with full flap:

'Right side-slip is full left rudder: about 60 lbs rudder force, right aileron force around 4 lbs, [elevator] pull force around 4 lbs, and about 12 degrees [of up aileron], and releasing [the controls]. There appears to be about 40 degrees of side-slip; seems rather excessive . . . very difficult to measure that.'

Dave tried a Dutch roll then went on to evaluate a most important feature of any training aircraft, its stall and stall recovery behaviour:

'Flaps up. Speed 65 knots, nose-up pitch 4 lbs [of elevator] push, and all the way up. I am going to put it into a stall . . . altitude 3000 feet, engine to idle, 56 knots, a little buffet; nose well up. Stalled, recovery, power on. [Dave then summarised that stall.] Stick force about 3 lbs, very slight airframe buffet; 51 [knots]; stall [stick forward], full power, and a very slight push forwards back to trim. Recovered wings level. Elevator [to re-gain level flight] is about 6 lbs. Fine.'

Dave Southwood then assessed the Manoeuvre Boundary of the Trago-Mills in the form of an accelerated turn, with the imposed g force rising to the maximum the tightest turn can generate. This is a very important test for a light aircraft which is primarily a trainer, for many civil pupil pilots do not realise and are often not warned that, because an aircraft has a stated stalling speed, typically 45 to 50 knots, that figure is very much dependent on the imposed load factor. A light aircraft in a steep enough turn will, like a jet fighter, display a lift boundary, stall and, as the RAF put it, 'depart from controlled flight' (which usually means a spin). The stall in a steep turn can occur at a speed well above the figure expected by the pupil, for the simple reason that the aircraft, sustaining some 3g, now has an apparent weight three times that which it has in level (1g) flight. The transcript of the in-flight recording continues:

'Now a recovery from an accelerated stall [turning] to the left. We are at 90 knots, holding 3.4g, buffeting at 3.4g, and it rolls to the right about 120 degrees, but [the roll] stops as soon as you move [the stick] forward. Quite a noticeable departure there, and that was at 90 knots. Elevator force about 6 lbs. I'll do one to the right, to see if there are any differences.'

There was little difference; the small aircraft behaved in much the same way in the right-hand turn as in the left. Dave concluded that it would flick roll 'quite noticeably', and awarded an HQR (Handling Quality Rating) of 6 on that part of the test. The reason for the aircraft rolling to the right, away from the direction of the turn when the maximum g was recorded, was that as the wings neared the stall one of them stalled before the other. This often happens with well-used club aircraft; one wing might have a small dent near the leading edge, there could be a minor rigging error, or the aircraft may have more fuel in one wing tank than the other. Engine torque can also be a factor, although the 100/120 hp engines powering light aircraft do not really have sufficient torque for that to happen. (In the case of the Trago-Mills, the engine torque, such as it is, was in the opposite direction; the turn would have been to the left.)

The final test in Dave Southwood's pilot assessment of the Trago-Mills prototype was spinning:

'5000 feet, all looks clear. I will be going to the left.'

A standard spin entry from near the stall was made: full applica-tion of left rudder and the stick fully aft, the agile trainer obligingly rolled over into a steep spin:

'One turn, two turns, [spin] stabilised after three turns, four, five: right rudder, stick coming forward, about three-quarters of a turn. Speed [of rotation] stabilised after about two turns, aircraft attitude was around 60 degrees nose-down, three-quarters of a turn to recover . . . rate of spin slowing down slightly on recovery.'

The above extracts from the transcript of the recording which was made by Dave Southwood while testing the trainer do not cover all aspects of his assessment but are sufficient to give an impression of the nature of the testing of even a straightforward light aircraft, and the professional approach of the newly trained test pilot. His subsequent report was favourable, bearing in mind that the Trago-Mills was the pre-production first prototype and would be the subject of further development work.

The Optica Exercise

Harry Fehl had, in some ways, a more difficult task confronting him for his Pilot Assessment exercise; the Edgley Optica. The Trago-Mills is a basic primary trainer and is therefore designed to be as docile and forgiving as is possible; it still required a trained test pilot to assess it, but it is a conventional low-wing monoplane and not difficult for a moderately trained pilot to fly. The Optica, on the other hand, is not conventional, far from it, and it is designed to be flown by professionals. Harry was to fly the aircraft from its factory airfield, Old Sarum. His tutor, who accompanied him, was James Giles:

'Edgley Optica; a number of differences from any aircraft that you have flown before, Harry, so what I want is quickly to go over the main points of your flight, in other words what you are planning, to make sure that you are going to pick up the main aspects of

Harry Fehl (*left*) is briefed by his tutor James Giles for his Pilot Assessment exercise on the unconventional Optica at Old Sarum (*B. Johnson*)

the aircraft. First thing is flying off grass [Old Sarum is a grass airfield], have you actually flown off grass before?'

'No. This will be the first time.'

'Well, things to watch on grass; obviously controllability, nose-wheel steering, what power requirements do you need? Probably more than on concrete. Also the landing: wet grass – brakes, landing roll and distance. This aircraft is designed as a substitute for a helicopter, so it is going presumably to be operating out of fields; so make sure you get notes of the take-off and landing distance on grass. That will be the first thing.'

Harry, the German student, was of course thoroughly prepared for his assessment:

'I took care of that during my flight preparation. I divided it: taxi performance, and ground handling in general on grass, and also [on a concrete runway] at Boscombe Down. I want to fly there to do a landing and a take-off and some taxiing, just to see how much power I need [as a yardstick to measure the same aircraft's performance on the grass at Old Sarum].'

'Fine.'

'That is the ground handling. I will also look, as you suggested, at the brake efficiency and response, which obviously will be different on grass and a hard surface. Moving along the mission: take-off. I will check the engine; how long it takes to run up to 100 per cent [power], and the actual rpm it will finally indicate.'

'Yes, what is of interest here is elevator effectiveness. As you know, the landing speed [of the Optica] is about 15 knots faster than the take-off speed. I think we should address ourselves as to why this might be. Clearly, elevator effectiveness is going to be part of it. Certainly, with the design of this aircraft, with a high tail running across the ducted fan exhaust, one could expect a possible pressure differential above the tail with the engine at full power [as on take-off], which may not be there when the engine is at low power [as when landing]. That is the sort of thing you need to address. And handling in ground effect. What is next?'

Harry replied that he would climb away and trim the aircraft for level flight to obtain an impression of the 'feel' of the aircraft's controls; find out the brake-out force of the stick; and assess any friction, backlash or lost motion in the control runs, which could make it difficult for a pilot to fly accurately, a most important consideration for an aeroplane designed for operations near the ground. Harry had heard that this prototype was not equipped with a self-centring stick:

'In the ailerons?' asks James Giles.

'Yes, in the ailerons. It might be important to look at this as well. Before I take any data, I just want to fly the aircraft. I am

going to make a high-speed run at about 120 knots, and then fly it at an altitude and at a speed which the aircraft is designed for [which is around 500 feet and as slowly as is safe]. I call this a 'road recce', just for five minutes; following a road to see what the flying qualities are like.'

James Giles agreed:

'Yes, just think of it as a helicopter; so do a line recce, in other words as if you are looking at a pipeline or overhead power lines, that type of thing. The field of view, all those things come in here certainly . . . The loiter configuration is obviously low speed, what speed will you be using?'

'Fifty-five knots.'

'That's fine, Harry. Remember at that low speed you are fairly near the stall, so you want to make sure in this type of aircraft that, if in the loiter you slow towards the stall, there are good cues, both in the position of the stick and the stick forces, maybe pitch attitude, that type of thing. In other words, pre-stall warning cues.'

'Yes. Moving on, I will check out the longitudinal instability. I will do that in the designed configuration for loitering; which will be at 55 knots with 10 degrees of flap. I will also check the static stability.'

Harry Fehl and his observer, the Company Chief Test Pilot Chris Chadwick, ex-naval test pilot and ETPS graduate, prepare for Harry's Pilot Assessment flight from Old Sarum (*B. Johnson*)

'Yes, and what in particular do you look for there?'

'I want to see if the pilot gets enough cues for speed loss from stick deflection and stick force, because it [any speed loss in the loiter] is going to be very close to the stalling speed of the aircraft; and if the pilot is in a turn, losing speed and pulling harder and harder, trying to observe a spot on the ground, he might lose control of his aircraft. So I want to check out if the stick displacement and the forces [the feel of the controls] are adequate, to give enough warning [of an impending stall].'

James Giles approved and pointed out that the stall warning cues were very much in his mind, for:

'You will be aware that there has been an accident, we don't know why at the moment, but we do know it was in that sort of manoeuvre, and that is an area you need to check on an aircraft like this. Always bear in mind what it is going to be used for, that is the key to getting the right answers from an assessment.

The question of accelerated and decelerated stalls was discussed as well as what Harry called the 'spiral mode': this, too, was part of the handling at low speed and height:

'I will look to see if the pilot can put on a certain amount of bank and leave the controls free, because he may have to take pictures, or be just looking around . . .'

'Exactly, in other words he is looking out at the ground, and what is the aircraft doing?'

This led Harry to his next test: accelerated turns, or the familiar Manoeuvre Boundary assessment:

Two Opticas fly past. The unconventional nature of the aircraft, which it is claimed can perform many of the duties of a helicopter at much lower cost, is apparent. (*B. Johnson*)

'The pilot might be in a tight turn, looking outside the cockpit, not concentrating on his instruments, and I want to check out what information he gets from the behaviour of the aircraft that he is approaching the stall . . . the speed at which the aircraft actually stalls and how it is characterised, and the recovery. Is it easy to recover? Difficult? In the pre-stall, is the actual stall easy to avert? Those are the kind of things I will be looking for.'

'OK. I suggest you set a level turn at, let's say, 1.6g in a 45-degree level-banked turn for example, and just let the speed come back; look out of the cockpit, so that you are not concentrating on the airspeed, because a pilot won't be all the time.'

Harry Fehl agreed for, as he put it:

'This aircraft actually invites you to look outside, you know, because of the almost unobstructed field of view. I will also check the roll performance, firstly with half aileron, then full deflection and check the time and the stick force to change a 30-degree or 60-degree angle of bank.'

'Yes, in other words manoeuvrability near the ground.'

The final tests in the Optica would be an instrument approach and landing at Boscombe Down to assess the control response in an instrument approach, and the landing run on a hard runway; then back to Old Sarum for a landing or two on grass. Finally, James Giles suggested that Harry should try to find out about the aircraft's high landing speed as compared with the lower take-off speed. (Most aircraft behave the other way round: the take-off speed is usually higher than that of the landing.) James suggested that Harry should:

'Just fly low in ground effect; about 5 feet, with power on, then gradually reducing the power and seeing how the control effectiveness changes.'

'If the elevator authority changes?'

'That is the sort of thing.'

'OK, what I have done already this morning was the flight control system . . . I also did a cockpit assessment and found some snags; now I am looking forward to the flight.'

With that, Harry Fehl, who was an F-4 Phantom pilot with the *Luftwaffe*, went out to make a visual inspection of this unusual aircraft, the Optica. He was to fly with Chris Chadwick, himself a graduate of ETPS and an ex-naval test pilot, now chief test pilot for the Edgley Company. It should perhaps be mentioned that the ETPS Pilot Assessment took place some weeks before the company went into receivership. One is pleased to report that, at the time of writing (summer 1986), the Optica Company, with a new management, is on its way to commercial health and has a number of firm orders for this unique and now revised aircraft.

The in-flight recording which Harry Fehl made while flying the Optica was in German and no transcript is available. However, the debrief which was conducted in James Giles' office, some ten days after the assessment flight, is interesting and gives a clear impression of the amount of work expected and executed by the hardworking staff and students of the ETPS courses.

'Harry, that is a very good report. Thanks very much. As you appreciated, that was a pre-production aircraft. It was a prototype and there were a couple of things that you probably were not aware of: the port wing was about 2 degrees out of alignment and was misrigged, which I'm sure accounts for some of the facts you have come up with in spiral stability and the stall. The other point was effectiveness of the elevators near the ground which you mention in your report. The company are working on that at the moment and the production models will have a revised elevator. You have drawn a number of very good conclusions and done a lot of work on one sortie. What do you think of it?'

'Well, I was surprised what you can get out of a single hour of flying. You know it is really amazing. I thought about it when I was preparing my test cards; the amount of work I was expected to do. I did not think it could be done.'

'What do you feel about the aircraft as it operates in the low-level, low-speed environment?'

'I was very surprised about the requirements [specifications] that were put on this aircraft: it should fly as a helicopter and it should also fly as a light aircraft, near the stall, which we found was about 45 knots, but without the pilot having any warning [of the approaching stall].'

'Harry, the aircraft has a bubble canopy, got an excellent field of view, like a helicopter. Any problems with this aspect of the design?'

Harry replied that the bubble canopy, although undoubtedly providing a superb field of view equal to many helicopters, did make it difficult for the pilot to fly the aircraft straight and level, owing to lack of the datum usually provided in conventional fixed wing aircraft by the engine cowling and cockpit combing. Harry found that to maintain level flight he had continually to refer to the artificial horizon, a situation which he found bad:

'. . . Because the pilot has to look out . . . and could end up in a climb which washes off the airspeed very quickly, which in conjunction with the stall characteristics made for me the aircraft unacceptable.'

'Yes, I agree with your comments about the stall absolutely, Harry. However, to be fair to Optica, the stall warning they have got, the audio warning, is under constant development . . . it is at an early stage of development and that is good because it is one of the things you see on a prototype that I am sure you will not see on a production aircraft by the time it has been fully certified. So it was good value, I hope. Thanks again for the report which is excellent, well done.'

The Chipmunk Exercise

Both the Trago-Mills and the Optica were prototypes; the Chipmunk, which was to be assessed at Middle Wallop by Robin Tydeman, was of course not. It was an interesting example of yesterday's technology: a piston-engined, tail-wheel aircraft. Squadron Leader Robin Tydeman, the senior student, had been flying Victor tankers before he began the ETPS course and it would be hard to imagine a greater contrast to the Chipmunk trainer. However, he was, he said, looking forward to the flight as any difficulties he might find in handling the aircraft would be no greater than those of a student flying it for the first time, and the course brief was to assess the Chipmunk for the role of an *ab initio* trainer. What was the profile of the assessment sortie?

'Take-off, transit to the area south of Salisbury, which will take about ten minutes . . . we will be doing some stability checks on the way and then, when we get there, we will be looking at the stalling characteristics of the aeroplane, which will take about another ten minutes. Five minutes or so of aerobatics, and then about fifteen minutes of spinning, some further stability checks on the way back and finishing with about twenty minutes in the circuit here [on approaches, landings and take-offs].'

That summary of testing was to be completed without any special equipment other than a force gauge for the stick, a knee-pad and stopwatch, and indicates the level of attainment achieved by

The Chipmunk flown by Robin Tydeman on his Pilot Assessment of the type (*B. Johnson*)

the students in eight months of intensive training. As was said at the outset of this account of the Pilot Assessment exercise, it represents more than a milestone; the end of the journey is in sight.

After the light aircraft Pilot Assessment there were a number of late exercises, mostly of a refamiliarisation nature. They included a dual flight in the Lightning to study energy concepts; take-offs and landings in the BAC 1–11 and Andover, followed by asymmetric flight in both of those big aircraft. The VSS Basset was also revisited, and there was night flying, again with the BAC 1–11. The fixed wing students sampled once again the delights of flying the school's helicopters, and the rotary wing men flew a 'Mini Assessment' in the Optica as well as their own specialised exercises, including a single-engine exercise in the Lynx. The ground school was kept busy with lectures with such gripping titles as 'Engine and Rotor Governing', 'Flight Control Systems', 'Active Controls', 'Automatic Systems' and 'Electronic Warfare'. The school made several visits to industry; all the students went to BAC at Warton, near Preston; the Rotary Wing were the guests of the electronic company Plessey, at Tichfield; while the Fixed Wing flew to Yeovil to see Westland helicopters. That last visit was made in the school Andover and the opportunity to practise short field landings on the small grass airfield is always accepted. (It is said the Westland men always enjoy watching: possibly they regard the performance as a convincing argument for helicopters.) This leads us to the high point, if that is the right word, of the many ETPS excursions: the annual visit to Studland Bay, which is made by parachute.

Vic Lockwood: 'We mount it every year, whether we need it or not. It often gets cancelled due to weather; we have a very narrow bracket, because if we don't get it in today we will not have the time for it later. I think everyone enjoys it. What we do is have a case of beer on the rescue boat and that is the incentive to get out of the aeroplane. Actually the plans have changed a little; we were going to jump from the Andover but [it was unserviceable] it is going to be the Chinook helicopter, which will be a new experience for all of us; it should be quite exciting . . . it is about 20 knots slower than the Andover and we go out of the rear cargo door so, instead of coming out of the side and whistling off to the left, we jump from the tail.'

All the staff and some of the students had made parachute descents before; for others this was their first and, many said, their last jump.

As they gathered in the ETPS crew room they were dressed in a motley collection of old clothing. Most of the staff were in the obso-

The Chipmunk's tail-wheel undercarriage makes it a rarity these days, when tricycle gear is all but universal (*B. Johnson*)

letc bright-red flying overalls which were withdrawn some years ago; some of the overalls bore traces of domestic distemper and paint which betrayed the mundane uses to which they had been put.

There was a good deal of excited chatter as people exchanged lies about their previous parachute jumps. It should be made clear that all the jumpees were volunteers but it seemed that most of the students had signed up. (One of the flying instructors said that he had spent many years avoiding having to jump out of aeroplanes and he wasn't going to start now in the evening of his career.) The annual jump is not confined to the ETPS; anyone at Boscombe Down can join in the fun and many did, including the A&AEE Commandant, Air Commodore Williams; the list was in fact over-subscribed.

The overseas students had to obtain written permission from their Air Attaché in London for clearance. One student, 'JT' from Singapore, was forbidden to jump. Since his government had just parted with nearly a quarter of a million pounds for his training, one could see why. The others seemed prepared to write off both money and student . . .

Serge Aubert: 'I jumped before: thirteen times and I don't know why I jump again.'

Les Evans: 'I've made four jumps: two from a balloon and two from a Hercules.'

Steve Moore, Harry Fehl and Dave Southwood were making their first jump; Dave thought it would be 'A bit of fun. Why not? It is part of the course.'

Steve Moore, for some reason, said he thought it was better to make one's first jump into water rather than over land. He was one of the few who felt positive about the fact that the dropping zone (DZ) would actually be in the sea.

There exists at Boscombe Down the legend of the student who, some years previously, changed his mind at the very door of the aircraft; it is said he completed the jump still grasping the door frame. The story gained a certain credence when, asked what would happen if anyone changed his mind at the last minute on this occasion, the tough sergeant jumpmaster, a veteran of twenty-seven years of parachuting, simply replied: 'They will be assisted out of the aircraft.'

The summer of 1985 was one of the coldest and wettest on record. The jump was fixed for 2 October in the hope that the sea would be at its warmest by then. This was to prove a false assumption. The weather on the day was set foul: low stratus cloud and driving rain. The minimum cloud base permitted for the jump is 1000 feet. The big Chinook took off (donated by 'D' Squadron at Boscombe Down) and set course for the dropping zone. The Royal Marines were providing the rescue boats; a large landing craft and a number of inshore inflatables to pick the men out of the freezing water. The Marines regarded the day as a valuable training exercise; it is not easy to get thirty or so men adrift in the open sea on which to practise rescue techniques. As the Chinook shook its way to Studland Bay the cloud base seemed to drop lower and lower and for a time it seemed that the jump would be cancelled for the third time in as many years. However, by an amazing stroke of luck, over the Bay the cloud base lifted to exactly 1000 feet. (Experienced observers in the helicopter later swore that the Chinook pilot must have had a substantial position error on his altimeter.) The first man to leave the Chinook was the 'Floater', an experienced military parachutist who assessed the wind drift to give the rescue boats a target area for the pick-up.

The jump was organised in sticks of five; after each stick the Chinook made a wide circuit over the Bay to allow time for the rescue. Eventually the tumbling figures had all jumped and the men had climbed on to the landing craft and reached for the beer. One of the first on board was Robin Tydeman; he simply said:

'It is the sort of thing that every BBC man should do.'

Harry Fehl: 'Never again.'

Bob Horton: 'Excellent; being sick on the way down was the best of it: really enjoyed it.' When asked if he really had been sick he confessed that he hadn't been but he added:

'A few of us felt a bit queasy, particularly the helicopter pilots; there is nothing worse than sitting in the back of a helicopter when you are used to flying them.'

Les Evans: 'It was tremendous. The best bit was knowing that your parachute was open; there is a great roar and then a bit of tumbling, then there is a big snap and it feels great; just sitting up there watching the world. It seemed quite a long time really; coming down, you can see the water coming; you know it is going to happen very soon but it always catches you out, so I was quite surprised when it hit me. It was colder than I was expecting as well.'

Someone said to the CO, John Bolton: 'Next time, let go of the aeroplane!'

'I wondered why he [the jumpmaster] wouldn't let me go; I was so angry.' (John was actually holding on to his static line which remains attached to the aircraft.)

Vic Lockwood: 'I must say I paused in the doorway for a second wondering what the hell I was doing.'

Everyone jumped, all were picked up, none was injured. The feelings of the parachutists were summed up in a note which John Bolton wrote to the CO of 'D' flight to thank them for loaning the Chinook; it ended: 'It was a pleasure to jump out of it.'

The Previews

The Pilot Assessment exercise was a qualifying round for the 'Preview'; the Finals of the course. The term 'preview' seems innocuous enough but it conceals a prize song of staggering difficulty as it means the assessment by the ETPS syndicates of the entire performance envelopes and fitness for purpose of a number of aircraft, fixed and rotary wing. These aircraft are not primary trainers but contemporary warplanes, including swing-wing 'state of the art' fighters, anti-submarine warfare carrier-borne aircraft, and exceedingly complex helicopters.

Preview, the rather puzzling title of the final test, is traditional; when a new military aircraft type is ordered, the manufacturer constructs his prototype to the Ministry specifications. The company test pilots will have flown the aircraft as discreetly as possible and the design staff will have made any modifications required to bring the machine 'to spec', or as near as possible. When they are satisfied that the aircraft is as near as it is ever going to be, or the due date is upon them, the prototype will be flown to one of the MoD Test Establishments for a 'Preview' by the Establishment's military test pilots, to verify that it is, in all respects, ready for production and service issue. With modern military aircraft coming within hailing distance of £10 million a copy, the assessment has to be correct and the responsibility on the young test pilots is heavy. If the aircraft is passed to the Services, other young men will have to fly, and possibly fight, in it. If it is rejected, the political ramifications are unthinkable. In contrast to the heady days in the 1950s when each annual Farnborough show produced a clutch of brand-new world-beating British prototypes (most of which remained just that), the appearance of a completely new type is, these days, rare; but there are also previews on a smaller scale: uprated engines, improved avionic fits, changes of armament, changes of role and other modifications to existing aircraft; all have to be assessed and evaluated before being 'Cleared to Service'. It is evident from this that the ETPS preview has to be taken very seriously, as indeed it is: fail the preview and you have failed the course; the coveted suffix 'tp' to your entry in the Air Force List is not for you.

The preparation for the Previews had been going on for some time; COs of operational units had been approached for the loan of their aircraft. There was some disappointment that it was found impossible to include a Harrier. The problem was simply a shortage of aircraft, due in part to the knock-on effect of the losses sustained during the Falklands war and the intensive training being undertaken as the lessons of that conflict are being applied. The aircraft were selected and included three types at the US Navy Test Center at Patuxent River in Maryland. (The students who do the Preview in America do so on a no-cost reciprocal basis: some US Navy students come from the Test Pilots' School at Patuxent to do their equivalent of the Preview at Boscombe Down on the school aircraft.) The allocation of pilots to aircraft was initially drafted in the office of the 'Boss': the CO of the school, John Bolton, and his Principal Fixed Wing Tutor, Vic Lockwood.

John Bolton: 'OK, Vic, it is time to sort out who is doing what on the previews. As you know, we have got the F-18 Hornet, the S-3A Viking, both at Pax River. We have the Tornado at Honington, the F-4 [Phantom] at Coningsby and Buccaneers at Lossiemouth. With a group of ten students that allows us [a syndicate of] two on each. To start from basic principles: we want to put the heavy guys – we have only two of them – on to the only heavy aeroplane, or reasonably heavy aeroplane, that we have got this year, the S-3 Viking, so they sort themselves out easily, Robin Tydeman and Nick Coulson.'

Vic Lockwood: 'Yes, that will work out well.'

The two names were entered against the S-3. It was agreed that in 1985, as in all past years, the traditional ETPS rules would apply: all the students would preview aircraft that they had never before flown. This is not always easy with the diminishing number of aircraft types available in this day of multi-role capability. It is one of the reasons for sending men to the United States to fly American types. It is also the reason for American Navy students coming to Boscombe Down. Although the students would not have flown the aircraft tested, they would be in the same category so that fighter pilots would in general preview fighters, which is why it was

The report writing
seemed endless,
especially for foreign
students like Serge
Aubert (*B. Johnson*)

easy to allocate the two multi-engined pilots to the S-3 Viking. The
conference continued.

Vic Lockwood: 'We are obviously not going to put them in
aircraft that they have flown before, but we will try to stick to role
compatibility, which I think might be a bit tricky this year.'

John Bolton: 'Right, if we look also at what they are likely to be
doing after they leave here, the sort of aeroplane that they are going
to be flying [as test pilots], then we can make some use for the
future of the preview . . . and, of course, we would like to place a
UK student in each preview but that may not be possible. Let's
look at the Tornado.'

Vic Lockwood: 'I am tempted to suggest Tom Koelzer for that,
though he is an air defence man and he should perhaps have gone in
the F-4 [Phantom], but I would have thought he would have flown
the F-4 in the States . . . my rationale is that the Tornado, being a
swing-wing aeroplane and Tom being an F-14 [Swing-Wing
Grumman Tomcat] pilot, we might be able to get some useful read
across on the Tornado. I don't know: how do you feel about it?'

John Bolton: 'Yes, he could have previewed the F-18, but there
seems little point in sending him back to Patuxent River to fly that,
so let's pencil him in for the Tornado. Anyone else who is likely to
be flying Tornados in the future?'

Vic Lockwood: 'Well, anyone who is likely to be going to "A"
Squadron [the Fighter Testing Unit at Boscombe Down]. Harry
Fehl, of course, when he goes back to E61 [Erprobungsstelle 61,

the German military test centre at Manching], it may help him to get on the Tornado project.'

John Bolton: 'Well, let's put that on one side for the moment . . . the three Brits we have left: Dave Southwood, Les Evans and Jim Ludford. Dave Southwood, he is pretty strong on the course . . .'

Vic Lockwood: 'It is the first time we have had an F-18; it might be good to put Dave on it because he is quite strong.'

John Bolton: 'He will do a solid, professional job on the F-18. I am quite happy to put him in there. Les Evans, he is bound for [the RAE] Bedford . . .'

Vic Lockwood: 'It might be a good idea to put Les in the F-4; he will get something out of the radar systems and that sort of thing.'

John Bolton: 'Right. The next one to look at is Jim Ludford . . . he has a Harrier background, going to 'A' Squadron, so really any fighter/bomber aeroplane would suit.'

Vic Lockwood: 'I think I would like to see him in the Buccaneer, I think he would do a good job; he is in the front seat there on his own, he is a reliable guy.'

John Bolton: 'He has to fly the Buccaneer as Captain [there are no dual-controlled Buccaneers]: quite happy to see him in there. We must sort out who will go with whom.'

Vic Lockwood: 'Can we pencil in Les on the F-4, and that gives us one student on each team? We can then go back and look at the other members of the syndicates, do you agree?'

John Bolton: 'Well, let's go and look at the non-UK students and see how we get on. We have Tom Koelzer pencilled in already and Harry Fehl thought about; let's look at Serge, his background is also Air Defence, the Mirage.'

Vic Lockwood: 'Well, he would make a good match on the F-4, because he is not likely to have flown it, and not likely to fly it back in France. Les being a Harrier background man, Serge will provide the Air Defence side of the preview; Les is very reliable and strong so that would be a nice balance I think.'

The next student to place was the big Italian, Mirco Zuliani, a difficult man to fit in, for as Vic said:

'It seems such a pity that his size is in the way all the time . . . I would be tempted to put him in the Buccaneer because it will give him a change; he has had a hard year because of his size; two aircraft he hasn't been able to fly [Lightning and Hawk] but he would definitely fit in the Buccaneer and he and Jim would make a good team and work well together.'

John Bolton: 'OK, so who have we got left? Steve Moore . . .'

Vic Lockwood: 'I have been impressed by the way Steve has come on this year. For a man with a helicopter and small fixed-wing background [BAC Strikemaster, an armed version of the Jet Provost] he has done remarkably well. He is a natural flier and I think that he would get a lot out of the F-18.'

John Bolton: 'He flew the Lightning well recently. He and Dave would make a good team.'

Vic Lockwood: 'As long as we can keep them out of the pub.'

John Bolton: 'Always the danger. We will have to keep his tutor out of the pub as well!'

That night, during the 'Happy Hour' in the Boscombe Down officers' mess bar, the list was revised to some extent. The final dramatis personae for the previews were as follows:

Patuxent River, Maryland: F-18 Hornet – Dave Southwood and Harry Fehl.

Patuxent River, Maryland: S-3A Viking – Robin Tydeman and Nick Coulson.

Honington, Norfolk: Tornado – Tom Koelzer and Steve Moore.

Coningsby, Lincolnshire: F-4 Phantom – Les Evans and Serge Aubert.

Lossiemouth, Scotland: Buccaneer – Jim Ludford and Mirco Zuliani.

The Rotary Wing's Principal Tutor, Mike Swales, and John Bolton also held a meeting and allocated the five helicopter students for their previews:

Patuxent River, Maryland: the soon to be controversial Black Hawk – Bob Horton and Gil Yannai.

Odiham, Hampshire: Boeing Chinook – Al Howden, 'Mike' Meiklejohn and 'J T' Koh.

As soon as they knew the aircraft allocated, the syndicates got down to work to pre-plan their respective previews. They had been allocated a total of only ten hours on the test aircraft, all of which were exceedingly complex. Each syndicate would divide the preview test programme between them, flying roughly five hours each, with the exception of the three-man syndicate at Odiham. It is obvious that the syndicates had very little time indeed to learn to fly the test aircraft; they had to combine that with the evaluation. In contrast, a pilot posted to an operational squadron could expect a fifty-hour conversion course before being considered by his flight commander as 'current' on the type. The amount of flying time available appears very short and John Bolton was asked about this aspect of the preview:

'As test pilots they are assessing the aircraft in specific areas: they are not using the aircraft operationally. The problem is to limit themselves, to look at only certain systems, obviously we want them to look at the handling of the aircraft because that has been a major part of their course throughout the year and [in the case of the Tornado and the F-18 Hornet] with so many combinations of wing sweep and flap angle and the various degraded modes in the automatic stability conditions at all speeds available, it would become very, very difficult . . . and the more they fly, the more they have to write; that is something that they should be doing as they go along. If they leave it until they get back to Boscombe Down, it is going to be a very large task. A very large proportion of our assessment of the students at the end of the course is based upon this exercise, both in the way they conduct themselves during the preview and also in the quality of their reports and the final verbal presentation.'

Each of the syndicates was accompanied to the base from which the previews are flown by an ETPS tutor. John Bolton was at Honington with Tom Koelzer and Steve Moore; he was asked what his (and the other tutors') role was:

'Well, my role is initially to supervise them from the test flying point of view to make sure that they are on the right lines; to make sure that they are not going outside their brief and also to get some experience [on the Tornado] myself, so that I can assess their report.'

The Buccaneer Preview

The tutor who travelled to RAF Lossiemouth with Jim Ludford and Mirco Zuliani was Squadron Leader James Giles. Although it is correct to describe James Giles as the ETPS tutor at the Lossiemouth Buccaneer preview, he, like the tutors attending the other previews, was really there in an administrative capacity: to act as *chef d'équipe*, to organise the aircraft, to be a point of contact between the host squadron and ETPS, thus relieving the two students of problems such as the availability of aircraft, the provision of navigators and other day-to-day operational problems. In addition, he would supervise, invigilate and, as Wing Commander Bolton said at Honington, get an hour or two on the test aircraft himself. The tutors on the previews were not there to instruct the syndicates how to test the aircraft; they had spent the previous ten months doing just that. Soon after the three men arrived at Lossiemouth, James Giles held a briefing in the Buccaneer OCU (Operational Conversion Unit):

'Right, here we are at the Buccaneer preview: the end of course exercise on which you will pull together everything you have been taught and hopefully learned so far. In eight sorties you have got to go around the envelope of the Buccaneer. It is an aircraft which has been in service for a long time [RAF Buccaneers are ex-Fleet Air Arm]. It has done, and continues to do, a very good job so it is up to you to find those areas of flight safety and operational importance

which would be relevant if we were buying the Buccaneer today to last for the next twenty years. Now remember, when you are flying you are bypassing the OCU conversion phase. You are going straight into an aircraft which has no instructor in the back seat, only a navigator, and you will be putting him into situations which it is probable he has never been in before; make sure you tell him what you intend to do before you do it, so that he is aware of what is happening. As I said, you are bypassing the conversion phase, so the moral is be careful; plan everything ahead; know what you are going to do and be sure to brief the guy in the back seat before you do it.'

The Buccaneer at first, or indeed second, glance appears a most formidable beast. Jim Ludford was asked how he felt about his forthcoming first and solo sortie:

'I'm looking forward to flying the Buccaneer. I think overall we are fairly well prepared for it: take a gentle approach to it and all should be OK . . . one thing the course has done is to tune us into getting from one aeroplane and becoming adequately familiar with another, to go up and do the sort of tests that we have got to do. We creep up on the limits rather than go straight to them. I think, to some extent perhaps, we are flying it more as an aeroplane than the guys on the squadron do. They do with it what they need to do, but we have got to find the corners of the little box within which you

The previews mark the last phase of the ETPS course. Mirco Zuliani walks with an observer to Buccaneer XX 899 at Lossiemouth. There are no dual controlled Buccaneers and Mirco confessed to 'feeling a bit nervous'. (B. Johnson)

can operate it. Maybe they take it that far, maybe they don't. I don't know on the aspects we are looking at. They are flying the Buccaneer operationally and we are flying it as an aeroplane.'

Jim Ludford, a Harrier pilot, and therefore used to a certain amount of assistance from the in-built 'black boxes' of that advanced aircraft, was asked what he expected to find deficient in the Buccaneer's somewhat dated design:

'There are deficiencies with all aeroplanes, you know that just by talking in mess bars and crewrooms over the years. There are some aspects of the low-speed flying control [of the Buccaneer] that need updating [and] automating rather than being left to manual control. The handling of the aeroplane is probably going to be adequate for the job, but there could well be other aspects that we haven't heard about which we will need to look at closely.'

Asked about the subsequent report, Jim Ludford was resigned:

'Well, there is that, yes. But we have become very good at writing reports over the past year; I think we are at the peak of our writing at the moment.'

On the question of reports, James Giles was asked how he was able to assess them on an aircraft which was not a type with which he was fully conversant:

'I happen to have got about fifteen hours on Buccaneers and I flew again here yesterday. So, whilst not being current on it, I have got myself refamiliarised with it. Really I sit here as an interested party. What I am looking for in a report are convincing arguments

Mirco does his visual checks before take-off, watched by his observer (*B. Johnson*)

that convince me – if I have never flown the aircraft – that it is worth spending a lot of government money on modifications, updating the systems and automating features, or whatever they come up with. So really, although it is good for me to know the aircraft, to make sure that the report is technically correct, it is not essential.'

The other half of the Buccaneer syndicate was the Italian, Mirco Zuliani, who was to have the first flight. How did he feel about the prospect?

'Oh, a little bit nervous but I think that the experience that we had during the course is the right preparation for an approach to fly a new aircraft. You know, a slow approach to each phase of our flight.'

Had he ever flown a similar aircraft in Italy?

'No, nothing similar, this is really completely different from other aircraft.'

One of the problems which confronts the overseas students is, of course, English. Mirco, like the other non-UK students, spoke good English but there is a vast difference between speaking collo quial English and writing a technical report which requires a high degree of precision of language. Had Mirco found it difficult to write reports?

'Oh, you will have to ask James that. It was really a hard time. It was not easy, mainly it was my fault for the lack of preparation of the [English] language . . . it was not easy to write reports in a foreign language. If you know a language it makes a difference to the way you present your reports and for some time it is difficult to write the correct way and therefore the tutors will not understand what you say . . . but towards the end, you try to forget what was the bad time and just remember the good times. I think the course is good and I think I have a good preparation for the future. But during the course there was really a hard, hard time, not only for me but the family; it was a hard time for them because we were so busy and no day out.'

Apart from a little initial difficulty which resulted in the premature shutdown of an engine on one of his early landings, Mirco successfully completed his half of the Buccaneer preview with his syndicate colleague, Jim Ludford. The weather, as so often is the case in northern Scotland, was very fine; the Wester Ross Highland scenery, over which some of the preview flying was done, was at its magnificent best. The roomy cockpit of the Buccaneer suited the big Italian, who quickly adapted to the twin-engined ex-naval fighter/bomber. Whilst the Buccaneer team was flying from Lossiemouth out over the Moray Firth which is virtually at the runway's end, over 300 miles to the south, at the Lincolnshire airfield at Coningsby, the members of another ETPS syndicate, Les Evans and Serge Aubert, had commenced their preview with the F-4 Phantom which, by coincidence, is also an ex-naval aircraft.

The Phantom Preview

The ETPS tutor nominated to attend the preview at Coningsby was Squadron Leader Tim Allen. Les Evans, Tim Allen and a very experienced F-4 instructor of the Phantom OCU at Coningsby, Flight Lieutenant Jack Dowling, who was appointed to fly in the rear seat of the Phantom as Les Evans's 'minder', were in a briefing room preparing for the sortie which Les and Jack were about to fly. The second member of the syndicate, Serge Aubert, was in his room in the Officers' Mess at Coningsby, already hard at work writing up the notes of his flight which had taken place earlier that same day. The transcript of the briefing reveals the roles of Tim Allen and Jack Dowling as advisers and shows that the tasking of the test flights was very much in the hands of the student syndicate:

Les Evans: 'The profile of the sortie is to get some air-to-air refuelling. Prior to that I want to look at some of the earlier points that we have already seen and to take them a bit further. In particular, I would like to do some wind-up turns. I will be looking at the stick force per g and also the lift, buffet, tracking and stall boundaries, all in the same wind-up turns.'

Jack Dowling: 'Similar to yesterday's sortie?'

Les Evans: 'That's right, Jack, yes. But we are going to do them at different speeds [the actual speeds and certain other performance figures relating to the Phantom preview are classified] and also

An F-4 Phantom in its hardened hangar at RAF Coningsby. Les Evans is helped to strap into the front cockpit while his observer, Flt Lt Jack Dowling, climbs in the back. The F-4, which Les has never before flown, is his subject for his preview with Serge Aubert. (*B. Johnson*)

go down to 5000 feet this time; yesterday we did most of them at 15,000 feet. With that in mind, we will set off for 15,000 initially and look at point nine wind-up turn which we didn't do properly yesterday; then we will come down to 5000 feet, do wind-up turns looking at the stick forces per g and the lift boundaries at a complete range of speeds.'

Tim Allen: 'Can I make an interjection here? Jack, it's your aeroplane, you are the expert on it, but knowing wind-up turns I can see that, at the higher speeds and the higher g levels, the aircraft is going to end up extremely nose low.'

Jack Dowling: 'Yes, you have a major safety consideration: if we are supersonic and getting more than 40 degrees nose-down at 5000 feet, you need 8000 feet to recover! So we will have to see how deeply the nose is going down.'

Les Evans: 'We saw yesterday how deep the nose does go at those high speeds. We will be starting those wind-up turns at 9000 feet, aiming to start taking data at 7000 and finish at 5000.'

Tim Allen: 'You have got to give yourself height because you can get carried away with the data taking and, at that minimum height, designate Jack to call it out and then always recover at that height.'

Les Evans: 'Thank you, Tim. Having done the turns, we will then look at some SPOs [Short Period Oscillation] and Dutch rolls. SPOs: damped and undamped; we have an indication already that it is a problem area for the aeroplane and that, without the stabs [automatic stabilisation system], the SPO period is quite long, which gives tracking problems. In particular, I want to have a look at them at 5000 feet at a spread of speeds. I will do the timing; I will tell you the number of overshoots and would you write them down, Jack? The Dutch roll we will do as well at the same speeds at 5000 feet. I will put in a rudder doublet and let the aeroplane snake and roll. I will do the timing of the period of it and if you could write that down I will count the overshoots. We will do that both damped and undamped [that is, with and without autostabilisation], OK? After that, when we get to our minimum fuel, we will give up and do the air-to-air refuelling; it's a VC-10 isn't it?'

Jack Dowling: 'Yes, he is on tow-line five.'

There then followed a discussion between Jack Dowling and Les Evans on the amount of fuel that the Phantom would uplift and the duration then available for the rest of the sortie.

Les Evans: 'OK, we will take the total amount he can give us, leave him and come back for more of those wind-up turns. I will aim to take the central hose first because that is the easy one, then we will ask for the starboard wing hose and that will be particularly interesting because we will then be doing the more difficult hose

Les Evans eases the big F-4 out of its hangar (*B. Johnson*)

with an aft C of G [the centre of gravity will be aft of the aircraft's datum due to the load of fuel just uplifted from the centre hose].'

Tim Allen: 'How high do you plan to do this, Les?'

Les Evans: '25,000. That is the tanker height and his speed will be 300 knots.'

Jack Dowling: 'If you want to vary the tanker height you can ask him . . .'

Les Evans: 'I'm happy with 25.'

Jack Dowling: 'Well, that tends to be an average height anyway; it's role-relatable for the assessment which you are making.'

Les Evans said that after the refuelling he would perform the remainder of the tests on his card, which included more wind-up turns, lift boundary assessment, SPOs and Dutch rolls at various heights and speeds. If in this account it appears that Les Evans seems to be repeating tests done before the refuelling exercise, that is perfectly correct: he has to, for the weight of the aircraft will be very much increased after refuelling and it is is essential to know the boundaries in that new condition, for a fighter might well have to be flown to the limit of its military performance immediately after flight refuelling. Having listed the tests, Les Evans asked Jack Dowling if he had any questions:

'No, but I think you will have run out of fuel after all that lot.'

Les Evans: 'Yes, fuel is going to be a problem, as it was yesterday; there are more test cards than I know we are going to have time for. It does not matter if we cannot get them all done; Serge can cover them next time.'

The briefing was over and Les Evans had a spare hour or so before the flight. He took advantage of the short respite to walk over to the Battle of Britain Memorial Flight which is also based at Coningsby. In the Flight's hangar some of the historic aircraft were being overhauled after the summer air show circuit. All the aircraft are maintained in an airworthy condition to a very high standard indeed, certainly higher than was possible in the desperate days of the high summer of 1940. The hangar is dominated by PA 474: the only airworthy Lancaster remaining out of a total of 7377 built. As Les Evans walked past the old bomber, one of its four Rolls-Royce engines was being worked on by a young servicewoman fitter; many WAAF (Women's Auxiliary Air Force) during the war years worked on Lancasters, and all aircraft in RAF service. The hangar in which the Lancaster is housed must have had many others over-hauled in it, for Coningsby was a wartime Lancaster base when it was part of No. 5 Group, Bomber Command. Coningsby is only one of many Lincolnshire airfields, most now derelict, with names that once were a roll-call of the nightly Lancaster raids on Germany: Fiskerton, Woodhall Spa, East Kirkby, Dunholm Lodge, Binbrook, Ludford Magna, Skellingthorpe, Syerston and many others. PA 474 remains a memorial to the 47,268 young aircrew of RAF Bomber Command who lost their lives during the Second World War. It is hoped to keep it airworthy into the twenty-first century.

As a fighter pilot, Les Evans approached another of the pre-served aircraft in the Coningsby hangar with awe: one of the Memorial Flight's Spitfires. Les looked at the Spitfire, dwarfed by

Coningsby is the base of the 'Battle of Britain' flight. PA 474, the only airworthy Lancaster in the world, is being overhauled after a busy summer season of air-shows. (*B. Johnson*)

the Lancaster, and sighed, 'I would give my right arm to fly this, I really would. It is a tremendous aeroplane.' He was asked what his opinion was of the men who fought in these aircraft in 1940:

'It is very high indeed. They were going into battle with very few hours of experience: I really feel for them because, to fly in battle with 200 hours total flying time, or something like that, must have been hard.'

Asked what he would expect to find as a test pilot if he were to fly the Spitfire, Les Evans replied:

'Obviously, very different from a modern jet fighter; directional control would be somewhat reduced from a fast jet; the propeller slipstream effects would be quite high, and you would expect some adverse yaw from the ailerons. I wouldn't mind betting the [all manual] control forces would be quite high too. But I'm sure any British test pilot or fighter pilot would love to get his hands on one . . . back to the F-4!'

Les Evans left the hanger with the Spitfires, Hurricanes and the Lancaster to enter the bunker which housed the Operational Conversion Flight. As Les dressed in his g suit and a survival suit, which is essential since most of the F-4 Phantom preview was to be flown over the North Sea, he was asked how the ETPS course had fitted him for the preview and final presentation:

'The course has been hard work but it is becoming really interesting now: this exercise in the Phantom is extremely good value from my point of view. I am finding it surprisingly easy to fly . . . after the course; you start to assess the aeroplane without even thinking about it.'

Les Evans and Jack Dowling went to the operations room, filed a flight plan, and discussed the question of UHF frequencies to enable them to contact the vital VC-10 tanker. Les Evans was holding a small force gauge which is used by test pilots to measure the force applied to the control stick during manoeuvres in the handling trials. The two pilots then walked to one of the many hardened hangars which protect the dispersed aircraft on operational airfields throughout NATO. The Phantom was checked in the hangar and taxied out under its own power to the long main runway at Coningsby. Once lined up, Les Evans selected full throttle augmented by reheat. The twin jet pipes became incandescent with bright orange flames as the two Rolls-Royce Speys developed some 50,000 lbs of thrust – equivalent to the power of a squadron of wartime Lancasters – and the borrowed Phantom shimmered into the air to climb rapidly away. The thunder of its flight was still heard long after the F-4 had disappeared into the overcast on its ETPS preview.

The published performance figures of the Spey-powered

versions of the F-4 indicate that the all-weather multi-role fighter is capable of an initial climb of 28,000 feet per *minute*, a maximum speed of 1500 mph (Mach 2.27) with a service ceiling of 60,000 feet. To be able to assess that sort of performance in just ten hours' flying, without ever having flown the Phantom before, underlines the quality of the ETPS course and students. It was a fitting finale.

Many of the RAF's Phantoms are ex-Royal Navy. Here is one in original ownership, an FG1, XT 857. (*via B. Johnson*)

Rotary Wing Preview: The Chinook

Far to the south-west of Coningsby, in Hampshire, lies RAF Odiham, which before the war was the base of Army co-operation squadrons flying silver-doped Hawker Hector biplanes. Today the aircraft operating from the old airfield are, in a sense, still working with the Army for they are engaged on troop carrying and supply missions. They are Boeing Model 114 Chinook helicopters; the big tandem-rotor machines are the largest rotary wing aircraft in RAF service and are unique to the RAF – neither the Navy nor the Army Air Corps fly them. It would be difficult to imagine a more marked contrast to the F-4 Phantom; the Chinook operates from 50 feet up to its normal service ceiling around 15,000 feet. The maximum speed is given in one source as 189 mph when moderately loaded. In the Falklands war, the ship ferrying RAF Chinooks (from Odiham) was the ill-fated *Atlantic Conveyer* and only one Chinook managed to take off from the ship before it was sunk by enemy action. Chinooks flew with great distinction with the American Army in the Vietnam conflict, over 550 Chinooks being deployed. According to reports, one of them, on a single flight, lifted no fewer than 147 refugees to safety.

As with all the aircraft previewed by the ETPS students, the details of the testing and performance figures are classified. However, it is possible to quote from the Chinook brief:

A Chinook with its rear cargo door open. An ETPS syndicate led by Al Howden did its preview on the big helicopter. (*B. Johnson*)

'You are to assume that the RAF will need to procure a medium Support Helicopter in the late 1980s to replace a proportion of its existing Puma and Wessex helicopters and to complement the existing Chinook fleet . . .'

The ETPS syndicate at Odiham to preview the Chinook was led by a Royal Navy lieutenant, Al Howden, the other members being 'Mike' Meiklejohn, from the Canadian Armed Forces, and the student from Singapore, 'JT' Koh. Al Howden discussed with his colleagues the sortie for the day:

'We will take a look at the single-engine flying. Now really all we want to do in the single-engine test is to throttle back nice and gently and look at the performance of one engine: so we are looking at maximum and minimum speed and also at the maximum manoeuvring bank. Now are we working to the ten-minute or the thirty-minute rating? OK. We will go for the ten-minute rating then, which is 850 degrees PTIT [Power Turbine Inlet Temperature].'

It should be explained at this point that although the Chinook has twin 60-foot rotors they are not individually powered by separate engines. In the first place the rotors intermesh, like an egg-beater, which, to say the very least, poses difficult problems of engine synchronisation; second, since the rotors are at the opposite ends of the 51-foot aircraft, lateral stability requirements demand that both the rotors keep turning! In the Chinook the two 3750 shp Lycoming turbines are clutched to a common drive-shaft which drives the rear rotor; a long shaft transmits the drive from a transfer gearbox to the forward rotor, keeping both in mesh. The tandem rotors rotate in opposite directions to cancel out torque effects without the need for the usual helicopter tail rotor.

The 'ten-minute rating' to which Al Howden referred is a power setting which a single engine can sustain for only ten minutes; a thirty-minute rating would have meant that the engine would have been operating at lower power and therefore for a longer period of time, the limiting factor being the turbine temperatures. The briefing continued:

'We will just look at the flying: see how fast we can go; see also how slowly we can go. Having achieved that, we will then reduce the airspeed back to 80 knots and see how fast we can climb all on one engine: maximum power, ten-minute rating. Mike will call the height and I will use the stopwatch to time it to 1000 feet. That will be the single-engine test completed. Happy with that? OK. Next the low-flying side of it, how are we going to get on to that?'

It was decided that, after the climb on one engine, the syndicate would make for a designated military helicopter low-flying area (LFA) to assess the control response of the big helicopter at minimum height; the exercise to culminate in a landing on sloping ground. 'JT' was to operate a video camera to record the aircraft's instruments for later analysis for the written report; a cockpit voice recorder was carried for the same purpose. A BBC television film crew also flew on the low level mission in the Chinook; the footage shot confirms that flying at around 170 knots at 50 feet over well-wooded country is quite an experience. This extract from the final briefing just before take-off gives some idea of what the test flight was going to be like:

Al Howden: 'One final thing, when we are at low-level what height are we going to fly down to?'

'Mike' Meiklejohn: 'We will be down to 50 feet minimum.'

Al Howden: 'Down to 50 feet: you are going to fly it, Mike, so you'll be able to look at control response and things like that. I will be navigating and obviously we will be weaving to avoid large trees and farms [!].'

'Mike' Meiklejohn: 'Yes, so we can see if the aircraft is capable of flying at 50 feet. Sounds good.'

Listening to that briefing one was tempted to intervene to enquire what would happen if the Chinook proved incapable of flying at 50 feet.

In the event, the low-level flying was achieved and proved to be spectacular, as the big helicopter weaved around trees and hugged the undulating ground of the low-level flying area. The abiding memory of the lay passengers, however, was the level of vibration created at high speed in the large unfurnished fuselage. The high-level handling, the low-speed testing and the landing on sloping ground were all conducted on the same sortie; the crew even managed to drop off a vital package at RAF Upavon before returning – at low level – to Odiham. There remained many other aspects of the Chinook's fitness to meet the specification drawn up by the ETPS staff, which formed the kernel of the preview task. Some eight hours of test flying remained, barely sufficient to accomplish the work involved. The Odiham syndicate was the only one operating on Boscombe Down's doorstep; the remaining three were a long way from home in the United States.

The US Navy Test Center at Patuxent River, Maryland, is the major test establishment dedicated to the requirements of US naval aviation; it is therefore a specialised equivalent to the A&AEE at Boscombe Down, except that the latter establishment is not confined to one service but is operated by the MoD Procurement Executive on behalf of all three of Britain's Air Arms. It should perhaps be said that the US Navy Test Pilot School is at least five times larger than the ETPS with many courses running concurrently; the briefing rooms at Patuxent River are rather better appointed, which is not to say better fitted for their purpose, than the rather spartan, though functional, equivalent at Boscombe Down.

As has been related, the Empire Test Pilots' School was formed at Boscombe Down in 1943 and was at that time the only such school in the world. Word of the success of the school seems quickly to have spread, for an American student from the AAAF was enrolled on the second course. (There was an American on the first course, Flight Lieutenant R. V. Muspratt, but he was in the RAF as a Member of the Eagle Squadron.) The first US Navy students attended Course No. 3 in 1945: they were Lieutenant Commander M. W. Davenport and Lieutenant Commander J. J. Davidson. After graduation, the two test pilots returned to Patuxent River where Rear Admiral E. J. Hogan takes up the story:

The badge of the US Navy Test Center at Patuxent river (*Colin Jones*)

'We sent some early test pilot students from Patuxent River in the late '40s to attend the Empire Test Pilots' School; then [in 1949] Lieutenant Commander Joe Smith, a young naval officer, went to the Boscombe Down School [in 1949 ETPS was at Farnborough] and came back here to Patuxent River and established our test pilot training curriculum, and that has grown over the years into the current Navy Test Pilot School. We have had a very close liaison with ETPS, both when it was at Farnborough and now at Boscombe Down, and [there is] a great amount of exchange; not only on matters of the curriculum but also on the philosophy of testing, and the technology involved in today's modern aircraft, so we are almost mirror images of each other. [As for] the other test pilot schools in the free world: Edwards [USAF] is separate and does not follow the same curriculum that we do nor do they have the breadth of application that we have, they are not involved in rotary wing testing as ETPS and the US Navy Test Pilot School are; the French school at Istres [EPNER] is somewhat similar to ours but it has a shorter curriculum and focuses more on the test team than it does on the individual. To sum it up: the United States Test Pilot School and the Empire Test Pilots' School are very close indeed; we are probably brothers rather than cousins.

'I am a graduate of the Empire Test Pilots' School [No. 19 Course] and when I came back from Farnborough to Patuxent River, I thought the Empire Test Pilots' School was the best. Now that I am in charge of the Navy School, I think that is the best! There may be some bias there. [Rear Admiral E. J. Hogan USN, is not only in charge of the Navy School, he is (in 1986) the Commander of the Patuxent River Naval Air Test Center, which includes the school].

'Basically, the product is very close. The quality of the individuals is almost the same: we have the same kind of individuals that want to become test pilots . . . it is a challenging environment and the young men and women that get involved in it are cut from the same kind of cloth: they are high achievers; they are aggressive; they are highly active; they have a professional approach to doing business. The products of both schools are, I think, close to equal.'

The Admiral enlarged on the close ties between the two schools, pointing out that each year there are US Navy students and usually a tutor who exchange with British students and staff, in addition to the preview students, which is another two-way exchange. In 1985 Course No. 44 had sent three syndicates.

Squadron Leader Robin Tydeman RAF and Flight Lieutenant Nick Coulson RAAF, as the CO, John Bolton, pointed out, were

Robin Tydeman did a preview at Patuxent River on the S-3 Viking, seen behind him. His syndicate colleague was Nick Coulson. (*BBC*)

both multi-engined pilots prior to joining the course and would therefore preview a 'heavy'; in this case a Lockheed S-3A Viking ASW twin-engined carrier aircraft.

The Viking Preview

The Viking must be one of the largest aircraft to operate from carriers and has folding wings which are essential to enable it to fit into the crowded carrier hangars. The wings fold just outboard of the twin General Electric turbofans, reducing the 68 ft 6 ins span to 29 ft 6 ins. The vertical tail fin also folds down to the left to reduce the height of the aircraft. The Viking's 53 ft 4 ins fuselage is the maximum that can be accommodated on the lifts of the carriers and is crammed with ASW equipment, most of it highly classified. A crew of four is normally carried: pilot, co-pilot and two weapon officers. The main feature of the Viking is its very long range; around 2900 miles, according to published reports. The Viking can also 'loiter' at low speed for over seven hours. This is the aircraft which the ETPS syndicate was about to assess. Robin Tydeman was asked about the first sortie that he and his partner, Nick Coulson, were about to make in the S-3A:

'We are going to have first of all a qualitative look at the aeroplane, just to see if it has any vices, and a major part of the sortie will be just gathering data in terms of its longitudinal stability. Then some asymmetric work [flying on one engine]. The last half-hour will be spent in the circuit, just looking at the various modes of landing the aeroplane. On subsequent sorties we will be gather-

The Viking taxies for take-off at Patuxent River (*Colin Jones*)

The Viking unfolds its wings. With Carrier aircraft the wing folding is essential in order to fit into the restricted space of a Carrier hangar. (*Colin Jones*)

ing a lot more performance data; looking at the stalling perform-ance and its lateral stability, and flying it in its role; that is at low level over the sea.'

The syndicate was soon immersed in the assessment of the Viking. A few days later Nick Coulson was interviewed as he pre-pared for the third sortie:

'What I am doing now is preparing the test cards to give us an outline of what we are going to do and to give us a reference to write things and jot down the numbers. We also have a voice recorder. It is a 2½-hour trip this afternoon and Robin and myself have spent yesterday, from 9 o'clock in the morning to 5 o'clock in the after-noon, plus two hours this morning so far; so there is a fair amount of preparation going into each flight. And that is just the basic preparation.'

'What will you be looking at this afternoon?'

'Firstly, it is a check of the inertial navigation system as it aligns itself on the tarmac.'

It is interesting to recall that the 'low-level' exercise which Nick Coulson flew with James Giles in the Jaguar at Boscombe Down was precisely the same, although the actual equipment will be different; it is a good example of the relevance of the ETPS sylla-bus. Nick Coulson continued:

'We will be doing ground handling and take-off data. We will then climb to 10,000 feet and look at the manoeuvre boundaries of the aircraft. After that we will look at the stability of the aircraft with different C of G positions, have another look at the stall, a few aerobatics: this aeroplane is capable of rolling, the only thing it can't do is a loop, and spins of course. We will throw the aeroplane about a bit: turn it upside down, to see what it is like.'

'What do you think of the Viking so far?'

'It is a little different to what I thought it would be; it's larger, but it handles quite nicely, and I think it is a good aeroplane for its job at this stage, although it does have, we think, maybe a few problems longitudinally; we expect some problems with a Dutch roll, but we don't seem to have come across it as yet. We have found a few minor things wrong with it, but overall it seems a pretty good aeroplane.'

'What do you find to be the main differences between operating here as opposed to Boscombe Down?'

'Apart from the American procedures . . . there is no real difference: the people here have been very helpful with us and have allowed us to do everything that we wanted to, so long as we fit in with their local rules. So there is no problem operating here.'

The Black Hawk Preview

One of the three ETPS previews at Patuxent River was the assessing of an American helicopter which was soon to be very much in the news in Britain: the UH-60 Black Hawk. The Westland controversy was still some months away as Captain Gil Yannai of *Heyl*

The canted tail rotor of the Black Hawk helicopter is well illustrated in this photograph taken at Patuxent River (*Colin Jones*)

Ha'Avir (Israeli Air Force) and Lieutenant Bob Horton RN prepared to preview the big battlefield assault helicopter. The Sikorsky UH-60 Black Hawk was, at the time of the preview, the newest battlefield helicopter in service with the US Army. Published performance figures give its maximum speed as 192 mph, high for a military helicopter, and a range of over 1000 miles. Not even its most devoted proponents would claim that the Black Hawk is, even by helicopter standards, pleasing to look at. It has a very long, squat fusclage which was dictated by the original requirement that it could be airlifted in a C-130 Hercules transport. That restriction on the size has reduced the number of fully-armed troops carried to about twelve; its twin 1536 shp General Electric turbofans could lift far more, but the UH-60 can and does carry a wide range of electronic warfare equipment. Bob Horton described some of the design aspects of the aircraft, just prior to test flying it at Patuxent River for his preview:

'The Black Hawk has a lot of unique design features; for instance it is covered with armour plating, the cabin windows slide back out of the way and they can stick a couple of 7.26 mm machine guns out of the side. It has got an extremely good undercarriage . . . the cockpit seats are crash resistant, so if the pilot gets the landing slightly wrong and arrives instead of lands, the seats will protect him from spinal injuries. It has also got a quite interesting tail rotor. The tail rotor is canted to about 20 degrees from the vertical. That is because once they had built the [prototype] aircraft

The Black Hawk undergoing its ETPS preview by Bob Horton and Gil Yannai (*Colin Jones*)

it had a very far aft C of G, that caused a number of problems. Some bright spark said why not just tilt the tail rotor so that it will produce an upward thrust moment as well as the conventional lateral moment.'

The tail rotor is required on single-rotor helicopters to balance the torque effect of the main rotors: to counteract Newton's Third Law: 'For every action there is an equal and opposite reaction', in other words to stop the helicopter going round the main rotor. The elegant solution to the problem of the Black Hawk's C of G by canting the tail rotor to provide some additional lift to the tail was not without some unwanted side-effects, as Bob Horton explained:

'The boffins think it provides about 2 per cent of the total lift in the hover, so it is holding up the back end to overcome this aft C of G problem, but it does lead to a few peculiar cross-coupling effects: whenever you put in a yaw input, it causes the aircraft to pitch up as well. They have had to have a sophisticated mixing unit to try to iron out these odd cross-couplings. Another unique feature of this aircraft is a Variable Incidence Stabiliser, called a Stabilator. Depending on your airspeed, by varying the Stabilator on the back, you can maintain the aircraft in a much more level attitude throughout its speed range.'

The stabilator which Bob Horton mentioned is really an all-moving tailplane which uniquely, for a helicopter, performs the functions of a fixed wing aircraft's elevators. On one of Bob Horton's flights, the Stabilator became jammed in the 'up' position, causing a nose-up angle of some 12 degrees; an unwanted demonstration of its effectiveness. During the ten hours of their testing, Bob Horton and Gil Yannai were to find other problems for their Boscombe Down presentation.

Hornet Preview

The third preview aircraft was in many ways the most advanced of any flown during the entire ETPS course: the McDonnell Douglas F-18 Hornet which is a maritime carrier-based fighter of the latest design. It is reputed to cost about $17 million a copy, which must have been at the back of the minds of the ETPS syndicate assigned to evaluate it: Hauptmann Harry Fehl of the *Luftwaffe* and Flight Lieutenant Dave Southwood, RAF. The F-18 which the ETPS syndicate had been allocated was resplendent in a non-standard, high-gloss red and white finish, with a large '02' on the nose and the legend 'REAR ADMIRAL HOGAN' painted just below the cockpit, '02' being the Admiral's personal barge. If the cost and the identity of the 'owner' worried Dave Southwood he did not show it; he said in a BBC interview that he found that particular Hornet interesting because:

'. . . this airframe is a fairly early development aeroplane – it was from about half-way through the F-18 development programme – so from the handling qualities side, there have been a lot of things we have found on it which have subsequently been corrected on the aircraft which are in service with the Fleet. Whereas before on the course we have always flown aeroplanes of a production service standard, this is an aeroplane to a pre-production standard; so there are a number of interesting features about it: the turn performance; the manoeuvring of it is excellent; and the systems are very modern state-of-the-art which we haven't had a chance to look at on any aeroplane on the course so far.'

The most advanced aircraft previewed by ETPS students was without doubt the F-18 Hornet. The preview was undertaken by Dave Southwood and Harry Fehl. (*Colin Jones*)

Dave Southwood was asked how the US Navy Test Pilot School at Patuxent River differed from ETPS:

'The schools in many ways have a lot of features in common, but the US Navy have a far greater requirement in terms of the number of test pilots for their service, so that the courses here are much larger. [There are] engineers and back seat crew attending the school as well, whereas at Boscombe they train virtually only test pilots and very few flight-test engineers.'

The first Flight Engineers' course at ETPS was in 1974. There was an engineers' course with one or two students in most subsequent years, running concurrently with the pilots' school, but no engineers in 1985.

Although Dave Southwood and Harry Fehl were pleased to be selected to test-fly the F-18 Hornet at Patuxent River, the trip was not without certain drawbacks:

Dave Southwood: 'It is quite hard coming out here, because the amount of information we had on the aeroplane before we left the UK was fairly limited. We did not get most of the information or see the manuals until we arrived on Monday, to start flying on the Wednesday. So we had a lot of work when we first arrived just to get familiar with the basic systems so we could fly the aeroplane. We then had to take an examination on the F-18 systems so we could fly it from the front seat, because many of the necessary controls are not duplicated in the back. It was quite hard work. On all the sorties we run a tape recorder, to put our comments on tape; that takes time to transcribe and, with the planning of the sorties and writing short reports for ourselves after each flight, there is a lot of work to do. Most of the work we do either during the day when we are not flying, or in the evenings and at weekends in the hotel, or come back here [the school briefing room] to work; whenever we can find the time.'

Unlike Boscombe Down, where American students from Patuxent River are put up in the Officers' Mess during their preview visits, the ETPS men are allocated rooms in the Patuxent Inn, just outside the Naval Test Center. That is no hardship for, like most permanent military bases in the United States, at the Test Center there is a swimming pool, a golf course and many other sports facilities available. There is also a Post Exchange – the PX – which is in reality an inexpensive supermarket for servicemen and their families. However, when Bob Horton, working late in his room in the hotel, talked about the amount of work confronting him each evening, it became obvious that none of the ETPS students had had the time for golf, swimming or even to browse among the glittering products of the American Dream available in the PX.

Bob Horton: 'As soon as we get back here each evening, the first thing that we will do is to go through all the data that we have col-

The F-18 Hornet about to begin the preview (*Colin Jones*)

lected from the day's flying, and that consists of analysing things like the data cards that have all the relevant "numbers" on them, and listening to the tapes from the recorder which we plug into the aircraft's intercom system. The trouble is that they record everything that is on the intercom, so we have to go through the whole tape transcribing it so that we can pick the bones out of it. Once we have done that, we can get the bits of data we may have missed on the cards, because you can only write at a certain speed, whereas the tape recorder picks up everything. When we have done all that and gathered all the data together, we have then to analyse it: discuss it together, try to relate what we have found to what it was like actually to fly the aircraft, and then also relate that to how the aircraft could perform in whichever role it has been designed for, or we are testing for. So there is a lot of discussion, analysing, and then of course writing it all up, which is a bit tacky, because it is an interesting thought that we generate an absolute plethora of data from just a single hour of flying. About a month ago at Boscombe Down on the Pilot Assessment exercise, where you go off for an hour and fly a small helicopter you have never flown before to gather as much information as you can on its stability and control performance, and then you have to write it all up: I wrote seventy-five sides of paper after just that one hour of flying. Nowadays, flying can never again be fun: you tend to go out there and as you get into the aircraft you think, "Don't like the cockpit: field of view isn't too hot; controls are a bit heavy", and so you are for ever analysing everything you look at now, from the moment you get into a helicopter: it completely changes your outlook.'

There is little doubt that all the students of the ETPS course would agree with that.

Bob Horton had some interesting observations on the difference between the British and American test pilot schools:

'I think the main difference here is that they seem to be a lot less flexible than they are back at Boscombe Down. There, if you want to change your planned sortie in any way, then it is not too much of a problem: you simply call up on the radio, or change the sortie just before you get airborne. Here at Patuxent River it is a major effort; for instance, if you want to come in and get a rotors-running refuel, that has got to be booked at least a day beforehand, and if you want to change your sortie details, or whatever it is you planned to do, it is a major problem to get it all sorted out. That is a bit frustrating when you are used to operating at Boscombe Down where things tend to be a lot slicker, I would say. They have many more aircraft here, of course, and it is a lot more congested, so that Air Traffic Control is more difficult: you have to listen out, certainly, and keep both eyes looking out of the cockpit all the time; there are an awful lot of aircraft flying around in different directions, and of course different types as well: helicopters and fixed wing.'

That mildly critical view of Patuxent River was balanced by the enthusiastic remarks of Harry Fehl when he landed, at dusk, after his first flight in the F-18: 'Fantastic! Really. It is amazing: the F-18 is a really new generation to what I have flown before: it is like Star Wars almost! It's a great, great machine.'

The three syndicates from ETPS each worked their way through the allocated ten hours, gathering data for the all-important presentation at Boscombe Down. It was not without incident: Dave Southwood had to use an emergency system to lower the undercarriage of his near priceless F-18 on his last sortie. Even Star Wars technology, it seems, is not infallible.

The three weeks allocated for the previews ended on 11 November and the students returned to Boscombe Down. The syndicates in the USA came back in a VC-10 of the RAF's transport fleet on one of its regular scheduled flights from Washington to Brize Norton. Jet-lag or no, the students had just ten days to write their reports for submission to the staff and, additionally, to prepare for the ultimate test: the presentation. In the married quarters behind the base, and the bedrooms of the Officers' Mess, the lights burned late indeed: some all night.

The Principal Tutor of the Fixed Wing course, Vic Lockwood, had the task of evaluating the reports of the two previews for which he had been the supervisor; the beautifully bound and very thick documents lay on his desk.

Vic Lockwood: 'The previews have been over now for ten days and we have just received these submissions on the S-3A Viking and the F-18 Hornet. They are fairly weighty tomes and for ten days' writing there is an awful lot in there. In fact, at this stage, the chaps are moving so quickly even the tutors would find it difficult to produce something of equal quality and volume in the time. I remember my own preview very well. I had many sleepless nights: some people on my course went through the whole final night to complete their report. I remember working through until two in the morning on mine, and I am sure that these men have had to do the same thing. It is now my job, as the principal marker, to read the reports in detail and, from my background experience, compare their findings with what I know about the aeroplanes. The reports are really a thesis on nearly everything they have been taught on the course but it is still part of the learning process and the last chance we, as tutors, get to put in some constructive input before they leave the course. So I mark it and give them my comments. The marking is, however, a two-tier process of grading, to ensure that one of us doesn't cheat and give his own preview team too high a mark. I will mark as primary assessor, give my comments to the syndicate, and then pass the report to another ETPS tutor who will read it to see if I have missed anything technically and also to compare my comments to what he knows himself.'

The reports, being critiques of current operational military aircraft, three of them belonging to the United States Navy, are classified. It is, however, known that they contain up to 100 pages of text supplemented by photographs, many specially taken; line drawings, including detailed representations of entire cockpit layouts, graphs and pages of appendices.

Although the preview reports are classified and cannot therefore be reproduced here, it is possible to give the reader some idea of the work involved. As a guide for the students, there exists a model report (see pages 247–53) of an imaginary preview assessment prepared as an appendix to a Flying Wing paper on report-writing in general, for which permission to reproduce has been granted. It is a preview on a mythical prototype advance trainer, the NGT Mk 1. Although the aircraft is imaginary, the report is similar, although much abbreviated, to the documents submitted to the tutors at the conclusion of the ETPS previews.

THE PRESENTATIONS

It should not be thought that the preview report is the sole basis of the presentation, far from it; as the Principal Tutor, Fixed Wing, Vic Lockwood, explained:

'The presentation will be based on the preview report but of course there is a lot of difference between writing reams of facts and figures and of getting those facts and figures across to a critical audience in the forty minutes that is allowed. It is a different technique, which is why we do a presentation: so that they can see both ends of their art; verbal communication and the written word.'

The presentations were to begin on 25 November and had to be prepared within the ten working days allocated for the preview writing. At that late stage, although it would have been technically possible to fail the course, the presentation would have to have been incredibly bad for that to happen. The presentations were to be delivered, not in the large lecture room in the ground school, but in the cinema in the A&AEE HQ building. This cinema is not used for camp shows but is a secure area for the showing of highly classified films of the testing of secret equipment and systems. The cinema is not large but is ideal for the purpose as it is equipped with slide and overhead projectors and has a small platform. The seats are comfortable but not soporifically so. The audience which attended varied with the presentation billed but all seemed to contain the COs of the three test squadrons at Boscombe Down and representatives from the Royal Aircraft Establishments at Farnborough and Bedford. There were a number of civilians: some undoubtedly 'boffins', to use that delightful wartime name given to scientists; some were 'Men for the Ministry'; others may have been contractors. All the ETPS staff attended the presentations, led by the CO, Wing Commander John Bolton. The senior officer from the A&AEE present was Group Captain Ron Burrows, the Superintendent of Flying and the 'owner' of all the aircraft at Boscombe Down, including the school fleet. Several of the 'Minders', instructors from the OCUs who had assisted with the preview flying, had gathered to see how their aircraft were reported on. All the ETPS students not making frantic last-minute revisions to their own presentations were also there, resplendent in well-pressed No. 1 uniforms which had only been seen on formal visits to industry, drab olive-green flying overalls being the usual dress. The Navy officers, in particular, appeared as if they had just walked out of Gieves in Portsmouth. Some of the overseas students looked quite exotic.

The syndicates had guarded the context of their presentations closely; they knew well enough that the manner of performance was just as important as the content of the programme. There were only two rotary wing presentations: the Chinook and the Black Hawk, and the rivalry between the two was intense. If Bob Horton and Gil Yannai had but known, their test aircraft would soon be the subject of press coverage in such depth that they could hardly have dreamed of at the time of the presentation. As it was, Bob and Gil Yannai had had the *chutzpah* to get the BBC film crew at Patuxent River to shoot a special sequence for the presentation of the Black Hawk. The rival helicopter syndicate, led by Al Howden, may or may not have got wind of the film; nevertheless, shortly before the presentation, they managed to persuade the present writer to let them use a short sequence from the BBC film of the Chinook tests; unfortunately this had been shot with a silent camera and the sound-track was not, at that early stage of the film-making, available. Although less effective, the Chinook film did, to some extent, dilute the impact of the Black Hawk footage. The competition between the two helicopter syndicates remained keen to the very end of the course.

The presentations were all classified 'Restricted' which means, in effect, that the quoting of performance figures is forbidden but permission has been granted to reproduce some of the content. Three of the presentations were filmed for the BBC series: the Chinook at Odiham, the F-4 Phantom at Coningsby and the F-18 Hornet at Patuxent River. The first was the Chinook, introduced by Al Howden.

EMPIRE TEST PILOTS' SCHOOL
STUDENT'S REPORT
on

NGT MK 1

PREVIEW ASSESSMENT

RANK & NAME
FLT LT H J KAY RAF
CAPT K L EMM RNLAF

COURSE No   44

CIRCULATION		
PASSED TO	ON(Date)	ACTIONED(Initials)
~~GROUND TUTOR~~		*(signature)*
SYNDICATE TUTOR	19 Nov	*(signature)*
STUDENT	22 Nov	*(signature)*
PRINCIPAL TUTOR	25 Nov	*(signature)*
OC ETPS	26 Nov	*(signature)*
INFO. GROUND TUTOR		
~~EXERCISE TUTOR~~		
~~SYNDICATE TUTOR~~		

EMPIRE TEST PILOTS' SCHOOL

TUTOR'S REMARKS

This was a very good report, and a good way to end your course. I particularly liked the way in which you brought your operational tasks into the paragraphs on flying qualities. Remember that it is no good getting all the right data and then being unable to put it into the correct context. I agree with your conclusions on the stall, but feel that you were not critical enough of the short period characteristics in configuration Land, as I think that the light damping will present the student with significant problems when landing in turbulence.

Nonetheless, well done; I hope that, in retrospect, you will have enjoyed the preview, and wish you all the best in your future career. *James*

PRINCIPAL TUTOR'S REMARKS

Well done all of you, I enjoyed your report very much indeed. It shows that you are well able to enter the field of test flying, and I wish you well *Vic*

OC'S REMARKS

Yes, a very good report and a fitting reward for all your labours. The very best of luck in your new profession

*This proforma must not be detached from the report.

NGT MK 1

PREVIEW ASSESSMENT

by

FLT LT H J KAY RAF AND CAPT K L EMM RNLAF

SUMMARY

A Preview assessment of the NGT Mk 1 was carried out to determine the
suitability of the aircraft for the advanced trainer role. Ten sorties
were flown to assess the aircraft's handling and performance at low, medium
and high altitudes, at speeds up to 500 KIAS/0.8 IMN. The NGT Mk 1 was
found to be crisp and responsive to fly throughout the envelope tested.
The field of view from the rear cockpit was excellent and would enable the
instructor to maintain a good lookout and to keep the touchdown point in
view at all stages of the approach to land. This was an enhancing feature
of the design. However, there was no unmistakable or timely warning of the
stall in the landing configuration and this might result in student pilots
inadvertently stalling the aircraft in the landing pattern. The stall in
this configuration was marked by a rapid wing drop to about 60° AOB, which
would be liable to cause accidents in student training. The main tailplane
trim switches were awkward to operate and made precise longitudinal
trimming difficult. There was no handhold in the rear cockpit to aid the
pilot during entry and exit; he might be tempted to use the HUD glass or
cockpit coaming to steady himself resulting in damage to these items. A
further 23 unsatisfactory features were identified which should be
improved. The NGT Mk 1 although considered to have good potential was
unacceptable for the advanced trainer role unless the stall warning in the
landing configuration was improved.

NGT MK 1

PREVIEW ASSESSMENT

References:

A   MOD, Defence Standard 00-970, Vol No 1, Issue 2
B   Operating Data Manual (ODM) AP 4105CE (AL 25)
C   Aircraft Servicing Manual NGT Mk 1, AP 4082 Chapter 10 (AL 62)
D   Aircrew Manual NGT Mk 1, AP 101B-1082 (AL 4)
E   ETPS Flying Wing Precis dated May 84

SECTION 1 - INTRODUCTION

1   PURPOSE OF THE TEST Following a Ministry of Defence requirement for an advanced training aircraft, a MOD(PE) test team was tasked to perform a Preview assessment of the NGT Mk 1. The aircraft was assessed to determine its suitability for the advanced trainer mission in temperate climate operations and to establish compliance with the requirements of Reference A. Additionally, the aircraft's performance was to be checked against the manufacturer's performance data in Reference B.

2   AIRCRAFT DESCRIPTION The NGT Mk 1 was a tandem-seat, single engine aircraft with low mounted, moderately swept wings. The aircraft was powered by a non-reheated Nadder Mk 101 Turbofan engine rated at 5000 lbf sea level static thrust. The ailerons and the all-moving tailplane were irreversible and hydraulically powered by 2 independent systems with no manual reversion capability. Artificial feel for the ailerons and the tailplane was provided by springs and the trim systems for these controls were electrically operated. The rudder was reversible with an electrically operated trim tab. The trailing edge flaps were hydraulically powered and could be selected to 3 positions. The aircraft had a retractable, tricycle undercarriage which was hydraulically operated. The brakes were hydraulically operated and incorporated an anti-skid system. Directional control on the ground was by means of differential braking. Other leading particulars and a photograph of the aircraft are presented at Annex A.

1

SECTION 2 - CONDITIONS RELEVANT TO THE TESTS

1   AERODYNAMIC CONDITION AND AIRFRAME HOURS The test aircraft were representative production aircraft in good condition with a standard RAF camouflage external finish. Total airframe hours for each aircraft are presented in Table 1.

TABLE 1 - AIRFRAME HOURS

SERIAL (a)	AIRCRAFT (b)	AIRFRAME HOURS (c)
1	ZZ 100	410
2	ZZ 101	515
3	ZZ 102	491

2   MODIFICATION STATES Aircraft modifications relevant to the test are presented in Table 2.

TABLE 2 - MODIFICATION STATES

SERIAL (a)	MOD No (b)	DESCRIPTION (c)	MODIFICATION INCORPORATED		
			ZZ 100 (d)	ZZ 101 (e)	ZZ 102 (f)
1	135	Fitted u/c operated ailerons stop	Yes	Yes	Yes
2	214	Aileron spring feel revised	No	Yes	Yes
3	235	Cam change to tailplane gearbox	No	No	Yes
4	251	Tail cone assembly conversion	No	No	No

3   WEIGHT AND CENTRE OF GRAVITY (CG) A graph of the change in AUW and CG during flight is shown at Annex B. The maximum CG movement during flight was 0% MAC and the tests were flown at nominal mid CG.

2

4   LIMITATIONS The limitations of Reference D were observed throughout the tests. The following additional limitations were imposed by Local Flying Orders:

a   Normal acceleration limits were +6.5g and -2.5g.

b   Minimum altitude for spin entry was FL 300.

5   WEATHER, TIME AND PLACE Ten sorties were flown from RAF Highfield during the period 29 Oct 84 to 7 Nov 84, as shown at Annex C.

7   TEST CONFIGURATIONS The configurations used during the test are defined in Table 3.

TABLE 3 - TEST CONFIGURATIONS

SERIAL (a)	CONFIGURATION (b)	UNDER-CARRIAGE (c)	FLAPS (d)	AIRBRAKE (e)	THRUST SETTING (f)
1	Cruise (CR)	Up	Up	In	Thrust for Level Flight (TLF)
2	Power Approach (PA)	Down	Full	In	As required
3	Landing (L)	Down	Full	Out	As required
4	Overshoot (OS)	Down	Full	In	Max
5	Glide (GL)	Up	Up	In	Idle
6	Take-off (TO)	Down	Half	In	Max
7	Climb (C)	Up	Up	In	Max

7   INSTRUMENTATION No special instrumentation was installed in the aircraft for the tests. Control stick and rudder deflections were measured on the ground and estimated in flight. Control stick forces were either measured using a handheld force gauge (0-50 lbf range) or estimated. All rudder pedal forces were estimated. A dual-sweep stopwatch was used to time the aircraft's dynamic modes. A clinometer and tape measure were used to measure cockpit field of view. Data were recorded on kneeboard cards and a cockpit voice recorder. All other parameters were taken from standard cockpit instrumentation.

3

8   CONTROL REFERENCE SYSTEM The flight control reference system showing maximum control column and rudder pedal displacements is presented in Table 4. Displacements of the control column were measured at the top of the hand grip and rudder displacements measured at the centre of the rudder pedals.

TABLE 4 - CONTROL REFERENCE SYSTEM

SERIAL (a)	CONTROL (b)	DEFLECTION (c)	UNITS (d)	DATUM (e)
1	Tailplane (column)	96 fwd 160 aft	mm	Controls neutral with zero trim
2	Aileron (column)	130 left 130 right	mm	" "
3	Rudder (pedal)	140 left 140 right	mm	" "
4	Tailplane Trim (switch)	4.6 nose up 3.5 nose down	gauge units	Zero (from tailplane gauge)
5	Aileron Trim (wheel)	78 left 78 right	degrees	Zero (from aileron trim gauge)
6	Rudder Trim (wheel)	45 left 45 right	degrees	Zero (from rudder trim gauge)

9   PILOT EXPERIENCE The experience of each member of the test team is presented in Table 5. Each pilot is designated by a letter which will be used in later sections.

TABLE 5 - PILOT EXPERIENCE

SERIAL (a)	PILOT (b)	TOTAL HOURS (c)	BACKGROUND (d)
1	Flt Lt Kay (Pilot A)	1700	700 hrs ground attack fighters 500 hrs basic instruction
2	Capt Emm (Pilot B)	1550	600 hrs air defence fighters 300 hrs advanced instruction

4

10 PILOT PERCENTILES Relevant percentiles of each pilot, based on the
Anthropometric Survey of 2000 RAF aircrew 1970/71, are presented in Table
6.

TABLE 6 - PILOT PERCENTILES

SERIAL	ITEM	PILOT A		PILOT B	
		DIMS (mm)	PERCENTILE	DIMS (mm)	PERCENTILE
(a)	(b)	(c)	(d)	(e)	(f)
1	Height	1760	40	1784	57
2	Sitting Height	924	34	941	57
3	Thigh Length	592	30	591	28
4	Leg Length	1085	47	1110	66
5	Functional Reach	791	40	836	84
6	Weight (kgs)	71	34	59.5	3

11 HANDLING QUALITIES RATING SCALE (HQR) The Cooper-Harper Handling
Qualities Rating Scale used in this report is shown at Annex D. The
ratings are presented as figures in brackets after the written assessments,
eg (HQR3).

12 VIBRATION ASSESSMENT RATING SCALE The A&AEE Vibration Assessment
Rating Scale used in this report is shown at Annex E. The ratings are
presented as figures in brackets after the written description of the
vibration characteristics, eg (VAR4).

13 AIRCREW MANUAL ILLUSTRATIONS Reference is made in the report to the
cockpit illustrations in Reference D using the convention (7.2) to indicate
Figure 7 item 2, for example.

14 TEST TECHNIQUES The test techniques and procedures used were in
accordance with those contained in Chapter 24 of Reference E.

15 DATA REDUCTION Data reduction was carried out on the Tektronix 4051
using ETPS program WFR-1.

16 FLYING CLOTHING ......

5

B-8

SECTION 3 - TESTS MADE

1 ENTRY AND EXIT

2 COCKPIT ASSESSMENT

3 GROUND HANDLING

4 CONTROL SYSTEM CHARACTERISTICS

5 TAKE-OFF AND CLIMB

6 LONGITUDINAL STABILITY AND CONTROL

7 LATERAL AND DIRECTIONAL STABILITY AND CONTROL

8 STALLING

9 SPINNING

10 MANOEUVRE BOUNDARIES

11 ROLE FLYING

12 APPROACH AND LANDING

13 PERFORMANCE

SECTION 4 - RESULTS, DISCUSSION AND CONCLUSIONS

1 ENTRY AND EXIT Entry to and exit from the NGT Mk 1 was by means of a
portable 4-step platform that included one additional small step for the
rear cockpit. The platform was of all metal construction and had a hand-
rail along the left side. Each step had numerous raised perforations to
allow water drainage and help to prevent the pilot's foot slipping during
use in wet conditions. Climbing the platform was easy for the pilot in
full flying kit.

a FRONT COCKPIT Entry to the front cockpit was easily accomplished
by stepping from the top step of the platform over the canopy rail and
onto the ejection seat cushion, using the windscreen arch as a handhold
to maintain balance while sitting down. Exit from the front cockpit
was easily performed by reversing this process. Entry to and exit from
the cockpit was satisfactory.

b REAR COCKPIT Entry to and exit from the rear cockpit required 2
additional steps to be made, first onto the additional small step on
the metal platform and then onto a small area of non-skid material on
top of the left engine intake. When stepping over the canopy rail, the
rear crew member had to lean forward slightly and there was no suitable

6

B-9

---

handhold to help him retain his balance. The most convenient areas to
hold during entry and exit were either the HUD glass or the flexible
plastic coaming, both of which were fragile. The pilot might use the
HUD glass or coaming to steady himself and this would be liable to
damage them. Lack of a suitable handhold in the rear cockpit was
unsatisfactory and a handhold should be provided.

2 COCKPIT ASSESSMENT

a TRIM SWITCHES Tailplane trimming was controlled by 2 switches
located on the top of the control stick in each cockpit (5.10). A
detailed drawing of these switches is at Annex H. The switches had 3
positions as shown; they were spring-loaded to the central position and
had to be operated together to run the trim motor. To operate the
trim, the pilot had to position his thumb precisely in the middle of
the pair of switches and overcome a high breakout force at an awkward
angle. It was frequently found in flight that only one of the switches
was activated resulting in no trim being applied. This was annoying
and distracted the pilot from other important tasks. A student pilot
would find trimming time consuming and distracting. This would lead to
him flying out of trim and make accurate flying more difficult,
particularly under instrument conditions. The operation of the main
tailplane trim switches was unsatisfactory and should be improved.

b FIELD OF VIEW

(1) The front cockpit FOV ......

(2) The rear cockpit FOV is presented diagrammatically at Annex
J. The forward FOV was unobstructed, down to 20° from the
horizontal which made it possible to see the ground to within
3.0 m of the nose of the aircraft. The rearward FOV was
unobstructed back to 23° from the tail. In flight the FOV from
the rear cockpit allowed a good lookout to be achieved and also
enabled the touchdown point to be kept in sight at all stages of
the approach to land, in all the configurations tested. This was
a valuable characteristic for the advanced training role and was
an enhancing feature of the NGT Mk 1's design.

4 CONTROL SYSTEM CHARACTERISTICS

a Tests of the flight control system mechanical characteristics were
made using an external hydraulic power supply on the ground and the
results confirmed in flight. These results are presented in Table 12
and Annex K.

7

B-10

TABLE 12 - CONTROL SYSTEM CHARACTERISTICS

SERIAL	CONTROL	BREAKOUT PLUS FRICTION (lbf)	BACKLASH (mm)	CENTRING (mm)	CONTROL COORDINATION
(a)	(b)	(c)	(d)	(e)	(f)
1	Tailplane	.75	2	1	3
2	Aileron	1	2	Absolute	2
3	Rudder	5	5	Positive	1

b Control systems oscillations in the longitudinal and lateral axes
were moderately damped during ground tests but these oscillations did
not cause any piloting difficulties in turbulent flight conditions.
The breakout and friction forces were small compared with control
forces when manoeuvring and control feel was good about the trimmed
position. The backlash did not affect the pilot's ability to track
accurately (±2 mil) a 15 ft ground target. The control system
characteristics would enable students to fly the aircraft accurately in
all phases of flight and were satisfactory for the advanced training
role. The flight control system characteristics complied with the
requirements of Reference A, Chapter 604.

8 STALLING

c STRAIGHT STALL - LANDING CONFIGURATION

(1) APPROACH TO THE STALL Three 1g stalls were performed in
configuration (L) with the power set at 80% RPM. The aircraft was
trimmed at 150 KIAS with the tailplane trim set at 2° nose up.
The aircraft weight for each of the 3 stalls was approximately
5000 kg, which gave a CG position of 15% SMC and a predicted V_s of
114 KIAS. The approach to the stalls was started at FL 250 and
using elevator alone the speed was reduced at 1 kt/sec. The
initial rate of descent was 500 ft/min and this reduced progressively to 100 ft/min at 116 KIAS. The deceleration from 150 KIAS
to 116 KIAS was easily controlled by progressive aft movement of
the stick; stick deflection was about 5 mm for a 10 KIAS speed
reduction. The pull forces during the approach to the stall were
small, of the order of 2 lbf at 130 KIAS increasing to 4 lbf at
116 KIAS. The deceleration could be stopped at any point during
the approach to the stall by moving the stick forward to the trim
position at 130 KIAS, and 15 mm forward of the trim position
(2 lbf push) at 116 KIAS. Light buffet was felt at 116 KIAS and

8

B-11

the aircraft became laterally unsteady with uncommanded roll oscillations of ±10° AOB at 1 Hz. At 115 KTAS there was a rapid wing drop to 60° AOB in approximately ⅓ sec accompanied by uncommanded pitch oscillations of ±10° at 1 Hz and moderate buffet. The rate of descent increased to over 4000 ft/min. A student pilot would be unlikely to recognise either the light airframe buffet or the wing rock as warning of the stall. Also, these symptoms occurred only 1-2 kts before the stall itself and with the high workload experienced during the approach to land, the lack of unmistakable and timely warning might allow the student to stall inadvertently. Moreover, the rapid and large wing drop at the stall could have catastrophic effects. The stall warning of the NGT Mk 1 in the landing configuration was unacceptable and must be improved before the aircraft is released to service. The stall warning did not comply with Reference A, Chapter 603, paragraph 3.3 in that there was no unmistakable and timely warning to the pilot of the approach to the stall.

(2) THE STALL The stall was defined as the rapid wing drop to about 60° AOB which occurred at 115 kts ......

(3) THE RECOVERY ......

SECTION 5 – RECOMMENDATIONS

1   The NGT Mk 1 was unacceptable for the advanced trainer mission unless the following essential recommendations are incorporated prior to release to service:

   a   ESSENTIAL

      (1) The stall warning in the landing configuration must be improved (Section 4, paragraph 8c(1)).

      (2) ......

2   The following recommendations should be implemented prior to release to service:

   a   HIGHLY DESIRABLE

      (1) The operation of the main tailplane trim switches should be improved (Section 4, paragraph 2a).

      (2) ......

9

B-12

---

   b   DESIRABLE

      (1) A suitable handhold should be provided in the rear cockpit to aid entry and exit (Section 4, paragraph 1b).

      (2) ......

3   The following further tests are recommended prior to release to service:

   a   ......

4   The following amendments should be incorporated in the Aircrew Manual (Reference D):

   a   Part 3, Chapter 2, new paragraph 7d:

      "Airbrake. Low speed handling characteristics with the airbrake extended are little different from those of a clean aircraft except that the buffet level is increased and tends to mask the buffet as speed is decreased towards the stall."

H J Kay   K L Emm

H J KAY   K L EMM
Flt Lt RAF   Capt RNLAF

ETPS
25 Nov 65

Annexes:

A   Rear Cockpit Field of View
B   Rates of Roll
C   Variation of Centre of Gravity with Fuel Usage

10

B-13

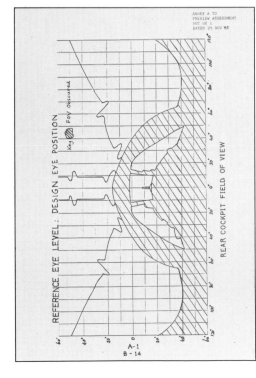

A-1
B-14

RATES OF ROLL

The rates of roll shown in Table 1 were measured at FL 50 using full aileron deflection.

TABLE 1 – RATES OF ROLL

SERIAL	LOAD NO/CONFIGURATION	AIRSPEED (KIAS)	TIME THROUGH 90° BANK (sec)		
(a)	(b)	(c)	1g (d)	2g (e)	4g (f)
1	1/CR	420	1.0	1.0	1.1
2	1/CR	350	1.0	1.1	1.3
3	1/CR	250	1.5	1.4	–
4	2/GA	400	1.0	1.1	1.2
5	2/GA	350	1.0	1.0	1.2
			TIME THROUGH 30° BANK (sec)		
6	1/PA	150	0.9		
7	1/PA	150	1.2		

(Author's Note: This data would have been better displayed in a graphical format with specification data included. The reader would then have been able to see roll rate trends and compare roll performance directly with the specifications.)

B-1

B-15

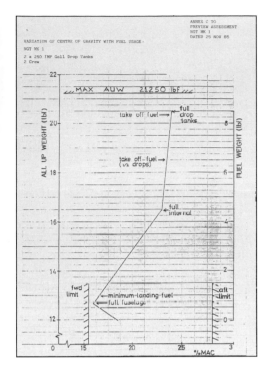

VARIATION OF CENTRE OF GRAVITY WITH FUEL USAGE -
NGT MK 1

2 x 250 IMP Gall Drop Tanks
2 Crew

MAX AUW 21250 lbf

take off fuel → full drop tanks

take off fuel → (½ drops)

← full internal

fwd limit

← minimum landing fuel full fuselage

aft limit

ALL UP WEIGHT (lbf)

FUEL WEIGHT (lbf)

%MAC

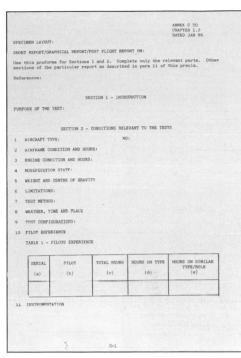

SPECIMEN LAYOUT:

SHORT REPORT/GRAPHICAL REPORT/POST FLIGHT REPORT ON:

Use this proforma for Sections 1 and 2. Complete only the relevant parts. Other
sections of the particular report as described in para 11 of this precis.

References:

SECTION 1 - INTRODUCTION

PURPOSE OF THE TEST:

SECTION 2 - CONDITIONS RELEVANT TO THE TESTS

1   AIRCRAFT TYPE: NO:

2   AIRFRAME CONDITION AND HOURS:

3   ENGINE CONDITION AND HOURS:

4   MODIFICATION STATE:

5   WEIGHT AND CENTRE OF GRAVITY

6   LIMITATIONS:

7   TEST METHOD:

8   WEATHER, TIME AND PLACE

9   TEST CONFIGURATIONS:

10 PILOT EXPERIENCE

TABLE 1 - PILOTS EXPERIENCE

SERIAL (a)	PILOT (b)	TOTAL HOURS (c)	HOURS ON TYPE (d)	HOURS ON SIMILAR TYPE/ROLE (e)

11 INSTRUMENTATION

C-1

SECTION 3 - RESULTS, DISCUSSION AND CONCLUSIONS

1   For the short report, write this section as in the full report. For the
graphical and post flight reports the content should be as described in paras 11c
and d of this precis.

SECTION 4   RECOMMENDATIONS

1   For the short report write this section as in the full report. In both the
graphical and post flight reports the content will vary.

Date   Signature Block

Annexes:

A
B

C-2

The Chinook Presentation

Al Howden: 'Good morning, gentlemen, welcome to our preview presentation on the Chinook helicopter. For those of you who do not know me, my name is Lieutenant Alan Howden. May I introduce to you Captain J. T. Koh of the Republic of Singapore Air Force and Captain Randy ['Mike'] Meiklejohn of the Canadian Armed Forces. For our preview exercise we were tasked with assessing the Chinook against specification. In order to assess the aircraft we were granted ten flying hours on the Chinook at RAF Odiham, and we flew the aircraft throughout its flight envelope from minimum to maximum all-up weight [AUW] and from central to fully aft C of G. The majority of the assessment was conducted with the aircraft's AFCS [Automatic Flight Control Systems] selected "on". A limited assessment was carried out

Al Howden and 'JT' begin their preview presentation on the Chinook; the last exercise of the ETPS course and, in effect, the Finals (*B. Johnson*)

with the aircraft's AFCS selected "off". [The AFCS smooths out the pilot's input and stabilises the aircraft by superimposing computer-generated signals on top of the pilot's, making the aircraft easier to fly.] In addition to the handling test, we flew instrument and night flying, and assessed the aircraft during tactical low-level operating, which included load lifting and [operations from] confined areas. Throughout the presentation we will concentrate on enhancing features of the design and on the unacceptable and major unsatisfactory items that we identified during the preview. Finally, we will conclude our presentation by outlining the main areas where the aircraft failed to meet the specification, and detail what further testing and manufacturer's advice is required. The presentation will last for forty minutes and is classified Restricted.'

The presentation went smoothly with the BBC film appearing on cue; the graphs and tables of performance figures were well presented. All three of the syndicate spoke, each handling a separate section of the preview. At the end of the presentation, the audience applauded and the meeting was then open to questions of a highly technical nature. After this the ETPS CO, Wing Commander John Bolton, congratulated the trio: 'A thorough investigation and a very, very good presentation. For you the course is over. Well done.' After the audience had left the cinema, the Principal Tutor, Rotary Wing, Lieutenant Commander Mike Swales RN, and the Rotary Wing tutor, Squadron Leader Iain Young (the tutor responsible for the Chinook preview), informally discussed the Chinook presentation they had just attended.

Iain Young: 'Overall it was a very good presentation. They displayed a good feeling for the aircraft, and the content and depth of knowledge shown in their written report came across very well, I thought. Timing was spot on, Mike, at forty minutes.'

Mike Swales: 'Excellent, yes.'

Iain Young: 'So for that they get an excellent mark. The visual aids. What did you think of the visual aids?'

Mike Swales: 'The slides were very good, and gave a good feel for the operation of the aircraft. My only area of concern, I think, was the use of the [BBC] film clip. That could have been relevant if it was talked over but it seemed that it was something that was just put in as an afterthought. The audience were left watching without any sound for about a minute, without any comment from the team at all.'

Iain Young: 'The content and understanding of the subject? I thought it came across quite well.'

Mike Swales: 'It certainly reflected their report and assured me anyway that they had a really good understanding of the aircraft and how it operated. Whether they actually chose the right things

The large audience is composed of ETPS staff and the COs of the Trials Squadrons at Boscombe Down, Farnborough and Bedford, in addition to men from the Ministry (*B. Johnson*)

to present is a subject of discussion but generally speaking they gave the whole audience a good feel for the aircraft, and from the applause at the end I think it was certainly well received in that respect.'

Iain Young: 'Yes, they had a good understanding of this difficult and complicated machine, didn't they? So, they get a good mark I think. The presentation?'

Mike Swales: 'Extremely well prepared, and they had obviously rehearsed several times: a slick presentation indeed and nicely divided up between the three members [of the syndicate]. All spoke with good, clear voices. Very good.'

Iain Young: 'Certainly came across well. So it is a good presentation mark. The question handling was very good. They were quite forceful; they understood the questions, which reinforces my opinion that they all understood the subject. Overall they get a very good mark. Well done, team.'

Mike Swales: 'I am delighted with the Chinook presentation that we have seen this morning. It reinforces our views I think, Iain, on exactly how much hard work they have put in throughout the year. It was a very, very professional presentation we have seen. A good report too, and they are well fitted now to go out into the world of test flying for their respective services.'

The Phantom Presentation

The next presentation which was filmed for the BBC series was that relating to the F-4 Phantom FGR 2. 'FGR' stands for Fighter, Ground Attack and Reconnaissance: truly a multi-role aircraft. The preview was conducted at RAF Coningsby. The two-man

syndicate about to offer their presentation represented two-thirds
of the team which had had a less than resounding success with the
earlier mini-presentation on the low-level sortie: Les Evans and his
French colleague, Serge Aubert. Les Evans described that occasion as 'a bit of a shambles' and added that Serge and he were fer-
vently hoping for better notices on this, far more important,
performance. The two young pilots had had a dress rehearsal in the
A&AEE HQ building cinema that morning and were now waiting,
with some anxiety, to start their presentation, as the knowledge-
able audience, including a lady 'boffin', filed slowly in. When the
senior officer, Group Captain Ron Burrows, arrived and was
seated, the meeting was opened formally by the ETPS CO, John
Bolton. Les Evans, exactly on time, stepped up to the rather
pleasantly carved wood lectern and addressed the august
gathering:

'Good morning, sir, lady and gentlemen. Following the Ministry of Defence requirement for a new Air Defence aircraft, a team
from the A&AEE, Boscombe Down, was tasked to perform a preview assessment of the Phantom FGR Mk 2. The team comprised
Commandant Serge Aubert, of the French Air Force, and myself,
Squadron Leader Les Evans. We were to assess the aircraft for its
suitability as an all-weather Air Defence aircraft, as an interceptor
and as an air superiority fighter. It is required to be capable of
worldwide operation by day and night; additionally, it should be
able to complete successfully a mission profile laid down by the
Ministry of Defence. During this presentation, which is classified

Les Evans begins his F-4
presentation. His
syndicate colleague was
Serge Aubert.
(*B. Johnson*)

Restricted, we will look at the performance of the aircraft and of its weapons systems. We will then discuss the aircraft's handling characteristics, followed by brief comments on the cockpit environment. I shall summarise our findings before inviting questions from the floor. Due to the brevity of the presentation, only the most desirable recommendations of the team will be presented. First thing, however, I will give a brief description of the aircraft. The FGR Mk 2 descended from the F-4B which was a carrier-based all-weather fighter for the US Navy and Marine Corps. The low-mounted mainplane had 12 degrees of dihedral at the wing tips, and incorporated leading and trailing edge flaps. Lateral control was provided by ailerons and spoilers and longitudinal control was by an "all moving" tailplane with 25 degrees of anhedral. The aircraft was powered by two Rolls-Royce Spey Mk 202 turbofan engines, developing approximately 12,000 lbs of thrust each in military power, and approximately 25,000 lbs thrust in full reheat.'

Les Evans then outlined the test programme and the techniques used to implement them. He then went on to discuss the figures, which are classified, as are the details of the weapon and radar fit presented by Serge Aubert. The team had taken advantage of a computer which had become available to the ground school, to make computer-generated graphics which were used throughout the presentation to illustrate a number of technical points, including the last part, in which Les Evans proposed to:

'. . . discuss the cockpit field of view and to summarise the presentation. The field of view from the front cockpit was measured on the ground and assessed in the air, both in close formation and in combat. This slide shows the horizontal plane field of view at the pilot's eye level. In the front sector, the front windscreen support, the angle of attack gauge took up prime space and arcs of 6-degrees width to the left and 10-degrees width to the right were obscured. Forty-degree cone to the rear was also obscured. The field of view directly forward was limited to 15 degrees below the horizon, whilst the view to the side was limited to 30 degrees below the horizon. The field of view from the navigator's position was similar to the rear and much worse forwards. In combat, the field of view was found to be very restricting and the large obscured area significantly reduced the look-out potential of the crew. This would make the aircraft vulnerable to a surprise attack and confer a serious disadvantage in close combat. The fields of view from both cockpits were unsatisfactory in an Air Defence fighter and should be improved. In summary, the Phantom FGR 2's good missile load, capable radar system, good endurance and rapid low-level subsonic acceleration made it acceptable for the Air Defence interceptor and Air Superiority roles. However, some serious . . . defi-

ciencies would significantly limit the aircraft's capabilities against the most modern Warsaw Pact fighter aircraft . . . that concludes our presentation. I will now invite questions from the floor which I would ask you to direct through me.'

Les Evans, Serge Aubert and Al Howden, their presentations over, join the audience for that given by Dave Southwood and Harry Fehl (*B. Johnson*)

There then followed a vigorous interrogation of a most arcane nature. At the conclusion of the questioning, the CO, Wing Commander John Bolton, closed the proceeding with a most complimentary summary in which he said:

'It is the first time I have seen computer-aided viewgraphs. I congratulate you on these. I also congratulate you on a very good presentation which was well balanced and told us a lot about the aeroplane. I would like to take the opportunity to thank all the course members for the effort put into these presentations. It is possible that they seem to be the last straw at the end of the course, but I thank you for the work that you have done, the effort that was put in and the standard of your presentations. Thank you very much and special thanks to today's team. Well done.'

The audience applauded and drifted out of the cinema. The syndicate was congratulated by a number of the tutors present and the opportunity to film their reaction to Les and Serge's efforts was taken by the BBC:

'What did you think of the show, Tim?'

Tim Allen (the preview tutor): 'I thought it was very good. Excellent use of viewgraphs. It is a very complicated subject and what they did was to manage to get the main things over at a reasonable pace during the presentation. The only thing I query about it was the order in which they did some of it but that is only a minor complaint. In the questioning they were able to show that they had got all the other points squared away well. Overall it came over very well indeed.'

Colin Wilcock: 'I thought they presented a balanced view of the aeroplane; to my mind they picked out the major problem areas of it. They appeared capable in the questioning and answering: overall I thought it a well-rounded preview.'

Perhaps the most telling accolade came from the hard-bitten 'minders'; the Coningsby OCU instructors, Jack Dowling and Flight Lieutenant Grant Taylor, who had no connection with ETPS other than flying in the back seat of the Phantom during the preview. As anyone who has ever taken a single flying lesson will confirm, instructors tend to find the glass half-empty rather than half-full.

Jack Dowling: 'It was very good. They must have put a lot of work into it . . . I was quite impressed with what they had picked up in the short time they were with us.'

Grant Taylor: 'They came up with terms while we were flying which I just could not believe, like "tight-closed loops" and things like that, which I now understand what they mean. They certainly picked up a lot more very, very quickly, than people who have been flying [the Phantom] for 1000 hours. I was quite surprised.'

'It rather justifies the course?'

Jack Dowling: 'I certainly think it does; their experience showed through.'

'How do you feel about it all, now that it is over, Les?'

Les Evans: 'Very relieved! It is a tremendous feeling to have finished the course and got it all behind us: it has been hard work but very rewarding.'

'How do you feel, Serge?'

Serge Aubert: 'I feel *heureux*!'

The F-4 Phantom preview was the last of the seven. The two accounts given are representative. Since all the presentations were, quite properly, subject to restrictions on grounds of security, there is little point in recounting the limited areas available; the object of the accounts above is to give the reader the feel of the presentations, rather than a detailed record of the proceedings. It can be said that in all seven cases, including the F-18, the preview syndicates recommended a number of improvements to the aircraft as tested. When one considers that all the aircraft were advanced contemporary operational types, none of which had been flown by the students prior to the previews, the depth and quality of the final presentations are a tribute to the staff and students of the Empire Test Pilots' School at Boscombe Down.

The Presentations marked the end of No. 44 Fixed, and No. 23 Rotary Wing courses. All the students had passed, not that there was anything remarkable about that, as James Giles pointed out:

'On the test pilot course which we run here, we are not looking at a man in terms of success or failure; our job is to teach him. If he cannot reach the standard of safety in the air and his credibility as a test pilot, then we would not pass him, but the issue is not by any means clear-cut. It is not a "pass" or "fail" in the classic sense of the words: historically, since I have been here, everyone has passed; that is, they reached the required standard. However, the selection procedure is such that the requirements we have virtually ensure that they should meet the standards.'

Although the selection of the students is such that their ultimate passing of the course is probable, it is not and can never be certain; for one thing none of the students interviewed by the BBC for the television series had thought that the course would be as unremittingly arduous as it in fact was.

Harry Fehl: 'I was at Manching [the German test establishment] before I came to ETPS, and I met a lot of test pilots there who had graduated from Boscombe Down. They told me, "It is going to be a lot of work, sleepless nights": you know, they didn't tell me half the truth; this has been an awful lot of work, and even if you go to bed early you can't stop your brain working. . . it takes a long time before you fall asleep [then] I dream in English! I have been to university, staff college, everything, but there is nothing to compare with it. If I am going to work this hard again I have to get a lot of money to do it!'

Dave Southwood: 'It has undoubtedly been the hardest working year that I have ever had. I have done more work this year than I did in three years at university. Everybody said when we started the course that it would be a very hard-working year and that you would sit there working until one, two o'clock in the morning. I didn't really think that it would be possible to work those sort of hours and get up and do a normal working day; from that point of view I have learned a lot about myself.'

'As an experienced fighter pilot, did you feel that the variation in the aircraft you flew on the course, the helicopters and heavy aircraft was of use?'

Dave Southwood: 'Excellent, excellent. That was one of the really big bonuses: I have flown nineteen types on the course, and done about 170 hours. There is nowhere else you could get that sort of flying experience other than the test pilots' school: it has been outstanding.'

'What is the role of the students' wives?'

Dave Southwood: 'To be very understanding. It is a hard year for the wives in many ways because although, on paper, we come to work at eight-thirty in the morning and are normally back at home at six in the evening, you get home and then work until midnight or later with a quick half-hour break for dinner. I just had to work all through the weekends as well, so it is a very difficult year.'

For those students with small children it was even more difficult, as Jim Ludford rather poignantly remarked:

'We [the pilots] soon slot into this way of life. You work all day, go home and eat, then work all evening. I think it is worse for the wife and kids because suddenly Dad is not around to go and play football and that sort of thing and there is not much else for them to do. It has been extremely hard work; a lot of good stuff, but I would never do a course like this again.'

Serge Aubert confessed, like all the others, that the course had been far harder than he had imagined, even though he, too, had spoken to test pilots in France who had been ETPS graduates. Mme Aubert did not speak English, Serge said, adding that she had made a good friend in Carla, Mirco's wife, but she had returned to a new job in Italy at the beginning of September so Mme Aubert was alone in the married quarters with one small son, and another attending a local school (where he rapidly picked up English with a Wiltshire accent) and Serge at work all day.

Although all the students selected for the course were above average pilots with their squadrons, most confessed to some doubt about their abilities, at least in the early days. Al Howden, Royal Navy helicopter pilot, certainly did:

'I arrived at Boscombe Down with a little apprehension about doing the job of a test pilot and I have certainly got enough confidence now to go ahead and give it a go. I think the course improves your flying abilities and your overall aviation ability by increasing your background knowledge.'

The most positive statement on the workload at ETPS came from the Falklands veteran, Bob Horton:

'I can safely say I am never going to work this hard again, because if I do I shall die!' Bob Horton, like the others, now knew where he was to be posted as a test pilot:

'Yes, they held what they call a Disposal Board here last week, and I have been disposed to the Royal Aircraft Establishment at Bedford. There is a lot of work going on there; among other things they are doing active control links, whereby they take out all the mechanical control runs and put in 'fly-by-wire' controls. There is a Wessex helicopter there with what they call a glass cockpit, which is a lot of cathode-ray tubes replacing all the old analogue instruments. There is still a lot of learning to do even when I get there: you are on the bottom rung when you leave here.'

Al Howden, the other Royal Navy helicopter pilot, was to join 'D' Squadron, just a few hundred yards from the ETPS hangar at Boscombe Down, to test fly helicopters for the A&AEE.

Robin Tydeman, too, was to stay at Boscombe Down to work with 'B' Squadron, the unit charged with the testing of multi-engined aircraft. He was to be a member of a team evaluating the RAF's newly acquired Trident Tanker/Transport.

Jim Ludford, the Harrier pilot, was joining 'A' Squadron to test fly developments on the Harrier GR5 and a Sea Harrier. There was a Buccaneer on the test squadron as well which he was hoping to fly, since he previewed the type at Lossiemouth. Dave Southwood, too, was destined for the fighter test squadron at Boscombe Down. Les Evans, on the other hand, like Bob Horton, was undertaking a tour with the RAE at Bedford.

The overseas students would all be going to their national test centres; the Canadian, 'Mike' Meiklejohn, to the one appropriately named Cold Lake.

The students from the UK have to sign an undertaking that they will serve as test pilots for at least thee years from the completion of the course. The reason is partly because of the cost of the training at ETPS but, as John Farley revealed, there is another (be it whispered) unworthy reason, due to the very quality of the ETPS course:

'The value of the education that a pilot is going to get at the Empire Test Pilots' School, as far as aircraft manufacturers are concerned, is invaluable: you cannot put a price on it. The opportunity that he has, not only to learn the theoretical and practical skills of his trade, but to fly many different types of aeroplane, to broaden his experience as a pilot, let alone to become an "under training" test pilot, is immeasurable . . . and only in very special circumstances would you, as a manufacturer, choose a pilot to join a test flying team who had not been to the Empire Test Pilots' School. There are always exceptions, of course, to all rules, and the reasons for the exceptions are quite straightforward. It may be just the man's particular background, especially in the military role, that the aircraft which you are designing and building is going to be used for; if there is a man who has great experience in that role you may well have him along as an adviser in respect of the operational matters, as opposed to the test flying matters. If, as time goes by, you find he can read and write well and can express himself, and turns out to be a good stick and rudder man, he may very sensibly be integrated into the team. But in general the nucleus of the manufacturer's test piloting team must be drawn from the Empire Test Pilots' School.'

The McKenna Dinner

Although the previews and the subsequent presentations are, in a sense, the finals of the course, they are not the culmination. That

Part of the formal official photograph of the McKenna dinner given to 'dine out' Course No. 44/23 in the Officers' Mess, Boscombe Down (*MoD (PE)/A&AEE*)

palm must go to the formal McKenna dinner held in the Officers' Mess at Boscombe Down. The building dates from the 1920s and forms a physical link with the wartime years and the founding of the course. The event is not only the dinner itself, for it is also the occasion for the presentation of the several awards that are annually competed for and, to the victor ludorum, the McKenna Trophy itself which can be awarded to any student on the course, from either the fixed or rotary wings. Officially the Trophy is presented to 'the most outstanding student of each course' but that requires qualification.

'James Giles: 'The McKenna winner isn't necessarily the man who is going to be Chief Test Pilot of the Air Force; it is very much of that year. I don't think that the students actually have the time consciously to think about it, they are too busy competing with themselves, just trying to keep on top of the work. The McKenna salutes the man who has done very well and come out on the top of the course overall, and we find that he is a worthy winner, and normally the other students say, "Yes. He is the man who should get it".'

In addition to the premier award, there are other trophies: the Patuxent Shield, awarded to the Fixed Wing runner-up to the McKenna winner; the Westland Trophy, for the Rotary Wing runner-up to the McKenna winner; the Edwards Award, for the student who most impresses the ETPS staff by his attitude and performance during the course; the Hawker Hunter Trophy, awarded to the syndicate which produces the best preview presentation; the Sir Alan Cobham Award, for the student who has consistently demonstrated the highest standards of flying in all the exercises of the course.

All these awards and the coveted diplomas, which testify that the recipient is a graduate of the ETPS school, are presented at the McKenna dinner, held annually at the conclusion of the courses.

Thursday 5 December 1985 was an exceedingly wet day. The weather was so bad that there was no flying from Boscombe Down. The rain lashed across the empty hardstandings and all the ETPS aircraft were in their hangars. For one member of the staff the day was to be the culmination of a great deal of hard work: Squadron Leader Mike Butt, the Rotary Wing QFI, was the project officer for the McKenna dinner. For months Mike Butt had been responsible for the organisation of the dinner; 125 guests had to be invited and all the myriad details of the evening to be arranged, from the wine list to the seating plan. There was a slight problem with the guest list: the air attachés of all of the overseas students graduating from the course are always invited. The Republic of Singapore did not have an Air Attaché in London so the First Secretary was invited, who turned out to be a lady: Madam Violet Loo. Now it is a tradition of the McKenna dinner that it is strictly a stag occasion and this gave rise to a difficult problem of protocol. Since the first McKenna dinner, held in 1945, the ladies, or more specifically the wives of students and staff, have been excluded with, one might add, growing and vocal opposition as the tide of feminism gathered strength. The alternative dinner for the wives, held elsewhere on the same night, did little to assuage their feelings but the ramparts of male chauvinism held until 1983 when a civilian A&AEE Flight Test Engineer, Mrs Valerie Shaw, graduated from No. 10 Flight Engineers' course and had to be admitted to the dinner as of right. (It is said that her husband insisted on *his* right to attend the all-female soirée of that year: no details of his evening are available.) As with the Law, precedent is everything and it was decided that the First Secretary of the Republic of Singapore would be accorded the status which protocol demanded, female or no. Thus the final guest list numbered 124 gentlemen and one lady.

The large dining room of the Officers' Mess at Boscombe Down was ready for the dinner. Mike Butt had every reason to be pleased with his work, for he and Mr Roberts, the Mess Manager, had created a setting worthy of the occasion. As the guests filed in from the ante-room, the RAF Salon Orchestra softly played. The long top table, and the others arranged in rows at right angles to it, were lit by dozens of candles in silver candlesticks; the candlelight was reflected by the gleaming cutlery and the spotless white napery. On the top table the trophies shone as they awaited the final ceremonies.

All the military guests were, of course, attired in mess kit. Nearly all had pilot's wings, some miniature decorations; a few of the young men wore recent decorations from the Falklands; some of the older officers, retired and heavy in years and rank, displayed the campaign medals and DFCs and DSOs of the Second World War, awarded when they were young men forty-five years ago.

There is a certain timeless aura about a formal dinner in a British Officers' Mess: only the large framed pictures of the monarch seem to change, every sixty years or so. The mess kit worn by the officers of the British Armed Forces owes nothing to fashion or style; like the mess itself, it is frozen in a time warp. The faultless place settings, the male company, the squadrons' silver, the badges, armorial shields, traditions, etiquette, the discreet servants; all have a timeless sense of order and continuity: Boscombe Down in 1985 could have been the mess of one of the many RAF outposts of the vanished Empire beyond the seas, at any time from 1920. It is a fact that nearly all RAF messes in Britain are built to exactly the same plan: once you know your way around one of them, you know them all, which clearly aids visiting aircrews. (It is not known if that, or economy, was the true reason for the conformity.)

The dinner got under way. At each candlelit table the conversation and the wine flowed. On the top table was the guest of honour: Admiral Sir Raymond Lygo, Managing Director, British Aerospace, who within a fortnight of the dinner was to become a reluctant public figure as the Westland affair unfolded. Another exalted guest was Air Chief Marshal Sir John Rodgers, Controller Air. From Patuxent River came Rear Admiral Jack Ready USN, the Commandant of the Navy Test Center. There were many distinguished airmen present, most of whom were graduates of the school; some had risen to the top of their profession, either within the services or in industry, which too had representatives present; and of course the only lady, Madam First Secretary Loo.

At the appropriate time Wing Commander John Bolton, the School OC, would rise to begin the speeches and the presentations. It might, at this juncture, be pointed out that, with one exception, none of the recipients of the various trophies knew they had won. The exception was the winner of the McKenna itself; by tradition he is told just before the dinner that he has won, because he is required to make a speech. He is, however, sworn to secrecy so all the remaining students know individually that they cannot be the winner, without any of them knowing who is.

Group Captain Ron Burrows, the A&AEE Superintendent of Flying, rose to speak:

'Mr President, Admiral Lygo, Air Marshal Rodgers, Commandant, distinguished guests, lady and gentlemen. Since 1945 the McKenna dinner has been held annually to celebrate the metamorphosis of the graduating course into fully fledged test pilots, and to present trophies to those who appear to have performed the wriggling act best. Over the years it has also become a pilgrimage for the converted, and a festival at which the most distinguished personalities in the profession of aviation may be seen from time to time, incorporating the spirit of what used to be the Industry dinner . . . Our guest of honour this evening is Admiral Sir Raymond Lygo who, during his professional life, rose from messenger boy on the staff of *The Times* to Vice Chief of Naval Staff and a period as First Sea Lord. In his time he has also been a fighter pilot, helicopter pilot, Squadron Commander . . .'

The Group Captain paid tribute to several senior officers departing from A&AEE, including the Commandant, Air Commodore Graham Williams. He then congratulated the graduating course,

The McKenna under way; Les Evans seems pleased that the training is over at last (*BBC*)

adding, 'It has been a pleasure to have such a lively group at Boscombe Down, and I wish you all a successful and happy future.'

Wing Commander John Bolton, the ETPS 'Boss', then spoke:

'Thank you, sir, lady and gentlemen. As Boss of this school I must ensure that I am properly dressed for the occasion . . . Mr Roberts, the "titfer", please.'

The 'titfer' referred to is a battered mortar-board academic's cap, which would be familiar to anyone in Britain who has attended grammar school or university. The hat duly donned, the 'Boss' continued:

'The titfer was presented to the school for use on such occasions by Air Marshal Sir Ralph Sorley in 1944. Sir Ralph was a distinguished test pilot in the 'twenties and 'thirties, and a previous Commandant of this establishment [see Chapters 1 and 2] . . . Tonight we graduate ten fixed wing, and five rotary wing test pilots. As you have heard, they have been a well-motivated bunch and were well-led by their senior student, Squadron Leader Robin Tydeman. It has been a pleasure to have them here. Amongst the group we have our first graduate from Singapore and, for the first time since 1945, we have a New Zealander on the course. Having listened to him, after a party, extolling the virtues of early aerodynamic research supposedly performed in Maori wind tunnels, I think it might be another forty-two years before we accept another one. Now the Americans are renowned for being laid-back. How is this for a cool test pilot?

The 'Boss', Wg Cdr John Bolton begins the after dinner speeches by donning the 'titfer'; a tradition which dates from 1944. To his right is the guest of honour, Admiral Sir Raymond Lygo. (*BBC*)

'Tom Koelzer came to me during the spinning phase of the course, in all seriousness, and said, "Boss, if the weather is bad tomorrow and I can't do that spinning trip, I am going to get married." It was and he did! . . . The graduates this year have achieved between 120 and 140 flying hours during the course. There is, however, one exception: Flight Lieutenant Dave Southwood, who is never out of his flying suit, and he has flown, would you believe, 173 hours in nineteen types. We were lucky again this year to be able to continue our exchange preview with Patuxent River. Six of our students went to America . . . we in turn provided previews for six US Navy students on the Jaguar, the Puma, the Lynx, the Hawk and the Gazelle. This arrangement with our sister school is working well. Customers at home and abroad [will] find that we maintained our high standards of graduate this year and they will, as our final preview exercise shows, be getting skilled and mature test pilots who can be trusted to do a professional job with complete responsibility. I ask you, sir, to honour the school by presenting the graduation certificates.'

Admiral Sir Raymond Lygo then presented the certificates, in strict alphabetical order, beginning with Commandant Serge Aubert and ending with Major Mirco Zuliani. After this, the first of the trophies was awarded:

'Next, the Edwards Award presented by the United States Air Force Test Center at Edwards Air Force Base, to the student who has most impressed the staff by his application and attitude and performance throughout the course. This evening we are very pleased to welcome Brigadier General Williams, Inspector General US Air Force Systems Command, who will present the award to Captain Randy Meiklejohn, the Canadian Armed Forces.'

The following award, the Patuxent Shield, went to Squadron Leader Les Evans as the runner-up to the McKenna. The shield was presented by Rear Admiral Ready USN.

Bob Horton took the Westland Trophy, awarded to the rotary wing runner-up to the McKenna; the Hawker Hunter Trophy for the best preview syndicate went to Les Evans and Serge Aubert which, in view of the 'shambles', as Les described their early preview exercise, must have given them great satisfaction. The Sir Alan Cobham Trophy for the fixed wing student who had demonstrated the highest standard of flying during the course was awarded to Dave Southwood and this left the premier trophy.

John Bolton: 'Finally, the McKenna Trophy which perpetuates the memory of Group Captain McKenna, the second Commandant of ETPS, who was killed in a flying accident while serving in that post. The Trophy is awarded to the best all-round student. I ask our Guest of Honour, Admiral Sir Raymond Lygo, to present this coveted award to Flight Lieutenant Dave Southwood, Royal Air Force.'

Dave Southwood accepted the Trophy to prolonged applause and made the short speech which tradition required. He began, 'I considered telling the normal jokes but at such a cosmopolitan function as this, the usual subjects of race, religion, politics and sex would doubtless have offended someone, and any jokes not involving such subjects would have offended the ETPS staff as they wouldn't have understood them.' The speech ended with references to the idiosyncrasies of the tutors. Toasts were drunk and the Guest of Honour told a long story about a well-known naval test pilot, 'Winkle' Brown, involving his attempt to smuggle from Gibraltar into Britain some illicit petrol at a time of rationing, only to find when he landed his Fury fighter, with the fuel in its drop tanks, that petrol rationing had ended.

The awards presented, the speeches made and the toasts drunk, the McKenna dinner of 1985 ended. So had the two courses: No. 23 Rotary and No. 44 Fixed Wing. In the ante-room the drinking would go on far into the night; there would be the usual mess games. The three trophies that are in the form of cups, including the revered McKenna, were filled with champagne – well, they are cups! and passed round the guests. The games became wilder and the chatter more animated. Harry Fehl's father was telling everyone that the last time he had seen London was from the cockpit of a Ju88; nobody knew if he was joking or not. Bob Horton, drinking from his Westland Trophy, was informing a senior manager of that troubled company what he thought of the helicopters they produced. There were many old friends meeting again for the first time in years; nearly all were test pilots or ex-test pilots: graduates of ETPS, Patuxent River, Edwards or the French school. They were from many nations: test flying is a small world, an exclusive international club. The young men of the graduating course were about to join; already they had, during the shared joys and sorrows of the past ten months, formed friendships which would endure: Harry Fehl had invited Gil Yannai, the student from Israel, to spend his end-of-course leave with him and his wife in Germany; Gil had accepted. Other similar invitations were made.

The party was in full swing and would continue into the small hours. The staff, too, were celebrating; for some of the tutors, this would be their last McKenna dinner as members of the ETPS staff. The Principal Tutor, Fixed Wing, Vic Lockwood, was leaving to attend the RAF Staff College; James Giles was to become Principal Tutor in his place. Mike Swales, who was Vic Lockwood's opposite number on the rotary wing course, was leaving Boscombe Down to command a training squadron at RNAS Culdrose; his

Bob Horton, in the anteroom after the dinner, drinks champagne from the Westland Trophy, presented to him as the outstanding Rotary Wing student on the course (*BBC*)

replacement was to be Iain Young. Two of the Ground School tutors were also posted: Andy Debuse was to take up another teaching appointment at RAF Halton, and Paul Ashmore was bound for the Ministry of Defence.

Although the staff would change, the basic character of the school would remain true, as it has throughout the history of ETPS, to the tenets laid down in 1943 by its creator, Air Marshal Sir Ralph Sorley.

Outside, the rain was still falling steadily; it was a very dark night, but the hardstanding between the gaunt hangars was lit by the bright security lights reflected in pools of rainwater. Inside the hangars, the ETPS aircraft, dimly seen, were waiting for ETPS Course No. 45/24: fifteen other young men, scattered as yet across the world, who in a few weeks would be at Boscombe Down, testing these aircraft and themselves to their limits. But on that night of graduation the only sounds were the hiss of the rain and the far-off celebrations from the distant Mess, as the outgoing school completed its traditional 'McKenna'.

NOTES

1 The exercise also served to familiarise the students with the controls and systems. Running concurrently were the flying conversion and instruments rating tests, the aircraft involved at this stage being the HS 748 Andover C1 turbo-prop transport XS 606, the BAC/Breguet Jaguar T2 operational trainers, XX 145, 830, 844, the Hawker Hunter T7/8 advanced two-seat trainers, XL 564, 612, and the Hawker Siddeley Hawk T1 trainers XX 342, 343.

   The rotary wing students had a similar programme, using their Westland Scout AH1 XP 849, a Mk 5 Westland Wessex XS 509 and a Sikorsky Ws-61 Sea King XV 370.

2 The two roles of pressure instruments cited are simplifications: the pressure sources are also used for the machmeter and, in many modern aircraft, for autostabilisers and autopilots, in addition to feeding information of height and speed to navigational computers, and carrying out other exotic functions.

3 Altimeters are calibrated to an International Standard Atmosphere (ISA) which postulates a sea-level pressure of 1013.25 mb, or 29.92 ins Hg, a temperature lapse rate of 1.98°C per 1000 feet from sea-level up to the tropopause at 36,090 feet (11,000 metres) at which point the temperature is regarded as remaining stable at −65.5°C.

4 It is usual practice in most countries to designate airfield runways by the use of the nominal magnetic heading in degrees of the runway in question. The heading is normally presented in an abbreviated form: '24' for '240', '06' for '060'. The normal convention is for a runway to have two possible directions of use, depending on the wind; thus a runway heading 240 degrees will have a reciprocal heading of 060 degrees: 240 − 180 = 060. This will be published as 24/06, as is the case with the main runway at Boscombe Down. The heading of a given runway is usually shown in large white figures at the beginning of each end of the tarmac. The figures are nominal since runways, being relatively permanent, cannot accommodate changing magnetic variation (though this is in fact a very slow process) and therefore are to the nearest ten degrees of the actual magnetic heading. Geographical considerations apart, the heading of an airfield runway is governed originally by the direction of the prevailing winds; in most of Britain this is westerly.

5 'Swept Wing Spin Training' in *Air Clues*, June 1985.

6 'Autorotation and Engine-Off Landing Training' in *Air Clues*, July 1985.

7 In aviation terms a 'loop' is an upward circular climb and descent in which the aircraft describes a perfect vertical circle or loop. Loops are made by the pilot pulling the stick backwards and holding it in that position. It is not dangerous (provided the pilot has allowed sufficient height for recovery) since the g forces in a loop on both pilot and aircraft are negative; if correctly performed, even a pilot not strapped in would not fall out of the aircraft due to the continuous negative g pressing him down in his seat. Unless the loop was very small, the applied g should be a moderate 3½ or 4, which a fit pilot should withstand without difficulty. A 'bunt' is an outside loop, that is a loop made by the pilot pushing the stick forward and diving the aircraft down and round the loop. This is a very dangerous manoeuvre since it subjects the pilot and the airframe to high positive g forces for which neither has been designed. Aircraft, other than fighters or specialised aerobatic machines, are stressed to withstand forces imposed in the main by negative g; i.e. pulling out of a dive, a steep turn or a normal inside loop. In the case of helicopters, positive g can result in the rotors becoming unloaded and, in some instances, striking part of the aircraft's fuselage with disastrous results. The warning given by Mike Swales to his student, Bob Horton, was a caution that in autorotated flight 'bunting', that is pushing the stick forward in level flight, would unload the rotor and cause it to slow down due to a reduction of airflow through it.

8 James Giles has kindly supplied an explanation of the 'Steady Heading' side-slip test technique.

   'Firstly rudder is applied, which causes the nose to yaw. Right rudder should make the nose of the aircraft go to the right for positive directional stability. Because the aircraft is yawing right, the left wing is moving faster and therefore producing more lift, tending to roll the aircraft to the right: the dihedral effect, therefore left stick is applied to balance all the forces while keeping the aircraft flying on a selected heading. That is the sequence which is usually found, but some aircraft actually roll away from the applied rudder; this may be caused by the configuration of the wing, or from a high rudder which itself produces a rolling moment stronger than that of the dihedral effect. There are also some aircraft which have a "rudder lock" at high side-slip angles, which makes them dangerous, since the pilot has to exert enormous effort to try to counteract aerodynamic forces which are making the aircraft go out of control. [The Halifax II suffered from this defect, and was the subject of a lengthy investigation at Boscombe Down; an A&AEE test crew lost their lives in the course of the inquiry. See A&AEE Report 760, quoted at some length in *A Most Secret Place: Boscombe Down 1939/45*, B. Johnson and T. Heffernan, Jane's, London 1982.] Since this side-slip manoeuvre is seldom used, why do test pilots have to learn it? The answer is that it is a method of generating side-slip angles which the aircraft will encounter in flying in turbulence, and by making sure, by testing, that the aircraft will always naturally tend to return to the direction in which it originally was heading; displaying a "weathercock" stability similar to an arrow in flight.'

9   Above 3000 feet all aircraft set their altimeters to the internationally agreed figure of 1013 mb, or to the American equivalent of 29.92 inches of mercury, to be independent of regional settings (QNH), there are 'Quadrantal Rules' which require aircraft above 3000 feet to fly at a given altitude plus or minus 500 feet, dependent on their magnetic heading, to ensure safe vertical separation.

APPENDIX I

Aircraft flown by Squadron Leader H. G. Hazelden on the first test pilots course at Boscombe Down

Date	Aircraft		Exercise	Time (hours)
21.6.43	Mentor	L4393	Partial Climbs 10,000–11,000 ft	1.50
22.6.43	Proctor	XV451	Ceiling Climb 16,000 ft	1.45
23.6.43	Warwick	BV296	Single Engine Take-offs	.20
23.6.43	Stinson	FK818	Ceiling Climb 13,000 ft	1.20
24.6.43	Master	W8573	Climb 17,000 ft	1.15
24.6.43	Beaufort	AW343	Handling	15
26.6.43	Warwick	BV295	Handling Experience	2.25
29.6.43	Halifax I	W9520	Handling Experience	1.20
30.6.43	Warwick	BV295	Handling Experience	1.00
30.6.43	Warwick	BV295	Handling Experience – engine cut and crash landing	.10
1.7.43	Anson	?	Partial climbs – A/c U/S for undercarriage	.15
2.7.43	Master	W8573	Handling – Stalling	1.15

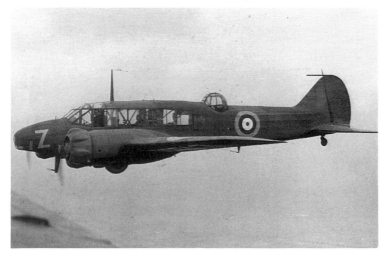

L7956, an Anson 1, one of the types on the school fleet which were flown by 'Hazel' at the time of No. 1 course in 1943 (*Flight*)

Date	Aircraft		Exercise	Time (hours)
5.7.43	Halifax I*	W9250	Handling – Taxiing, Take-off and Landing	.55
6.7.43	Halifax I	W9250	Ditto – A/c U/S – Pilot's Hatch blew open	.35
7.7.43	Hurricane II	Z2399	Handling Experience	.30
13.7.43	Albemarle	P1523	Handling	.30
14.7.43	Beaufort	AW343	Handling, Take-offs and Landings	.50
16.7.43	Halifax	W9520	Handling	1.00
17.7.43	Oxford	HN272	PE Trials	1.30
20.7.43	Oxford	HN782	Climb and Levels	1.30
24.7.43	Oxford	HN581	To Weston Zoyland	.30
26.7.43	Oxford	HN782	Climb and Levels	1.25
27.7.43	Halifax	L9520	Oil Cooling Levels	1.45
28.7.43	Lancaster III	ED565	To Ringway	1.15
28.7.43	Oxford	HN581	From Ringway	1.15
29.7.43	Warwick	BV224	Low Power Levels	2.40
30.7.43	Warwick	BV224	Low Power Levels	2.40
2.8.43	Hurricane	HD264	Handling	.40

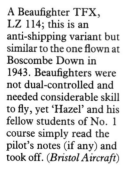

A Beaufighter TFX, LZ 114; this is an anti-shipping variant but similar to the one flown at Boscombe Down in 1943. Beaufighters were not dual-controlled and needed considerable skill to fly, yet 'Hazel' and his fellow students of No. 1 course simply read the pilot's notes (if any) and took off. (*Bristol Aircraft*)

*W9250 was never issued, being a missing 'security' block number in a series used for Hurricane 1s. L9250 was a Halifax II known to be on charge to the A&AEE. In correspondence with the author 'Hazel' confirmed that the 'W' may have been a slip of his pen.

Date	Aircraft	Exercise	Time (hours)
4.8.43	Oxford	HN581 Directional and Lateral Stability	1.30
5.8.43	Mitchell	FL215 Handling	1.10
6.8.43	Hurricane	HD264 Directional and Lateral Stability	1.00
7.8.43	Beaufighter	EL292 Handling	1.15
9.8.43	Oxford	HN782 Handling to 270 ASI – A/c U/S – Petrol Leak	.30
9.8.43	Oxford	HN782 Ditto – OK	.45
10.8.43	Hurricane	Z2399 Fuel Consumptions	1.00
12.8.43	Hurricane	HD264 Climb to 34,000 ft	1.00
13.8.43	Mitchell	AD688 Handling	.45
14.8.43	Hurricane	HD264 Oil Cooling Levels – Oakley and Return	1.30
16.8.43	Warwick	BV225 G-AGFJ } Air Test	.40
17.8.43	Warwick	Ditto Range Test	9.05
18.8.43	Warwick	BV301 Oil Cooling Levels	1.20
19.8.43	Warwick	BV225 G-AGFJ } Consumption Levels	.40
23.8.43	Hurricane	Z2399 Consumption Levels	1.10
24.8.43	Anson	DG717 To Yatesbury and Return	.45
24.8.43	Hurricane	LD264 Climb to 33,000 ft	1.15
26.8.43	Fortress	FK192 Meteorological Flight to 35,000 ft	2.00
27.8.43	Master III	T8886 Spinning	1.05
30.8.43	Mitchell	FL215 To Oakley and Gt Massingham	1.30
30.8.43	Oxford	HN581 Gt Massingham – Snailwell	1.10
31.8.43	Master	W8573 Climb to 20,000 ft – Landed at Lasham	1.15
31.8.43	Oxford	HN581 Return from Lasham	.20
1.9.43	Warwick	BV225 Farnborough and Brooklands	.30
1.9.43	Anson	? From Brooklands to Boscombe Down	.30

Date	*Aircraft*		*Exercise*	*Time* *(hours)*
2.9.43	Oxford	HN581	Measured Take-offs and Landings	.30
2.9.43	Lancaster	L4115	Handling – Port Outer Engine U/S	1.15
4.9.43	Hurricane	LD264	Aerobatics	1.00
6.9.43	Halifax	?	Flare Dropping – Lyme Bay	2.10
7.9.43	Hurricane	Z2399	Climb – A/c U/S	.20
7.9.43	Hurricane	LD264	Climb to 25,000 ft Levels 22,20,18,17,16	1.40
8.9.43	Oxford	HN782	Single Engine Partials	2.30
9.9.43	Sea-Otter	JM743	Handling	1.40
10.9.43	Oxford	HN782	Formation	.30
10.9.43	Hampden	AE439	Photography of Firebrand	.40
17.9.43	Halifax	LV304	Air Test	.40
20.9.43	Whitley	D4149	Handling	1.00
11.9.43	Hampden	AE439	Photography	.50
23.9.43	Beaufort	AW343	Handling	1.00

APPENDIX II

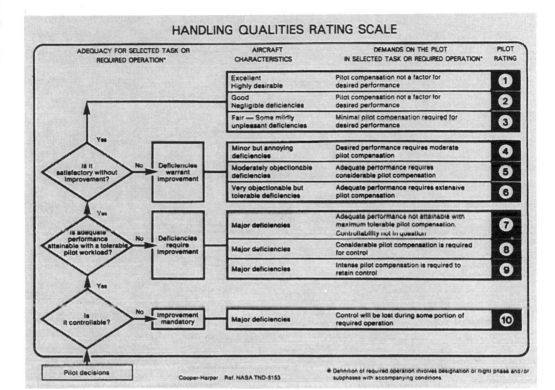

GLOSSARY

A&AEE	The Aeroplane & Armament Experimental Establishment
ADF	Automatic Direction Finder
AFCS	Automatic Flight Control Systems
AMSL	Above Mean Sea-Level
AOA	Angle of Attack
APU	Auxiliary Power Unit
'Arm T'	Armament Testing
ASI	Airspeed Indicator
ASW	Anti-Submarine Warfare
AUW	All-Up Weight
CAA	Civil Aviation Authority
CCIP	Continuously Computed Impact Point
C of G	Centre of Gravity
DFC	Distinguished Flying Cross
DZ	Dropping Zone
EGT	Exhaust Gas Temperature
GCA	Ground Controlled Approach
HQR	Handling Quality Rating
HUD	Head-Up Display
IAS	Indicated Airspeed
IFDF	Intensive Flying Development Flight
IMC	Instrument Meteorological Conditions
JPT	Jet Pipe Temperature
KIAS	Knots Indicated Airspeed
LFA	Low-Flying Area
MSD	Mean-Sea Datum
NAVWASS	Navigation and Weapon-Aiming Sub-System
NCU	Navigational Control Unit
N_G	Gas Generator
N_R	Rotor Speed
OCU	Operational Conversion Unit
OTU	Operational Training Unit
P1	Pilot in Command
PAR	Precision Approach Radar
PEC	Pressure Error Correction
'Per T'	Performance Testing
PMD	Projected Map Display
PTIT	Power Turbine Inlet Temperature
SPILS	Spin Prevention and Incidence Limiting System
SPO	Short Period Oscillation

STOL	Short Take-Off and Landing
TRE	Telecommunication Research Establishment
UHF	Ultra High Frequency
VHF	Very High Frequency
VMC	Visual Meteorological Conditions
VOR	VHF Omni Range
VSS	Variable Stability System
WAAF	Women's Auxiliary Air Force
WAMS	Weapons-Aiming Mode Selector

BIBLIOGRAPHY

op indicates the book is out of print

EMPIRE TEST PILOTS' SCHOOL
Ground school notes: Books A and B and *Flying wing précis: chapters 1–8* ETPS, RAF Boscombe Down, Salisbury, Wiltshire SP4 0JF.

GIBBS SMITH, C. H.
Aviation: an historical survey from its origins to the end of World War II HMSO, 2nd rev. edn pbk 1985.

GUNSTON, B.
The encyclopedia of the world's combat aircraft Hamlyn, 1976. op.

GUNSTON, B.
Modern combat aircraft Treasure Press, 1985.

JOHNSON, B. and HEFFERNAN, T.
A most secret place: Boscombe Down 1939/45 Jane's, 1982.

PENROSE, H.
No echo in the sky Cassell, 1958. op.

ROBERTSON, B.
British military aircraft serials 1911–79 Cambridge: Stephens, 1979. op.

STINTON, D.
The design of the aeroplane Collins, new edn pbk 1985.

SWANBOROUGH, F. G. and BOWERS, P. M.
United States military aircraft since 1911 Putnam, 2nd rev. edn 1977.

THETFORD, O.
Aircraft of the Royal Air Force since 1918 Putnam, 7th rev. edn 1979.

WOLFE, T.
The right stuff Cape, 1979; Bantam, new edn pbk 1981.

INDEX

Numbers in italic refer to illustrations